Economic Control

First published in 1955, this book offers a detailed history from the past to the mid-20th century on economic control. The book examines economic competition, particularly regarding the British economic system, and Fogarty looks at its scope, as well as its limits. This analysis considers working conditions in the mid-20th century, examining the impacts of industry on the life and work of the British agricultural population. The book first examines production decisions, arguing that a systematic and periodic overhaul of control mechanisms are required. Fogarty goes to give a detailed analysis on decisions about industry objectives. Ultimately, a broader look is given on the wider economic setting, and the definition of the economist is itself examined, taking into account the wider role that economics played in 20th century society.

T0270873

Economic Control

Michael Patrick Fogarty

Routledge
Taylor & Francis Group

First published in 1955
by Routledge & Kegan Paul

This edition first published in 2018 by Routledge
2 Park Square, Milton Park, Abingdon, Oxon, OX14 4RN
and by Routledge
711 Third Avenue, New York, NY 10017

Routledge is an imprint of the Taylor & Francis Group, an informa business

© 1955 Michael Patrick Fogarty

Publisher's Note
The publisher has gone to great lengths to ensure the quality of this reprint but points out that some imperfections in the original copies may be apparent.

Disclaimer
The publisher has made every effort to trace copyright holders and welcomes correspondence from those they have been unable to contact.
A Library of Congress record exists under ISBN: 55002687

ISBN 13: 978-1-138-31055-1 (hbk)
ISBN 13: 978-1-315-14386-6 (ebk)
ISBN 13: 978-1-138-50057-0 (pbk)

ECONOMIC CONTROL

Michael P. Fogarty

ROUTLEDGE & KEGAN PAUL LTD
Broadway House, 68–74 Carter Lane
London

First published in 1955
by Routledge & Kegan Paul Ltd
Broadway House, 68-74 Carter Lane
London E.C.4
Made and printed in Great Britain
by William Clowes and Sons, Limited
London and Beccles

CONTENTS

*

v

CONTENTS

PART IV

ECONOMICS IN ITS WIDER SETTING

LIST OF TABLES AND CHARTS

vii

viii

LIST OF TABLES AND CHARTS

ix

LIST OF TABLES AND CHARTS

Part I

THE PROBLEM

Chapter 1

FOREWORD—THE PROBLEM
OF CONTROL

THE means of producing wealth have passed in modern times through three ages. The first was, to borrow the language of Patrick Geddes and Lewis Mumford, eotechnic. Its characteristic materials were wood and stone. It used increasing quantities of power, derived from wind, water, and, thanks to the invention of the horse-collar, from the more skilful use of the horse. Inventions came comparatively slowly, but included (especially if re-inventions, or popularisation, of discoveries of the Ancient World are also counted) many of the first importance: the clock, glass, printing and paper, scientific method, the university, the factory. The eotechnic phase lasted, with variations from country to country, from the Middle Ages to the middle of the eighteenth century. It was followed by a palaeotechnic phase, the age of coal and iron, steam and the railways, continuing to the first quarter of the twentieth century. The rate of major inventions and discoveries leapt forward: from a bare forty or fifty in the fifteenth century and little over three hundred in the seventeenth, it rose for the nineteenth century to over two thousand. These inventions were more particularly in the fields of natural science, technology, and economics; the other social sciences had yet to come into their own.

Finally, in the twentieth century there opens a neotechnic phase, the age of electricity and atomic power, motors and aircraft, the telephone and radio, alloys and synthetic materials; of the technician, as apart from the man who has learnt from experience alone; of automatic as apart from craft production; and of the rise alongside natural science of the science of human relations. The pace of change quickens still further: the rate of inventions rises to new peaks.

In the conditions of life which have accompanied this sweeping and accelerating advance towards the mastery of the world, good and bad have been mixed. The growth in productivity through the palaeotechnic and early neotechnic decades is recorded in Table 1. An Indian or Japanese worker in the last quarter of the nineteenth century was earning 3 (1925–34) cents an hour; by 1944–5 an American worker was earning on the average 98 cents of the same

3

TABLE 1. Value of the product of an hour's work, U.S. cents
per hour, prices of 1925–34

(1) FOR THE ECONOMY AS A WHOLE

	U.S.A.	Great Britain	France	Japan	India	U.S.S.R.
1688	—	13½[1]	—	—	—	—
1800–1	23	17	7	—	—	—
1840–9	23	15	8	—	—	—
1860–9	26	23	13	—	3½	—
1884–93	34	31	17	3	—	—
1895	—	—	—	—	4½	—
1911–14	55	37	21	5	—	17
1925–9	78	49	32	12	8½	16
1937	92	55	37	19	—	15
1940	—	—	—	—	—	18
1944–5	98	61	—	18	9½	—

(2) BY SECTIONS OF THE ECONOMY
(a) Agriculture, forestry, etc.

Increase		From	To
1870–1943	U.S.A.	10	30
1867–1938	Great Britain	12	20
1860/4–1935/9	France	7	17
1897–1934	Japan	64[2]	148[2]
1928–1938	U.S.S.R.	108[2]	127[2]

(b) Manufacturing

Increase		From	To
1869–1938	U.S.A.	21	107
1870/6–1938	Great Britain	12	36
1861/5–1937	France	6	32
1913–1938	Japan	9	17
1913–1936	U.S.S.R.	12	22

(c) All other, including services and small-scale manufacture

Increase		From	To
1870–1939/41	U.S.A.	43	124
1860/9–1937	Great Britain	26	67
1860/9–1938	France	16	42
1928–1938	U.S.S.R.	33	22

From Clark, *Conditions of Economic Progress*, 1951 ed.

[1] England and Wales
[2] $ per man per year

value. Workers have moved steadily (Table 2) from the less productive, over-manned occupations to those, in manufacturing or the service trades, carrying higher rates of pay. Advances such as these have opened dazzling perspectives for human welfare.

TABLE 2. Percentage of working population in each industry or occupation

	U.S.A.		G.B.		France		Japan		U.S.S.R.	
	1870	1940	1881	1938	1866	1946	1872	1930	1926	1939
Agriculture, forestry, etc.	53	19	13	7	43	21	85	50	81	58
Mining	1	2	4	5⎫			0	1⎫		
Manufacturing, building				⎬	38	35		⎬	6	17
ing	21	30	46	42⎭			5	19⎭		
All others	25	49	37	47	19	45	10	30	13	24

Clark, op. cit.

It is not surprising that many of those who saw the early successes of the palaeotechnic age missed its darker side. The contrast between the palaeotechnic and the older eotechnic environment was in fact by no means uniformly favourable to the former. Table 3 records the result of a present-day comparison between conditions of life and work in urban and rural areas in Great Britain. The farmer and farm worker, living in a landscape and buildings and even using techniques dating largely from the eotechnic age, have the advantage in air, light, and beauty of surroundings and in physical health; in the stability and solidarity of their working group and local community; and generally in mental health and balanced personality. The townsman, living in an environment and working at occupations created for overwhelmingly the greater part since the Industrial Revolution, has the advantage in income, choice of consumption goods and public utility services, and in choice of occupations; as also in facilities for education and training, and that rather limited range of intellectual qualities (one is sometimes tempted to label them slickness) measured by intelligence tests. The difference is not only between townsman and farmer. One might also point the contrast between the careful soil-conservation practice of the British and, generally, the European farmer, resting on eotechnic traditions, and the soil-mining methods which made a dust-bowl of American prairies, opened up in the palaeotechnic age with the help of the

5

TABLE 3. Conditions of life and work in which the agricultural population of Great Britain was on the whole at an advantage or disadvantage over and against townspeople, 1950

Advantage	Difference	Disadvantage
Overcrowding (workers)	Housing	Pay (workers)
Garden	Services (neigh-	Transport to service cen-
Landscape	bourhood	tres (workers)
Density of development	centres)	Water
Atmospheric pollution	Transport to	Electricity
Primary working group:	service centres	Drains
variety and responsi-	(farmers)	Radio and T.V. reception
bility of work	Pay (farmers)	Services (main centres)
Cohesion of neighbour-		Contact with neighbours
hood		(including telephone)
Integrated culture		Isolation of working group
Physical health		Limited range of roles avail-
Absence of mental disease		able (choice of jobs and
Fertility (may indicate ad-		social connections)
vantage in psychological		Insularity of culture
characteristics other		Intelligence, mental de-
than intelligence)		ficiency

From Fogarty, report to Nuffield Foundation's Agricultural Policy Group on Rural Life and the Family Pattern, 1951 (cyclostyled).

railway, the steamship, and the reaper and binder. The contrast between town and country would have been even more marked had it been drawn before the beginning of the neotechnic age; in the 1830's, when poverty produced the Labourers' Revolt, or the 1840's and 1850's, when the degradation of the palaeotechnic town was immortalised in Mayhew's *London* or Engels's *Condition of the Working Classes in Britain in 1844*. The palaeotechnic revolution increased individual income and opportunity. It promoted the education needed to cope with its own problems and the remedial services needed to relieve its own worst defects. But it failed lamentably under such headings as stability, social solidarity, conservation, or town and country planning.

Today, in the neotechnic age, we are trying to combine the achievements of the eotechnic period in creating a satisfactory environment and of the palaeotechnic age in multiplying individual income and opportunity. The most important conclusion of the above-mentioned survey of town and country is not that there is

6

still a gap between the two, but that the gap is being narrowed from both sides. The income gap has closed for the farmer and half closed for the farm worker since the war. The countryman is rapidly acquiring his electricity, water, and drains, and his transport (public or personal) to shopping, educational, and service centres. The towns have rediscovered the virtues of full employment and town planning, and are beginning to understand the importance of the neighbourhood or the primary working group. A time can be foreseen, two or three generations ahead, when the gap may have closed so far as to cease to count.

But why did it open originally, and why is it at this particular moment that it is being closed? One influence has certainly been that of technology itself. It is, for instance, evidently far harder to plan towns well in a world of steam engines and open fires, one where the people of big towns must be packed close because transport is by horse or by steam railway, than in the age of electricity, light, power, and transport, of the telephone and radio, the bus and the delivery van. But this is hardly the whole or even the major cause. Nothing in the technology of the nineteenth century made it essential to build houses back to back or in the monotonous rows known to the town planner as 'by-law' housing; or to allow the population of Greater London to swell to eight million. Planners today are beginning to see, from experience of the more generous modern standards of eight or twelve houses to the acre, that the close packing of population on the land may actually have had social advantages to offset the additional difficulties which it put in the planner's way. Nor, as the experiments of Robert Owen showed, was it essential to thrust the problems of human relations in industry and the neighbourhood to one side. Booms and slumps, likewise, were not more inevitable then than now.

A second contribution to the palaeotechnic failure came from a philosophy, a set of cultural norms, which deliberately left aside certain characteristic values of the eotechnic age: notably aesthetic values or those associated with leisure. But it would again be nonsense to maintain that this inadequate conception of what the aims of individuals and society should be was the sole or perhaps even the main cause of failure. No one deliberately willed the degradation of mid-nineteenth-century London or Manchester. Often it was the same men who were unconsciously responsible for it, or members of the same new industrial class, who were most horrified when eventually their handiwork was brought to their notice. If they were not, it was commonly because they themselves had grown in and from this environment and were in a sense its victims; for economic

7

and social events shape cultural norms as well as being shaped by them.

The point was rather that, in the rush of events at the beginning of a dynamic age, changing more swiftly than in any previous human experience, society had lost control. Any one invention—the car, for instance, or radio—may have revolutionary repercussions throughout the social system; let alone the flood which has poured over the world since the end of the eighteenth century. In the face of the new speed of events nineteenth-century society, however excellent its intentions, no longer knew how to translate intentions into reality. The recovery in the neotechnic age has been due not so much to a new philosophy—whether there is such a philosophy, and what its value may be, is problematic—as to the invention of increasingly effective methods of social control.

But what sort of control? It is useful to make a twofold division. How, first, are needs diagnosed? How are detailed decisions arrived at about what to consume, how much to provide for the future, what to do about the economic relations between different geographical areas? Then, secondly, supposing that these decisions have been made, how best can it be ensured that they are carried out?

Then control of what? This book is concerned with *economic* relationships. The common-sense definition, which is also the best scientific definition ever given, is Pigou's. Economics is concerned with any and all human relationships in so far as they have been, or can be, brought into relation with the 'measuring rod of money'. Wherever money and monetary standards penetrate, or could penetrate, the economist follows. He is concerned with whatever influences—and in so far as it influences—the size, nature, and distribution of the national income.

It is useful to distinguish here between social relationships which *immediately* involve money and those which merely *influence others* involving money; for it is with the former that economists are chiefly concerned.

The most fundamental factor of all in the size and nature and distribution of the national income, as in every other type of social relationship, is of course ethics. Decisions about what needs to be done depend in the last resort on people's ideas of right and wrong; their *cultural norms* or *ethical standards*. Cultural norms represent actual current beliefs and motive patterns: whereas ethics are the more absolute standards to which these tend to approximate. Ethical standards are in part—at their most basic level—fixed, and apply always and everywhere: such broad and universal rules as 'love your neighbour as yourself'. But there is also the level of what

8

might be called 'middle principles', which are concerned with rules applicable to a given society at a given time. One might, for instance, reason as follows:

'In a modern industrial society people are particularly likely to suffer from unemployment or from the breakdown of their family and community life. Therefore the general rule "love your neighbour as yourself" requires us here and now to give special attention to the problems of full employment or of marriage guidance or neighbourhood planning.'

At this level, obviously, the norms of action will vary greatly from one society to another. What needs to be done depends on the *personalities concerned*, the *social structure*, and the *physical and technical environment*. It depends on who people are, on the families, communities, and social classes they belong to, the industries they work in, the surroundings they live in, and on the wealth, knowledge, and qualities of mental and physical health they have available.

So far money, and therefore economics, does not immediately or necessarily come into the picture. This is the background to economics; it is not economics itself. But there is still another level of action: that no longer of principles—not even 'middle' principles—but of the machinery through which they are applied from day to day. Basic social norms, the social structure, and the environment decide among other things which *sanctions* and *mechanisms* a society will use to induce its members to make (from its point of view) the right decisions, and to carry them out. This is the level of *social process* as apart from the *social framework*. And it is here that the economist appears on the scene; for here money directly comes in.

As a first approximation, it may be said that a man is persuaded to reach a certain decision or take certain action by sanctions of one of three kinds:

(i) Political—that is, formal authority, such as that of Parliament or of a manager or supervisor.
(ii) Social—that is, informal authority, such as the pressure of public opinion.
(iii) Economic—that is, authority expressed in money form, as in buying, selling, or taxation. The economic sanction may be said to apply wherever and to the extent that any relationship involves or may involve a gain, loss, or exchange customarily measured or measurable in money terms. Very roughly, therefore, it applies to all those activities whose results are summed up in the concepts of national income and capital: 'roughly',

9

that is, because these concepts do not in fact cover all activities (housekeeping, for instance) whose results can be partly or wholly measured in money terms.

These sanctions take effect through mechanisms, which likewise are of three main types:

(i) Competition. People, or groups, are left free to do as they think fit. But what is done will have to be justified after the event by reference to fixed standards.
(ii) Direction. The action to be taken is prescribed in advance.
(iii) Consultation. Action is neither free (before the event) as in competition, nor prescribed in advance as in direction. But those concerned consult in advance, with no binding obligation, and agree if possible on the course to be taken.

Of course, what one nearly always meets in practice is a combination of several sanctions and several mechanisms at once. For instance, the board of directors of a firm, deciding on the annual distribution of dividends, is under:

(i) The formal authority of the law and the shareholders' meeting.
(ii) 'Social' authority. For instance, the pressure of financial opinion (expressed in the financial Press), of public or trade union opinion, and so on.
(iii) The economic pressure of customers, suppliers, and the trade unions.

And these pressures (among others) take effect through such varied channels as:

(i) Competition, which determines what constitute 'reasonable' prices, wages, or dividends.
(ii) Directions under the Companies or Finance Acts, or from the shareholders' meeting.
(iii) Consultation with all manner of people and groups both in and out of the firm.

I have said that personality, social norms, and the social structure and environment 'decide' which sanctions and mechanisms are to be used in a particular case. But influence also flows the other way: the sanctions and mechanisms used are likely to modify a society's personality patterns, structure, and norms for the future. A society may, for instance, choose to rely largely on competition, because that corresponds best to its particular personalities, structure, norms, and environment. But, having chosen competition, it is liable to find—as Britain has done in the last two hundred years—that through the working of competition its most cherished beliefs are turned upside down; its social structure is remodelled from top to bottom, new types of personality arise to fit new opportunities, and it ends up living (or possibly being reduced to radio-active dust) in an utterly different environment. It is a circular process, like the hen and the egg, with personality, structure, norms, and environment modifying sanctions and mechanisms, and being in their turn modified by them.

It is nevertheless useful to remember that personality, environment, norms, and social structure change relatively slowly, and may therefore correctly be called the 'social framework'. Sanctions and mechanisms ('social process'), on the other hand, change or can be changed relatively fast. And this distinction is particularly useful in economics, since economics is primarily concerned with 'social process'. The sections of the hen-and-egg circular process which are first and foremost relevant to economics are:

(i) The *economic* sanction.
(ii) As applied through the *mechanisms* of competition, direction ('economic planning'), and consultation.

Enmeshed as he is in a social process in which everything determines everything else, an economist must of course pay attention also to what is happening outside his immediate field. He has to remember, and study, the social framework in which he works, and which economic processes in their turn are engaged in modifying. He cannot afford to neglect the efforts of colleagues who are busy with other (political or social) aspects of the 'social process'. But his first job is to cultivate his own garden. He must study the working, and the advantages or disadvantages as a means of social control, of the economic sanction: that is of competition, direction, and consultation in so far as these are concerned with and affect the size, nature, and distribution of the national income.

And that is what the two following parts of this book propose to do. I have distinguished above between control over decisions about what is to be done and control over the execution of these decisions. The latter is in some ways a more straightforward problem, and will be taken first. The order of the book will thus be:

PART II. *The control of production.* Supposing that the necessary decisions have been made about what is to be done, how effective is the economic sanction, combined with each of the various mechanisms of control, in ensuring that it gets done? 'Production' for this purpose will include not only what is ordinarily understood by that

11

term—manufacturing, for instance—but also distribution and the evolution of the labour market.

PART III. *The control of decisions about what is to be done.* The effectiveness of the economic sanction for this purpose will be examined under three headings: consumption-savings decisions; investment decisions; and decisions affecting inter-regional and international relations.

Finally, Part IV will come back to some of the wider or external implications of the economist's task, outside his own immediate field. Parts II and III will touch incidentally on some consequences of the fact that the processes the economist studies operate within, but also modify, a certain social framework. Part IV will be the place to consider this at more length.

See Further Reading List, p. 300.

Part II

PRODUCTION DECISIONS

Chapter 2

THE SCOPE AND LIMITS OF ECONOMIC COMPETITION

I. IMMEDIATELY SIGNIFICANT DECISIONS WITHIN A GIVEN SOCIAL FRAMEWORK

HOW effective, in the first place, as a means of control over production, is economic competition; that is competition sanctioned primarily (though never in practice exclusively) by ability to attract customers' money?

It is essential to remember in answering this question that economic competition, and indeed any other combination of sanctions and control mechanisms, operates within a given framework of norms, social structure, and personality. Answers will be valid only within the given social framework, in this case that of Great Britain and, with reservations, other more or less similarly structured Western countries. Social action does ultimately change its own framework. But it will not be at all surprising if a given combination of sanctions and controls is more (or less) effective in bringing out conformity to conditions set by the social framework than in changing that framework itself. There is no *a priori* reason why effectiveness for these two very different purposes should be the same. In the case of economic competition it is as a matter of fact very different. It can also very well happen that, if competition fails to give satisfactory results, the fault lies with the surrounding social framework rather than with competition itself.

The effectiveness of economic competition will be illustrated here by reference to markets of three main types: those for manufactured goods, retail goods, and labour. Its discussion can be brought conveniently under three heads:

(*a*) The effectiveness of economic competition in enforcing decisions about consumption, investment, or inter-regional and international trade and investment, in so far as the factors involved are understood by and of immediate importance to the parties to each competitive transaction; and taking the social framework as given.

15

(b) Its effectiveness for doing likewise with remoter or more diffused claims, still taking the social framework for granted.

(c) Its effectiveness in altering the social framework; personality, culture, and institutions.

If it succeeds—if it is 'full', in the sense defined below—economic competition as a process for enforcing immediately significant decisions within a given social framework produces results of five kinds:

(1) *Consumer Sovereignty.* The production of goods and services is adjusted between different lines so that, given consumers' existing habits and incomes, no further adjustment could make them better off.

(2) *Minimum costs and prices.* Prices are just enough to cover the costs of production, and provide whatever the society in question accepts as a 'normal' profit, in a representative firm. By this is meant a firm with the lowest costs attainable in a given line of production by managers of high but common ability (disregarding cases of exceptional genius), using the best accepted standards of technology, on sites or in circumstances of a sort equally available to other concerns, and operating to a normal capacity. It will be a firm efficient as efficiency is understood in the given society, working to a standard which others can also hope to attain. Not all firms will necessarily be of 'representative' efficiency. But they will have to charge prices as low as those of the representative firm, and make do, if necessary, with a sub-normal profit.

The costs minimised here are 'opportunity' costs. The value set on each service costed is that of the highest price or wage it could earn in any occupation after adjustments described under this and the preceding and following sub-heads are completed.

(3) *Fair pay and maximum incomes.* Men, money, and natural resources are used so that no worker, or unit of land and capital, given workers' and owners' existing tastes, could become better off by moving into another line of production. This incidentally implies equal pay for equal work, and that men or units will be paid the equivalent of their marginal contribution to production. A worker's wage, for instance, is equal to the amount by which production would fall if the number of workers of his skill and grade were reduced by one.

(4) *Precise, quick, and extensive coordination.* Precise and quick control is maintained over transactions even when they are very numerous. Control through the pricing system, on which economic competition relies, is precise, highly differentiated—capable, that is,

16

of registering small differences in needs or costs—and self-registering and self-enforcing, without the intervention of any higher authority. It works very quickly—in the best organised markets, indeed, almost instantaneously. And it causes expected as well as immediately prospective changes in the market, or in accepted standards of efficiency, to reflect themselves instantly in current prices.

(5) *Decentralisation.* Deliberate decision-making, as apart from the automatic processes of the market, is decentralised.

Common sense tells us that these are all desirable results. Let us leave for the moment the question of how and why they are desirable and whether there are others, also desirable, which competition does not attain. The whole question of what mediaeval writers called the Just Price will have to come up again later. Here we have simply to ask how, and how regularly, competition does what it is said to do if it succeeds.

How far the results of 'full' competition are achieved depends on the prevalence, or lack of prevalence, of certain conditions.

(1) *The continuity of competition.* Factors affecting this are:

(*a*) Continuity in time, place, and product. Does the business man (or with appropriate changes, the worker selling his labour) feel competition pressing upon him in respect of all his products, in every period and at every place at which he sells them?

(*b*) Reversibility of goodwill. Does competition come from products, not necessarily identical with those the business man sells, but such that a customer who changes from Firm A to Firm B will feel the same goodwill for product B against product A, as he once felt for A against B? Heinz beans, for instance, are not the same as Waveney; but a customer may feel the same goodwill for Heinz to the exclusion of Waveney as for Waveney to the exclusion of Heinz. The same argument applies, with appropriate changes, to competition between factors of production.

(2) *The freedom of competition.* It is not necessary, in order for competition to work perfectly, for there to be available at a given moment enough capacity in efficient firms to take over the whole of inefficient firms' demand. But the efficiency of competition depends very much on:

(*a*) Whether there are or are not *absolute* bars to a competitor trying to enter and take over a particular part of the market. 'Absolute' is vital. One of the commonest mistakes in economic analysis is to suppose that the existence of *brakes* on entry, as

2   17

apart from absolute barriers, is inconsistent with full competition. Why this is so—why competition can be effective even though action is delayed—will be shown in a moment.

(*b*) If there are merely delays to entry, not absolute bars, how great the delays are.

'Entry' may mean either that an established firm edges into a market, or that new firms are set up. Barriers (absolute or merely delaying) may include:

(i) *Technical difficulties.* To compete in producing a given class of goods involves employing a certain number of men and investing a certain, possibly deterrent, sum of money in buildings, plant, and working capital. The opportunity to invest may arise only at intervals, as with the farmer who needs to absorb a neighbour's farm in order to create an efficient unit. Transport costs may make it uneconomic (as with gas and electricity) for more than one producer to serve one market; or, as with coal, or retailers, may limit the range over which a group of producers can compete. Skilled labour, research facilities, or financial, technical, or marketing facilities may be centralised in a certain area, or effectively available only to certain (usually large) firms. Time also counts: change and development cannot be accelerated beyond a certain speed without causing disorganisation.

(ii) *Market difficulties.* A market may be in the hands of one or two big concerns; if potential competitors are small, it may be possible to prevent retailers handling their goods, or to wear out their limited resources in a price-cutting war, or otherwise to make their way hard by devices which have nothing to do with relative costs, or with efficiency in meeting consumers' needs. Buyers or (notably in the labour market) sellers may be ignorant, sluggish, or even deliberately misinformed.

(iii) *There may be legal barriers to entry*, as for instance the monopoly conferred on the nationalised industries. There may also be private restrictions to the same effect, organised by trade associations.

(3) *The prevalence of long views.* It often happens that the factors making competition effective operate over rather long periods. The notice taken of them will therefore depend very much on whether business men take long views, or discount the future and insist that a bird in the hand is worth two in the bush.

These factors take effect—whatever their effect may be—by

18

influencing competitors' hopes of future income. The essential question is whether, looking ahead for whatever period seems good to him, the seller of any article or service is or is not led to conclude that he will do best for himself by fixing his price at the level of the costs of an efficient or 'representative' competitor; or whether he sees the chance of profit by raising his price above that level, or failing to lower it to it. The former state may be called one of 'full' or 'effective' competition.

The conditions in which he will conclude that it is most advantageous to charge the competitive price—or, of course, to keep his price the same but make corresponding changes in the quantity or quality of what he sells at it—are grossly overstated in many current text-books. It is certainly true that a business man will be kept to the competitive price if his customers are so well informed and free from personal attachments (that is, from goodwill), and if alternative supplies are so copious and so instantly expansible, that if he swerves by a hair's breadth from the competitive price his entire custom will be taken over in a flash by other firms. That is very close to what happens in certain highly organised markets for standardised products, notably the Stock Exchange. But these are not the only conditions in which it will pay a seller to keep to the competitive price. Typically, in the market for manufactured goods, in retail trade, and in the labour market alike, sellers can, because they are not all replaceable at once or are protected by goodwill, raise their prices in the short run and exploit their customers. But if the pressure of competition, however slight, is continuous, if there are no absolute barriers to entry, and if goodwill is reversible, the seller of, say, a certain manufactured article will have to calculate as follows. By raising his price in the short run he can make an extra profit. But he will lose, let us say, 10% of his customers this year, 10% more the next, and so on. The drain will continue. The time will come when, thanks to this drop in the number of his customers, he is making no more profit than he would have done had he left his price competitive. And still the drain goes on. He must stop it or face bankruptcy. He can do so by dropping his price to the old level. But that will not get him back his old customers. The goodwill which once protected him and held his customers in spite of high prices is reversible. It has been transferred to other businesses and now works to his disadvantage. Lost customers will not return merely because he is now charging no more than his competitors. Either, therefore, he remains content with fewer customers at the old price—and this means that in the end he will be worse off than if he had charged the old price all along and kept his original number of clients—or, to get

19

them back, he cuts his price below the old level and lives for a time on the fat of his monopoly profits; which, goodwill being equal and opposite and his old customers being still slow to return, are drained dry in the process.

He may well, indeed, find it impracticable even to do this. Since goodwill exists, he cannot expect to win back his lost customers at once. On the other hand, he will normally find that when he cuts his price his competitors match him step for step. If his cuts were justified by lower costs, he could afford to laugh at them. But if not, the effect of his cut will merely be to exhaust his reserves without bringing his customers back.

It may not even be necessary for competitors to be able to supply all an inefficient or monopolistically minded firm's customers with 'perfectly reversible' goods, nor need they be able to enter, even in the long run, the whole of its market. In competing with an established firm, where overheads are already given, it is enough to be able to drain off enough customers to make it impossible for the firm to cover its current cash costs; or in the rather longer run these plus depreciation. A new firm, or one reorganising, can of course arrange to do without the marginal customer and charge a higher price for a smaller output protected by a barrier of irreversible goodwill, or some other absolute bar to competitive freedom. But costs, for the smaller output, will probably also be higher. The excess may well eat up the extra profit.

The symbol of full competition, in fact, is not the flash of avenging lightning but the slippery slope. It is open to most sellers to exploit customers, or rest on their oars instead of driving ahead to new achievements, in the short run. But if the conditions mentioned prevail, they will find in the end that they have played the fool to their own undoing. One would expect intelligent sellers to appreciate this.

This must be qualified not only for the fact that all sellers are not intelligent—and in some primitive markets rather few are—but also for people's tendency to discount the future. If the pressure of competition is so light and the barriers to entry so sticky that the loss which ultimately falls upon the monopolist is deferred to a time very remote, he may discount it and proceed with his monopolistic activities none the less. The tendency in that case may well be for firms in an industry where this outlook prevails to end up with, typically, rather few customers and relatively high costs, but only normal profits.

How far do the conditions in which market competition is effective actually prevail? The most complete check, where it is available, is in terms of the results which competition achieves. The neatest and subtlest terminology in which to analyse these is that usual in economics, namely marginal analysis. This cannot usually be applied to results from an individual firm, since business men commonly do not and cannot know the key quantities in marginal analysis. They do not know the shape of the demand curve for their product; the net revenues to be expected from additional production allowing for competitors' reactions and for the lower prices at which it might have to be sold, a key question in the exploitation of monopoly; or even, at times, the cost of producing this extra product. For individual firms, it is necessary to stick to the less precise language of accountancy.

Marginal analysis can, however, be used on data from large numbers of businesses, taken together. Data taken in the right form are only now, since the Census of Production of 1948, beginning to be available in this country. For certain British Dominions (Canada, Australia, New Zealand, South Africa) they have been available much longer. For the United States they were available from 1889 to 1919. Paul Douglas has used these figures to discover whether, in manufacturing industry in these countries, under the control mainly of market competition, prices have actually been just sufficient to cover the costs of a representative firm operating at its normal capacity, and the factors of production have actually been paid the value of their marginal products. He secured some 2,185 observations of American industry from 1889 to 1919 and 1,373 from the Dominions from 1912 to 1937. The factors of production, he found, were in general paid about the equivalent of the value of their marginal products. In 75% of all cases the relation between prices and costs was as predicted by the theory of full competition; or diverged by no more than could be accounted for by errors of calculation. In 20% of all cases there was a marked but not massive divergence. In 4-5% of all cases the divergence was large. These large divergences included cases of the unduly slow working of competition in expanding or contracting trades, and of sweated industries, as well as of straightforward monopoly. These cases are referred to again below.

There are no such full data yet for Great Britain. It is necessary to rely on an alternative approach, consideration of how far each of the conditions affecting competition actually prevails, with only rough qualitative estimates of the results achieved. For this approach it is convenient to take separately evidence on :

(1) the continuity of competition, technical barriers to free entry, and the 'market' limitation which consists of control of the market by one or a few firms ;

21

(2) the other type of market limitation due to customers' ignorance and the existence of goodwill;

(3) legal barriers and voluntary restriction, as by trade unions or trade associations;

(4) the prevalence or otherwise of long views.

See Further Reading List, p. 300.

Chapter 3

THE SCOPE AND LIMITS OF
ECONOMIC COMPETITION

II. IMMEDIATELY SIGNIFICANT DECISIONS WITHIN A GIVEN SOCIAL FRAMEWORK— TESTING THE EFFECTIVENESS OF COMPETITION IN BRITISH CONDITIONS

(A) CONTINUITY, TECHNICAL BARRIERS, MARKET DOMINANCE (NOT DUE TO LEGAL OR VOLUNTARY RESTRICTION). (1) MANUFACTURING INDUSTRY

A FIRST rough test of the continuity of competition, the likelihood that a firm will feel pressure all along its front from businesses similar enough to be able to turn out products meeting the condition of reversibility of goodwill, is the number of firms with similar products, equipment, and business experience present in a given market. For British manufacturing industry, mining, and public utilities the necessary statistics are available from the Census of Production. From the same source it is possible to illustrate market dominance and some of the technical barriers to entry. The investment, for instance, required by a typical firm in each trade can be measured in terms of workers to be employed and horse-power per worker. A first indication of where transport costs are liable to limit the radius of competition, either by tying firms to one of a few sources of materials or by making products costly to distribute, is the weight of materials and fuel used in an industry per worker. The Census statistics of the number of sellers in a given market obviously also illustrate the possibility of market dominance by one or two firms.

Data of all these kinds for British manufacturing industry in 1935 are summed up in Chart I. It seems that about 9% of the employment in *manufacturing* industry in firms employing eleven workers or more in that year was in 'highly concentrated' trades, and a further 17% in trades which were 'weighty' but not highly concentrated. There was 74% in trades with neither of these characteristics.

23

CHART I

British Manufacturing Industries, 1930-5

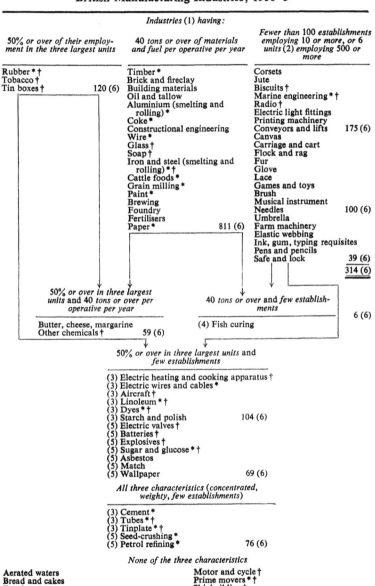

Industries (1) having:

50% or over of their employment in the three largest units	40 tons or over of materials and fuel per operative per year	Fewer than 100 establishments employing 10 or more, or 6 units (2) employing 500 or more
Rubber * †	Timber *	Corsets
Tobacco †	Brick and fireclay	Jute
Tin boxes † 120 (6)	Building materials	Biscuits †
	Oil and tallow	Marine engineering * †
	Aluminium (smelting and rolling) *	Radio †
	Coke *	Electric light fittings
	Constructional engineering	Printing machinery
	Wire *	Conveyors and lifts 175 (6)
	Glass †	Canvas
	Soap †	Carriage and cart
	Iron and steel (smelting and rolling) * †	Flock and rag
	Cattle foods *	Fur
	Grain milling *	Glove
	Paint *	Lace
	Brewing	Games and toys
	Foundry	Brush
	Fertilisers	Musical instrument
	Paper * 811 (6)	Needles 100 (6)
		Umbrella
		Farm machinery
		Elastic webbing
		Ink, gum, typing requisites
		Pens and pencils
		Safe and lock 39 (6)
		314 (6)

50% or over in three largest units and 40 tons or over per operative per year	40 tons or over and few establishments
Butter, cheese, margarine	(4) Fish curing
Other chemicals † 59 (6)	

6 (6)

50% or over in three largest units and few establishments

(3) Electric heating and cooking apparatus †
(3) Electric wires and cables *
(3) Aircraft †
(3) Linoleum * †
(3) Dyes * †
(3) Starch and polish   104 (6)
(5) Electric valves †
(5) Batteries †
(5) Explosives †
(5) Sugar and glucose * †
(5) Asbestos
(5) Match
(5) Wallpaper   69 (6)

All three characteristics (concentrated, weighty, few establishments)

(3) Cement *
(3) Tubes * †
(3) Tinplate * †
(5) Seed-crushing *
(5) Petrol refining *   76 (6)

None of the three characteristics

Aerated waters	Motor and cycle †
Bread and cakes	Prime movers * †
Furniture	Shipbuilding †
Motor repairs	Silk & rayon †
Packing	Apron and overall

Retail bespoke tailoring
Shoe repair
Wholesale bottling
Brass finishing
Leather tanning, etc.
Saddlery
Wooden crates
Chain, nail, screw
China and earthenware
Cotton spinning *
Cotton weaving
Hat and cap
Mackintosh
Scientific instruments
Shirt
Tool
Wholesale tailoring
Wool and worsted
Cocoa and sugar confectionery †
Machine tool †
Newspapers
Wholesale bespoke tailoring †
Electrical machinery †

Bacon curing
Cardboard boxes
Miscellaneous hardware
Plate and jewellery
Linen †
Copper and brass *
Preserved food
Hosiery
Printing and bookbinding
Textile machinery
Cutlery
Holloware
Drugs
Plastic materials, buttons, etc.
Rope, twine, and cord
Shoes
Stationery
Textile finishings *   3,204 (6)

	'000's firms employing 11 or more	Establishments employing 0–10
GRAND TOTALS		
Total employed, Census of Production trades, 1935	7,203	827
Of which:		
Public utilities	698	10
Mining and quarrying	845	10
Building and contracting	502	270
Manufacturing	5,157	537
Manufacturing industries employing 4,000 or more (sample in the Chart)	4,779	
Of which:		
Highly concentrated (50% in three largest units)	428	
Weighty, not highly concentrated (40 tons or over)	833	
Few establishments, not weighty or highly concentrated	314	
None of these characteristics	3,204	
Public utilities †, mining and quarrying †, highly concentrated or weighty manufacturing	2,804	
Rest of sample, building	4,020	
Balance of manufacturing not included in sample in Chart	378	

Sources: Leak and Maizels, 'Structure of British Industry', *Journal of the Royal Statistical Society*, 1945. Sargant Florence, *Investment Location and Size of Plant*, C.U.P., 1948.

(1) All manufacturing industries (i.e. excluding mining, building, public utilities) employing 4,000 or more in 1935.
(2) As defined by Leak and Maizels, *Journal of the Royal Statistical Society*, 1945. A firm or group of firms under one ownership or controlled through majority shareholding.
(3) Under 100 establishments employing 10 or more.
(4) Under 6 units employing 500 or more.
(5) Under 100 establishments *and* under 6 units.
(6) Employment, 1935, in '000's.

* 3·0 h.p. or more per worker. In America in 1909 (Florence, p. 99) the capital invested was about:

3½ times the annual wage bill in industries with   0–0·99 per head.
4½   ,,   ,,   ,,   ,,   1·0–1·99   ,,
7   ,,   ,,   ,,   ,,   2·0–2·99   ,,
10   ,,   ,,   ,,   ,,   3·0 †   ,,

† Mainly establishments employing 500 or more. The numbers of large-plant or heavy-investment industries in the Chart which are *also* concentrated or weighty are:

	Concentrated	Heavy	Both together	Neither	Total
3·0 h.p. or more per worker	9	10	19	7	26
Mainly establishments employing 500 or more	15	3	18	14	32

Steel, which was then merely 'weighty', has since, through national-isation, become highly concentrated as well. So has coal, the biggest source of employment in mining and quarrying. In the *public utilities*, competition in any one locality has always been severely limited by transport costs in the sense not, of course, of the weight of materials or products but of the cost of mains and connections for gas, water, or electricity, which brings it about that only one supplier can economically supply each area. In addition to these main data of the Census, an allowance must be made for the 827,000 workers employed in 1935 in *workshops* with ten employees or less. These of course go to swell the proportion of employment which is not 'highly concentrated'.

It seems on balance that in 1935 the highly concentrated and weighty sectors of the Census of Production trades, together with public utilities, accounted for about 35% of the total employment in these trades. The highly concentrated sector alone, plus the later nationalised industries, together with the public utility trades, accounted for between 25% and 30%.

The various indices of concentration and of barriers to entry tend to focus on one comparatively small area of industry. Nineteen of the 26 industries marked as requiring more than three horse-power per worker are weighty or highly concentrated, as are 18 of the 32 large-plant industries; 15 of the large-plant industries are in the small 'highly concentrated' sector alone. The highly concentrated and weighty sectors are drawn chiefly from the chemical and electrical industries, and from those producing semi-finished materials, together with coal and public utilities. The finishing end of industry is relatively free.

These figures are only first indications of where to look for difficulties in the path of competition. Qualitative studies show that trades dominated by two or three firms may, in fact, be highly competitive. Even two firms may provide each other with complete and vigorous competition all along the line, and the desire for prestige, or to offer a full line of products, or to spread risks, or to create openings for promising young managers, are strong inducements to big firms to branch into many lines. An analysis based purely on national statistics ignores the effect of competition from imports, or, still more important, the need to compete in overseas markets. Sales abroad accounted in 1950 for 23% of the gross domestic product of the United Kingdom, and for much higher proportions in many manufacturing trades, or in shipping. Many apparently monopolised trades appear in quite a different light when set in their international context. Much competition also comes from substitutes, not from within an industry as defined by the Census. The Hoover competes with the brush, rayon with cotton, electricity with gas.

On the other hand, apparently close and competitive relationships may conceal wide divisions within an industry. The textile machinery industry contains sections so thoroughly non-competing that an official enquiry can speak of 'a virtual monopoly'. Rolls-Royces only rather remotely compete with Austin Sevens, though both belong to the motor industry. Differences of this sort should not be exaggerated, for what actually happens is that the Seven is in continuous competition with the Somerset, the Somerset with the Devon, the Devon with the Sheerline, and so on up to the top. A shift of prices at one point in this inter-related system will affect custom all along the line. Nevertheless, breaks in continuity within industries exist; there are few trades where the market has no chinks.

Transport costs must also be examined rather closely. Even in the 'weighty' industries these costs are rarely in Britain, which is after all a country of small distances and good communications, so formidable as to limit a market of necessity to one or two firms. The public utilities are by far the most important exception. Allowance must be made for the fact that many by no means weighty small service industries—garages, dressmakers, bakers—have for convenience to operate near the consumer. But in spite of their dispersal, the number of competitors in any one market for these small service trades usually, as will be shown in a moment in discussing retailing, remains quite large. The same is true of the supply of houses.

Heavy investment per worker, or large size of plant, may make it necessary for new firms, or firms undertaking a major expansion, to proceed by wide and expensive steps. The cost for example—to take an extreme case—of the steel strip mill completed in 1951 at Margam, with all its accessories, was £60,000,000. But this need not prevent vigorous competition between already established plants. Even, also, where the final investment for mass production in a certain line is large, the cost of initial experiment and penetration into the market may be small. A firm usually has a small margin in hand over and above its normal working capacity as reserve against breakdowns, short-term fluctuations, withdrawal of plant for repairs, or simply future needs. This can be used for experiment, and any extra plant needed in the early stages may be small. The United Steel Company spent, at the prices of the 'thirties, between a quarter and half a million pounds at the time when it moved into stainless steel on a large scale. But the initial investment was only a little over £9,000.

27

In many trades the risk of the first steps in a new line can be reduced by hiring all-purpose buildings and services from a trading estate company. The experimenting company commits itself only to pay rent for a time; the estate company knows that vacant buildings can always be re-hired to other firms.

The discontinuity of entry due to the fact that land or mineral resources only occasionally fall vacant is, like that due to the size of plants and largeness of the unit of investment, usually an obstacle to the emergence of new firms rather than to competition between those already established. If the number of these is enough to ensure continuity of competition, and they have reserves of land or resources, competition may be fully effective. But there are one or two important cases in which the sheer physical impossibility of obtaining a base for expansion has seriously impeded competition even between established concerns. This may have happened to some extent in farming, though the evidence is conflicting. It certainly happened in coal-mining before nationalisation; this was, in fact, the main technical justification for nationalisation. In building and town planning it has long been recognised that there is a problem of 'blighted' districts in the older built-up zones just outside the centres of big cities. Buildings in these areas are convenient to the centre and cannot always be effectively competed with by those on land further out. They could be competed with by new buildings in their own neighbourhood. But the land is built up; and without a compulsory purchase order a builder can often obtain a tract of land large enough for satisfactory redevelopment only by paying a monopoly price to the owners of existing obsolescent property. Competition between existing property owners continues, and may quite well keep down rents to the level appropriate in the case of efficiently managed property of that type. But it is competition at, so to speak, a low level of technique, and the entry of those who wish to apply a higher technique is barred.

Market and scientific research facilities, advisory services, capital, and skilled labour and management are and have been unevenly available to firms of different sizes or in different parts of the country; information on this will be given in later chapters. Their quality has often also been unnecessarily low. In this section of this chapter, however, we are concerned with the effectiveness of competition *within* a given social framework, so that what is relevant here is the unevenness, not the absolutely low standard. For the already established and fairly substantial firm this unevenness is not today in general—as usual, there are many individual exceptions—a major barrier to expansion. The districts where new development in a trade naturally originates are those where the trade is already fully established, and skilled men of the right type are likely to be found. The problems of finding and training them elsewhere no longer loom as portentously as they did before the location of industry was taken seriously in hand and modern methods of training developed. Co-operative research associations, canalising scientific knowledge to even the small firm, were by 1947 by way of becoming 'a major influence' in British industry. State and private advisory services, similarly available to all comers, have increased and multiplied. The institutions of the capital market have become steadily more capable of providing for even the small firm.

The new, unestablished firm is in a much more difficult position, particularly over capital. The improvement of the market has not kept pace, so far as this class of firm is concerned, with the State's progressive draining of the main traditional source of capital for the new business, its own ploughed-back profits. It is broadly true that where Chart I shows the number of established and especially of substantial firms to be enough, *prima facie*, to ensure full competition, defects in the supply of money, skill, or knowledge will not make this competition markedly less effective. But these factors have probably prevented the emergence of a certain amount of useful new competition.

The last factor—deliberate control apart—which may prevent competitors from building up their capacity so as to compete effectively with the dominant firm in a market is the time required for growth and change; that is for construction, development, and the associated adjustments in human relations within a firm. Paul Douglas's American and Dominion studies show that this can have real importance. Several of the cases recorded by him in which prices, wages, and profits diverged markedly from competitive levels could be accounted for in this way. But the delay in these cases would be only temporary. This factor is one which affects only the speed at which competition develops. It can rarely if ever impair its final effectiveness.

As a rough working rule, it may be assumed that in British manufacturing industries which are neither weighty nor highly concentrated, the conditions so far discussed are not such as to prevent effective competition. In the trades outside these categories, it would seem that normally:

(1) Competition is continuous.

(2) A firm has to sell its products against others in relation to which its goodwill is 'reversible'.

29

(3) Firms are not so few as necessarily to lead to concentrated control of the market.

(4) Technical conditions may be such as to slow up expansion or the entry of new firms, but are not such as to set any absolute barriers to it, nor to make the steps by which entry proceeds very wide or expensive.

This is not of course to rule out that the competition which these conditions permit may be, as it sometimes is, made ineffective by the others to be discussed below. But so far as the factors hitherto discussed are concerned, competition in these industries, outside the 'weighty or concentrated' sectors, would seem to be effective. The same judgement would apply to building, which does not appear in the body of Chart I. In the weighty or concentrated sectors it is impossible to generalise: the evidence must be judged case by case.

(B) CONTINUITY, TECHNICAL BARRIERS, MARKET DOMI-
NANCE (NOT DUE TO LEGAL OR VOLUNTARY RESTRIC-
TION). (2) RETAILING

A rather similar analysis of the number of sellers and the technical obstacles to entry can be made for the retail trade. Large plants, concentrated control, and heavy capital investment are not features of the retail trade. Though large units exist, small independent shops control three-fifths of the trade. Lack of skill, knowledge, and capital have been marked, but have certainly not operated to stifle new competition. Competition from new firms alone has been massive. In the 'twenties and 'thirties 50–100,000 new names a year appeared in retail and small service business, or 10–12$\frac{1}{2}$% of the existing number in the trade.

Transport costs in retailing—the mobility of the housewife—do on the other hand count a great deal. How far must one, because of them, think of entry into the local groups of competitors as limited? What is the actual number of firms in each competing trade and group, that is the number which the housewife regards as being in easy reach? Is it enough to ensure continuity of competition?

A mass of information on this has been collected in recent years by geographers and town planners. The maximum travelling time beyond which a shopping centre will be regarded as 'inconvenient' seems to be typically 10–15 minutes for local shopping and 20–25 minutes for main centres. Nine out of ten of the town population of Britain live in or around the edges of towns having a 'full' range of shopping services, and most even of the country and small-town population of the Midlands and South live within Saturday shopping distance of them. The bare minimum shopping facilities which town planners regard as convenient in such towns, if newly built in present circumstances of austerity, taking the main centre and one local centre together, may be illustrated by the proposals of the Manchester Plan for a new suburb of about 50,000 inhabitants. In the two centres, the housewife would have access to about a dozen apiece of butchers, bakers, grocers, newsagents, and shoe or shoe-repair shops; half a dozen or more greengrocers, drapers (or women's outfitters), cafés, hardware stores, and cycle, pram, and electrical shops, together with three or four each of a number of others. In a fully developed town of the same size, such as Worcester, these numbers would be three or four times as great. Once again, it is necessary to look carefully at the actual continuity of competition in time, place, and product; the actual reversibility of goodwill, within each market. But it seems that for the urban housewife, at least, the competing group is usually quite substantial. There may be an exception to this in the case of local shopping in suburban areas. But delivery services reach out into even under-equipped suburbs, and 'neighbourhood-bound' shopping, in which main centres compete to only a very limited extent with local, is characteristic only of the poorest and most isolated estates. In the country, the growth and very extensive use of bus and delivery services has meant that for many purposes village and market town form one competing unit. It is chiefly where the number of competitors in the market town itself is small, in what A. E. Smailes classes as 'sub-towns' (perhaps also in his 'towns'), as in Central Wales, that for ordinary shopping the combined total of sellers falls so low as to give *prima facie* ground for assuming that competition is not continuous, or that control of the market is highly concentrated.

(C) CONTINUITY, TECHNICAL BARRIERS, MARKET DOMI-NANCE (NOT DUE TO LEGAL OR VOLUNTARY RESTRIC-TION). (3) THE LABOUR MARKET

In making a similar analysis of the labour market, it is important to remember the limits of the present discussion. The question is always whether competition is effective *within* a given social framework. Is it effective, that is, given existing levels of education, existing class structures, and so on? The importance of this reservation for the labour market is obvious. It is also assumed for the moment that 'remote' or 'diffused' problems, beyond the control of the parties to individual competitive transactions, have been satisfactorily disposed of. Among these is the problem of unemployment. It is

31

assumed—the assumption will be removed later on—that demand is kept high enough to make the number of vacancies at least equal to the number of men looking for jobs.

There is no lack of sellers of labour, except in the most specialised grades or in the most isolated districts; though the number offering skilled labour has, as will be shown in a later chapter, been kept unnecessarily low by lack of facilities for education and training. Sellers' ignorance of openings in other trades and districts has been greatly reduced over the last generation by the Ministry of Labour's various services; though there is still a great deal of it, especially among young workers starting their career. The question, in the labour market, is much more of the number of buyers to whom a seller has access.

The very great majority of semi-skilled, unskilled, and general clerical workers, who make up about 70% of the total in Great Britain, live, in this small and heavily populated country, within daily travelling distance of a considerable number of possible employers, with many more accessible at the price of a change of district. When the economy is fully employed, enough of them are on the move to ensure that an unsatisfactory employer's labour force drains away rather quickly. A fairly large proportion of both factory workers and miners have long accepted as natural journeys of upwards of half an hour each way to work, particularly in the large towns and some of the older mining districts. The equivalent of 25–30% of all men and boys in factory trades, and 40% of women and girls, change their jobs each year. About two-thirds of this movement, in the case of men, is represented by causes other than retirement or dismissal. About 10% of the population moves from one local government district to another each year, even in a time of acute housing shortage. That there are many workers reluctant to move, especially those who are older or have family ties, is shown clearly when big structural changes in the economy are under way, as in the coalfields or cotton districts in the 'twenties and 'thirties, or more generally during the war. The movement required in those cases went far beyond the 'mobile margin'. But that margin is wide enough nevertheless to make competition in the labour market very 'full'. There are few employers of any size, even one as apparently monopolistic as the National Coal Board, who do not have to reckon from year to year with a proportion of mobile workers great enough to be a considerable nuisance if the feeling spreads that they are not being fairly treated.

More specialised workers, and managers, are sometimes more and sometimes less favourably placed. The market for services is often nation-wide—as with teachers or local government officials who move from authority to authority—or may even be international. But the skill of the specialist, and particularly of the foreman or manager, is often largely in the ways of one firm or department, or at any rate of one industry. The farmer is not qualified for a position of similar responsibility, pay, and prestige in any industry but farming; this by itself, apart from any special satisfaction he gets from his position as a farmer, would account for the fact shown by surveys that farmers have little interest in changing their job, whereas farm workers are as willing to move to a new trade as workers of any other class. The farmer can, however, at least change his farm, whereas the company secretary, the superintendent, the foreman, the senior clerk may be tied in effect to one firm. This is all the more so as these senior workers are more often entitled to benefits, as, for instance, under firms' pension schemes, which will be lost if they move. The mobile margin in these higher occupations often consists largely of new entrants: and entrants' choice is still often limited by lack of education or information.

Nowhere, however, except perhaps in farming, do sons follow fathers regularly enough to allow a profession to ignore problems of recruitment altogether. Recent experience suggests that in Britain today there is, as a matter of fact, a rather high degree of continuity of competition between prospective employers of at any rate the commoner types of higher-grade labour, as for instance between the Civil Service, business, the universities, and the professions; or between teaching and social service on the one hand and production and administration on the other. But, because the channel through which the pressure of competition takes effect—the margin of workers on the move—is so often narrower than in the case of the less skilled workers, competition tends to work much more slowly here than with lower grades. This is illustrated by the difference in the rate of adjustment to inflation in the pay of higher and lower grades respectively. Thus wages in 1949, before deduction of tax, averaged 136% above 1938, but salaries only 74%.

(D) CUSTOMER IGNORANCE AND GOODWILL—MANUFACTURING, RETAILING, THE LABOUR MARKET

The remaining 'market' barrier to entry is lack of information on the part of buyers; or, conversely, the goodwill which attaches to sellers whose customers' experience makes them certain of good service.

With known and standard products goodwill may count for little.

3   33

A 3% price difference was enough in the late 'twenties to enable the new Appleby Mills to break down the goodwill of existing sellers of steel plates. In the great produce markets, or on the Stock Exchange, goodwill may not count at all. On the other hand, United Steel's stainless steel rolling mill was installed though 'it was thought probable it would be anything from ten to fifteen years before it would be fully justified by its market'. In general, the significance of goodwill in the market for manufacturing and mining products is limited by the fact that buyers are normally other businesses, and therefore highly skilled.

In retailing, where the commodity as actually sold (an article plus certain services) varies from shop to shop, even in the case of standard goods, goodwill evidently counts very heavily indeed. Retail buyers are also less expert.

In general they buy reasonably, having regard to their own interests as these are understood in their class, time, and place; that is, to that framework of personality, social structure, and social norms which we are for the moment taking for granted. The idea that they are bamboozled by advertisement into an artificial standard of living cannot in general be upheld. The average expenditure on advertising direct to the consumer was, for nine-tenths of the goods and services passing through retail trade in 1938, just over 1% of manufacturers' costs. Consumer information is not a costless commodity; some expenditure is needed simply to make known the presence of goods on the market. The facts seem to indicate that advertising generally stops at this. It takes, that is, the form that theory indicates it would under full competition. Firms spend what is needed to put their products in the picture. If it is suggested they should spend more, they react as if to the suggestion of a price-cut. They recognise that competitors will match their expenditure, step for step; and, as they have no further advantage to offer to customers, beyond what they have already made known by their 'informational' advertising, the result will be more expenditure but no increase in sales. They stop, therefore, at the informational level. This purely informational level will of course be much higher in the case of a new product, building up its goodwill, than with established goods. Advertising does certainly create some bias in favour, for instance, of 'commercial' as apart from 'cultural' goods; but this must be attributed to the inadequacy of information about the latter rather than to too much information about the former. This will be reconsidered in Chapter 11.

There are, however, sections of retail trade where there is real danger of irrationality. Eleven per cent of the sales in retailing in

34

1938 were 'substantially advertised', to the average extent of 6% of manufacturers' cost, and only part of this can be explained by the newness of the product, or other factors consistent with full competition. Largely overlapping with this is a sector where buyers cannot normally be expected to accumulate enough experience. Examples are fast-changing lines in toilet preparations; patent medicines whose results cannot be thoroughly verified by the ordinary user; goods such as heavy furniture, which are rarely bought. These probably account for more than 5% but less than 10% of consumers' expenditure. A small but significant part of general expenditure also goes through the hands of problem families, newly-weds, and the inexperienced male.

In the labour market, goodwill obviously plays a very great part, and more and more so as increasing attention comes to be paid to human relations in industry. It is also often irreversible; the man who has spent years with one firm or regiment will often never feel the same about any other. But ties of this kind have not prevented the existence of the considerable 'mobile margin' of workers referred to above. They must probably be regarded as a delaying factor in competitive adjustment rather than an absolute barrier. Labour exchanges were established before the First World War, and professional personnel management has grown up since. Customers' (hirers') information about the labour available is thus now often good, at any rate in medium to large concerns. Selection procedures have been improved, and sources of supply, under the pressure of full employment, are combed far more thoroughly than in the past. Though defects remain, they must be regarded as brakes on competition rather than absolute barriers.

(E) ORGANISED RESTRAINTS ON FREE ENTRY—MANUFAC-
TURING, RETAILING, AND THE LABOUR MARKET

There has grown up, especially in the last two generations, a vast mass of restraints on free entry into all three of the types of market examined here. Some are imposed by the Government or by local authorities, others by private trade associations or trade unions. The creation of new capacity is limited by capital rationing, building licensing, and town planning or location of industry control. It may also be prevented by legal monopoly, as by patents; or the nationalisation Acts; or the legalised cartels in coal and agriculture before the war; or by trade associations, with or without State encouragement falling short of the grant of legal powers. Existing capacity may be eliminated, as happened in several industries in the 'thirties. This may be done by law, as in cotton under the Spindles Act of 1936, or by private arrangement, as in flour-milling or shipbuilding. The volume of production or sales may be limited by quotas, as in consumer rationing or import and export quotas, and under many trade association agreements. The type of product may be fixed, as in the war and immediate post-war schemes for 'utility' production of clothing and a wide range of consumer goods. Prices may be fixed or raised under trade association agreements, or by tariffs or specific taxation, or by collective bargaining. The supply of raw materials or components may be restricted or cut off under a State allocation scheme, or to enforce a trade association policy. The staff to be employed may be limited by insisting on professional qualifications; and the conditions under which they may be employed are restricted by collective bargaining and the Factory and Public Health Acts.

These restraints are all-pervasive. There are, for example, close on two thousand trade associations concerned with labour matters alone, and trade association and trade union practice extend into every nook and cranny of the economy. Retail prices were fixed before the war for about a third of all goods entering into retail trade. The proportion may well be higher today.

These restrictions, impressive as they are, do not, however, *necessarily* make competition ineffective. The intention, or at least the official intention, of most of the controls in this long list is to leave competition active enough to achieve the results outlined on p. 16. As always in this chapter, we are trying to find out here not whether competition is effective for any and every purpose but whether—a much more limited objective—it is effective in enforcing conformity to standards established *within* a certain social framework, and in cases where any 'remote or diffused' needs have been provided for in other ways. It is a fact, as will be shown in the next chapter, that competition takes only a fitful account of remote or diffused needs and of needed changes in the social framework. And most of the controls mentioned are designed, at least ostensibly, to make good this deficiency. Only in extreme cases, such as coal under nationalisation, do they try to replace or bar market competition altogether. In less extreme cases they may bar competition between existing sellers in a certain market, but leave the market open to competition from imports, or from substitute products, or even from newcomers to the trade. Alternatively, as in the case of certain pre-war controls in agriculture, or of war-time or town-planning controls in retailing, they may bar new entrants but leave the road open to competition among those already in the trade. Let us leave aside for the moment the question whether the various controls over competition do

36

actually succeed where competition fails, that is in dealing with remote or diffused needs or with changes in the social framework. The question here is: do they in fact leave competition free enough to do its day-to-day work of enforcing conformity—as defined on p. 16—to accepted standards within the existing social framework, when no remote or diffused needs arise?

The evidence on this is neither adequate nor up to date. We have not, in particular, adequate information on the effect of the Government and trade controls introduced since 1939. But a broad impression might be something as follows.

First, those who have undertaken the widest investigations in the last twenty years have concluded that there is little evidence that public or private restraints have in general made prices, or wages, or the distribution of production between different lines diverge markedly—more at any rate than they would otherwise have done —from the norms outlined on p. 16, except in the war and immediate post-war years: the years of rationing and really severe and general State controls. Studies by Lucas in the generality of industry, Andrews in manufacturing (including its labour market), Carr-Saunders and Wilson in the labour market of the highly organised professions, and the National Institute of Economic and Social Research in retailing all point the same way. So, on the whole, do the conclusions of the post-war working parties in manufacturing industries and of committees investigating trades such as cement or electric lamps, or practice under the patent laws—cases where marked divergences from competitive norms had been suspected.

There is, for example, little sign that the patent system here has been abused as it has been in America. There is much evidence of trade associations' success in preventing prices from falling as far below the competitive level as they would otherwise have done in the years of depression, or in particular depressed trades. But there is also much evidence that associations become ineffective once they try to raise prices above the competitive level. There is evidence that the standards of the most advanced firms have failed to go forward as quickly as they might. But this is a matter of change in the norms or standards of industry, that is in the social framework. It is not a question of conformity to already established standards.

But a general rule is not a universal rule. There is much evidence of at least minor divergences from competitive norms. There is some evidence, as in flour-milling or electric lamp manufacture in the 'thirties, or in the areas of retailing covered by resale price maintenance, of major divergences. And it can be shown that these divergences, major or minor, would have been much more serious had it not been for forces other than economic competition: the sanctions of public opinion and of the law—or the threat of the law. The Monopolies Commission have found this to be true, for instance, of the electric lamp industry. Many divergences, furthermore, are of a kind which are liable to become worse as time goes on. Restraints are usually imposed in the first place with some regard to competitive prices and production patterns. But even the initial relation between controlled prices and competitive prices is often rather loose (quite apart from any question of malicious intent), since the standard of a representative firm, as defined on p. 16, is not always easy to ascertain; especially where, as in retailing, the service rendered varies greatly from case to case. Intent is, in fact, often malicious. The less efficient firms in a trade will often find ways of resisting the adoption of a standard of efficiency as high or of prices as low as those of a 'representative' firm.

The effort needed to overcome these difficulties may be forthcoming at the start, but not when it is a question of altering prices once fixed. Prices therefore tend to become rigid. This has long been pointed out as a danger with tariffs and quotas in international trade, or wages under collective bargaining. It has recently been shown to be the main danger of price-fixing in retailing and manufacturing, as it certainly proved to be in pre-war price-fixing and production quota schemes in mining and agriculture. Other examples of rigidity have been the slowness of building by-laws to adapt to new techniques, and the difficulty met during and just after the war, in schemes for producing utility shoes, textiles, clothing, or furniture, in combining flexibility with precise standards. This danger of rigidity should not be exaggerated. The flexibility of the British economy in the last generation, a period of rapidly spreading public and private controls, has, in fact, been astonishing. Of eleven million insured workers in 1923, five million were in trades whose employment over the next fourteen years rose by more than 50% or fell by more than 25%. But the danger of inflexibility always exists; and it remains to be seen how far the greatly increased prevalence of public and private controls since 1939 will affect the capacity of the British economy for adjustment in the long run.

As the evidence so far stands, it can be said that legal and private restraints on free entry have not on the whole, in peacetime, made economic competition ineffective in enforcing accepted standards where no remote or diffused issues arise. But there are important exceptions, and cases where exceptions would quickly arise were it not for non-economic pressures.

(F) THE PREVALENCE OF LONG VIEWS

The last great group of factors affecting competition, the prevalence of long views, has been the special study in recent years of the Oxford Economists' Research Group. At the end of the 'thirties this group showed that it is normal business practice to adopt pricing rules which override the possibilities of *short-run* exploitation of markets, and insist that, if disaster is to be avoided over the *total* of a firm's life, prices must be equated to the average costs of a 'representative' firm. Some confusion arose because the Group simultaneously showed the need, when analysing firms' policies, to use the language of accountancy, in which business price policies are framed, rather than that of marginal analysis. Were they really adding something new to the storehouse of knowledge, or simply inventing a new terminology? The later work of P. W. S. Andrews, the Secretary of the Group, made it clear that they were, in fact, adding a new set of conclusions; including that on the normal length of business men's views. The 'spiv' business exists in the minor chinks where the continuity of competition is broken. There are also short-sighted business men, bound for their own undoing. There must somewhere, in trades where the entry of competitors is slow, come a point at which one monopolistic bird in the hand seems more profitable than two of its competitive brethren in the bush; though where, and in what trades, such a point is found has not yet been enough explored. But the dominant impression of the evidence —and one, after all, which merely confirms common sense—is that most business men are in business to stay, and take a correspondingly long view. It is not simply the competition apparent today that matters to them. The competition which may become apparent tomorrow, or three or four years ahead, matters as well. Where an outlook of that kind prevails, competition can be rather highly effective. And the evidence on trade union policies, notably as summed up in a massive recent study by J. Driscoll, points the same way.

(G) CONCLUSION.   THE ROLE OF COMPETITION AND THE MONEY SANCTION

It would be rash to draw general conclusions from evidence for one country, and much of it out of date. But it is clear that as a means of enforcing accepted social standards, and of providing for immediately sensible needs—and remember that it is *only* with these that we are so far concerned—economic competition has in Britain been, and still remains, a powerful tool. In British conditions a high degree of continuity of competition and of reversibility of goodwill are often found. Entry is commonly braked or restricted, rather than absolutely barred. Legal, trade union, and trade association restrictions tend to steady competition round its trend, or make its operation slower, rather than to distort the trend itself. Views are prevalently long, as 'full' competition requires. Economic competition as at present found in Britain can, moreover, as will be shown in later chapters, be improved by removing a number of the obstacles to its efficient working. There is a monopoly sector in British business, and even outside this sector many traces of monopoly can be found. It cannot be seriously argued that economic competition is the only sanction and control mechanism needed. But over a wide area of manufacturing, retailing, and the labour market alike it seems capable in British conditions of securing a fairly close approximation to the results outlined on p. 16.

It does this—to separate for once its two elements—as a result equally of its competitive and of its economic character. Competition between sellers permits precise and diversified adjustment to demand or potential demand. The use of money makes it possible for buyers to express their desires precisely, in a medium such as to register the decisions of millions of buyers immediately, comprehensively, and unmistakably; to deliver the means of further service directly into the hands of those who serve buyers well; and to withdraw them from those whose service is bad—and to do all this without the overhead costs (to be examined in Chapter 5) of deliberate planning, organisation, or control.

It is possible to have the one element without the other. When the top management of a firm fixes the budget for a certain department, that represents monetary control without competition. Competition, in its turn, can be for social prestige or political power as well as for money. These, like money, are measures reflecting an overall verdict on competitors' efficiency. Efficiency may also be measured more directly and in detail in terms of the physical realities underlying this overall verdict. The telephone operator's efficiency, for instance, may be compared with that of her colleagues by her reaction time or the number of her mistakes. There are cases where any or all of these alternatives to economic competition may be needed to supplement or replace it. We come to these cases in the next chapter.

But these observations merely qualify, without contradicting, the main conclusion here. In the field so far covered, of *immediately* felt needs arising out of a *given* social framework, competition and money measurement together offer a unique combination of qualities. They provide an exact, comprehensive, and above all self-registering, self-enforcing, and decentralised measure of good service to society and incentive to provide it. They offer a mechanism of control capable of coordinating, swiftly and precisely, vast numbers of simultaneous transactions in markets as wide as Great Britain, or, indeed, as the world. And over a wide area of British industry, competition works like this not only in theory but in realised fact.

Chapter 4

THE SCOPE AND LIMITS OF ECONOMIC COMPETITION

III. WHERE COMPETITION IS LESS EFFECTIVE

COMPETITION AS A PROCESS CONCERNED WITH LESS IMMEDIATE CLAIMS

BUSINESS MEN, workers, and even consumers in a country like Britain do, as has been said, take a fairly far-sighted view of the decisions they have to make. Even so, among the reasons for making a certain decision there may always be *some* which have their impact very far in the future. However important such reasons may be for humanity in general, they carry little weight with firms or individuals who have to make their decision here and now, or with their competitors. So also a decision may have effects diffused over many people and a wide area. But those immediately involved in making it may have no very compelling reason to give these effects attention appropriate to their actual importance for human welfare.

Even in relation to these 'remote' or 'diffused' cases, competition serves a useful purpose. It sorts out transactions and reduces them to order. It thus creates an orderly background against which the remoter and more diffused issues can be more clearly distinguished. This, for instance, was why Lenin, in the first chaotic years of the Soviet revolution, dropped his first attempts at detailed planning, and restored competition over most of the Soviet economy under the title of the 'New Economic Policy'. Only when competition had sorted out the chaos was it possible to begin the series of Five-Year Plans. Competition also allows freedom to experiment and feel the way when needs are not yet clear. It is often easier and safer to learn how and where competition needs to be supplemented by letting competition run and learning from its experience than by jumping to conclusions from the start.

But this is merely to say that, when 'remote' or 'diffused' effects are present, competition may clear the ground for their consideration. It may dispose of other problems and so make it easier to pick

42

these particular issues out. And it may throw up hints about how they might be dealt with. But, if it is really the case that a particular issue has effects so remote or diffused that individual competitors or competing firms cannot be expected to appreciate their full significance, a situation has arisen with which competition cannot deal. And, in fact, there are four chief types of remote or diffused need which have everywhere to be provided for by some other means.

The first case is the distribution of incomes and wealth. Theoretically, the parties to (say) a wage agreement might stipulate for all the conditions of a just wage, as these will be outlined below in Chapter 8. They could demand:

(1) Equality between the wage and the value of the work done.
(2) Due regard to the worker's cost of living as an individual, a family man, and one expected to be fit for a certain job.
(3) Due regard for the effect of income distribution on employment, or on capital accumulation and the class structure.

But in practice the second and third conditions are too remote. In British industry wages are fairly closely related to work, but only roughly (by way of differentials in favour of men) related to family needs; they are only slowly beginning to be related to national needs at all. The distribution of capital is barely beginning to be a matter for collective, let alone individual, bargaining. As regards both family and national needs the State, with its income tax, its family allowances, and its occasional efforts to provide guidance on national wage or profit policy, has had to step in to fill the gap.

Secondly, there is the general case of basic services, including those whose benefit (or disadvantage) is felt either over longer periods—the case of the conservation of men and resources—or over a wider area than people engaged in current transactions usually take into account. Short and narrow views are particularly dangerous if they involve the neglect of services on which other development depends, or the destruction (or prolonged alienation or impairment) of human life or natural resources. If endowed with the eye of history, the small boy licking a poisonous ice-cream would no doubt prefer to remain alive; but he may have no second chance to gain the experience without which competition can lead to no good results. The individual farmer in East Africa or in the Middle West of America might in theory have studied the genesis of dust-bowls and decided of his own accord to plough along instead of across the contour. It is a matter of history that he did nothing of the kind, and his land was destroyed. Individual citizens of London might have boycotted the firms and government offices which poured in through the last generation to increase overcrowding. They might have refused to buy the bungalows which each year ate further and further into the Green Belt and the market-garden land of Middlesex, and committed the community for two or three generations to come to bad layouts and community design. But these considerations also were too remote, with too little impact on each individual in each short space of time, to be given their due weight without some form of public or cooperative control. Roads, water supplies, smoke prevention, and health and education services are other cases falling under this head.

Services such as these will usually be provided in *some* form under competition. Examples are: private water companies, toll roads, privately financed railways, or nursing homes. It is desirable that some of them should be provided competitively, at least in part; this is true of education. But rarely, if ever, are they or can they be provided under competition in sufficient quantity and quality.

Thirdly, stability, a state of affairs in which expectations are realised, is essential to human welfare. It may have to be enforced against gangsters and speculators, who have an interest in instability. But experience shows it to be unreasonable to expect even the more law-abiding citizens to foresee the consequences of their own actions, as individuals or groups, clearly enough to guarantee stability fully. That—as well as the gangsters—is why it is part of the traditional function of the State to maintain law and order and undertake defence. The importance of a similar steadying influence in the economic field was well understood in earlier ages, but has in recent generations had to be re-learnt. The housewife prefers steady prices even at the risk that they may be higher. The shopkeeper dislikes not only the big stores which undercut him on the basis of lower costs, but also, more justifiably, the other small man next door who upsets the market for a standard article by using it as a loss leader, or cuts prices below costs in a desperate effort to avoid bankruptcy. The worker's whole way of life is coloured by whether his wage is casual or—even though lower on the average—is steady, and by the degree of stability and 'due process' in his relations with colleagues or supervisors. The farmer sells goods whose demand and supply are neither quickly nor easily changed; in the absence of control, demand and supply easily get out of balance. The balance is restored, under economic competition, only by prolonged and violent fluctuations of farm incomes. And farmer, worker, shopkeeper, and housewife alike fear slumps or inflation.

Instability is evil in itself, and reacts on demand and production.

Less is sold at retail of goods whose prices are erratic. 'Stick and dog' rather than high farming is the safest bet in the face of unstable markets. The manufacturer's labour or customer relations are built up over long periods; the disruption caused by a war, or slump, or price-cutting campaign may set back for years the slow, step-by-step process of improving or cheapening the product. The technique of a trade may be such that certain physically productive types of equipment are worth using only if there is the certainty of a fairly steady demand. Both a firm and its customers, trade or retail, in any case usually find continually changing prices and wage rates a nuisance.

So also the threat of unemployment blights the will to work, and inflation and easy profits may loosen the grip of competition and make it ineffective as a means of control. Inflation by itself, the mere fact that buyers' incomes have gone up while the amount of goods and services to be bought remains the same, will not, it is true, make competition ineffective if all prices are instantly adjusted to the new situation. But this does not happen in a country where long views are prevalent and pricing practice is of the kind typical in Britain. There tends to be a time-lag. Prices are not increased until costs of production rise, or business men are satisfied that the increase in money demand is permanent and likely to be reflected in costs in due course, so that they put themselves at no disadvantage by adjusting to it. Until that happens, demand tends to press against the physical limits of capacity and buyers are ready to pay higher prices to marginal firms. These firms are able to keep going instead of having to close down in whole or part, and release men and materials for their more efficient competitors. Inflation, in short, creates monopoly; free entry is limited by the lack of a free exit. Since the time-lag is often more marked in one field than in another—rail fares, for instance, rise more slowly than greengrocery prices, and salaries and pensions more slowly than wages or profits—inflation also distorts the distribution of incomes, and twists the production pattern away from that preferred by consumers in the long run.

Competition does itself lead to a degree of stability, though not a sufficient degree. Shopkeepers, for instance, often find it profitable to observe conventional prices, and adjust to them the quality of what they sell. So do builders in a free market, and, indeed, businesses of all kinds. Much more important, the order which competition imposes on transactions, being based on a large number of independent decisions, is subject in its broader features to the law of large numbers. Statisticians can study and make reliable predictions about it, whether the purpose of these be, as usually with a firm, to adapt policy to the market, or, as often with governments, to devise ways of correcting the market's misdeeds. The trade cycle itself is statistically predictable. This quality of predictability will of course apply much less to particular markets, or sectors of markets, where the number of sellers may be small. But it is found strongly in major markets and the market economy as a whole, and gives economic competition one of its most important advantages over other forms of control.

Fourthly and finally, there are functions which have to be collectively performed because their significance lies precisely in the fact that they are collective. The ceremonial functions of a president or the Royal Family are an example of one sort. A collective bargain is another; it is valued as an expression of solidarity, as well as for the detailed changes it makes in wages or conditions. Separate social insurance schemes, adjusted to occupational risks of sickness or unemployment, were rejected in the Beveridge Report, and in the National Insurance Act of 1946, in favour of the principle 'that men stand together with their fellows'. The common school is similarly a symbol of social solidarity overriding differences of class or race. The family, the neighbourhood, the profession, the works as a social unit, represent other solidarities of this kind.

In cases of group solidarity like these, economic competition plays an ambiguous part. It makes it easy for even small groups to become conscious of their identity and take collective action. There must be some control over the activities of these groups in the interest of the larger communities to which they belong. But competition provides this in such a way as still to leave each small group in a very real sense master of its own fate. The group has to adjust to the impersonal forces of the market. But it, and it alone, makes all the conscious and deliberate decisions involved. To that extent, competition is the charter of the small group's freedom. But competition is also the charter of individual freedom, and individualism often leads also to the disruption of existing solidarities. And by failing to provide for other remote or diffused needs competition may aggravate this: by permitting bad town planning, for instance, or a wrong distribution of industry, or unstable or wrongly distributed incomes.

The effects of disrupting existing solidarities, of ignoring the problems of conservation and basic services and the need for stability, or of a wrong distribution of incomes, are liable to be cumulative. The rich, because they are rich, also get the best and most profitable chance in life. The sweated worker, because he is underpaid, cannot live well enough to keep his skill and strength, and is therefore paid less. To live at all he accepts longer hours, draws in his wife and children, and becomes still less able to resist oppression. The trade cycle, once started, is self-perpetuating. A defect in the balance of payments with one country may, unless specific steps are taken to seal off that country, lead to a contraction of trade all round, in order incidentally to close this one gap. The wheat farmer, when his income drops, grows still more, and this causes the price to drop (since the demand for food is inelastic) even more than in proportion. It was thus that Britain, as an importer of such primary products as wheat and an exporter of finished goods, was able during the depression of the 'thirties to enjoy a rising standard of living at the primary producer's expense. And the disruption of social groups may lead to a degree of 'social poverty' such that people no longer even feel the need to preserve or add to those that they have left.

It does not necessarily follow that, because there are remote or diffused costs and claims to consider, some conscious or deliberate mechanism of control, or deliberate sanction, must be brought in to supplement competition in respect of them. The supplementary sanction may be public opinion, not politics; the supplementary mechanism of control may be consultation, not direction. Business practice in Britain looks more to the long run and the common interest than that of an Eastern bazaar. That is due to differences in public opinion even more than in the law. The conclusion is simply that there must in these cases be *some* supplement to competition: that implies nothing as to what the supplement is to be.

COMPETITION AS IT AFFECTS THE SOCIAL FRAMEWORK IN WHICH IT OPERATES

Economic competition has been considered so far as a process operating within a certain framework of personality, social norms, and social structure, and a certain physical and biological environment. This 'social framework' sets the standards which the market enforces. But what of the question, not of enforcing standards or using the existing social structure, but of building new structures and of setting the standards to be enforced? Remember that in all this Part we are considering problems of production, and assuming that decisions about what is to be produced have already been taken. The 'standards' and 'structures' in question therefore concern such things as the qualities to be expected by a 'representative' firm of its executives, the introduction of new techniques, the raising of norms of output, or the establishment of new firms or plants. What, in fact, does economic competition contribute towards changing the social framework of production, so as to make it better fitted to do what society wants of it?

The social framework determines the social processes within it; but the social processes continually reshape the social framework. Economic competition, as a form or part of social process, makes its contribution to this. But it is a rather erratic contribution. It arises out of the wide freedom which competition leaves to competing individuals and groups to experiment and choose their own road. There is much evidence from both industrial and general sociology that imposed changes tend to meet more resistance than those which people are left free to work out and decide for themselves. By leaving them this freedom, competition smooths the path of change. On the more positive side—as apart, that is, from merely removing obstacles to change—freedom to experiment is an essential element in all genuinely new development, whether in scientific research, in business, or in the public or voluntary social services. Leaders must be free to feel their way forward, and so under competition they are. Since there is no sharp dividing line between routine administration and structural change, they may, and often do, by this piecemeal and tentative advance, complete and install new standards without any further action being required.

But to permit is not to cause. Economic competition *forces* firms to conform to the prices indicated by the best technical standards of the day, or else to go out of business. But it only *encourages* them to undertake the development of new standards, in the hope that by breaking through the continuity of competition into a temporary and (perhaps) patent-protected monopoly extra profits may be earned, or extra prestige obtained. The inducement is relatively weak. The loss motive, as has often been pointed out, is usually a far more powerful incentive than the profit motive, or even the motive of public service. The hope of profit itself becomes less the nearer competition comes to the 'full' standard and the quicker and more continuous the follow-up of new developments by competitors. There is such a thing as the 'competition of dullards', which enforces low existing standards, and is in that sense 'full', but fails to provide an effective inducement to advance to new and higher standards.

It is not enough to invent a new standard or technique; someone must do the expensive and risky work of applying it and developing it to the point at which it becomes a matter of routine. He may also have to take the unpleasant step of rendering obsolete existing capital or workers' skills, and to face the laborious though no doubt pleasanter task of building up a new firm or institution. Once the ball starts to roll, there may be little difficulty; if a new practice is sound, competitors will have to fall into line. But it is precisely with the 'threshold costs' or risks, or social frictions, that the difficulty arises. Patents, or some other inducement from outside the competitive system, are often needed to persuade the pioneer to take the first plunge.

This is all the truer since, over and above the difficulties peculiar to and arising directly out of changes in the social framework, the effects of these changes are often remote or diffused; and their remote or diffused repercussions will not always be favourable. The benefit, for instance, from installing basic services in an under-developed country—roads, water supplies, schools—is often too remote to be attractive as a commercial proposition. The innovator is as likely as not to be something of an individualist and a danger to group solidarity. He upsets the existing ordered rhythm and stability of life, and spreads the penetrating fear that 'something may happen'. He may touch off a short- or long-term boom or slump. He is as likely as not to upset the distribution of incomes, or, in his enthusiasm for immediate success, to ignore good conservation practice. And all these disturbances may prove cumulative, as with other remote or diffused influences. Marx was wrong in maintaining that the social disturbances let loose by the Industrial Revolution must necessarily cumulate to the point where 'the capitalist husk bursts asunder. The knell of capitalist private property sounds.' But it would have been perfectly correct to expect this to happen if these forces were left to work themselves out under competition alone.

The special difficulties of change in the social framework in itself, as apart from its remote and diffused effects, may be illustrated from any of the three fields of social (including technical) norms, social structure, and personality. Taking first social norms, it can be shown that in 1935-9 output per man-hour in American manufacturing industry was nearly three times as great as in Britain. But experience shows that, since American firms only indirectly and to a limited extent compete with British, the mere knowledge that these superior technical norms exist does not necessarily lead to their rapid adoption in Britain. Some agency, such as, from 1948 to 1952, the Anglo-American Council on Productivity, is needed to see that ideas are fed from the one system into the other. A major factor in American superiority is heavier investment per worker. The State, in Britain, therefore found it necessary to intervene to increase the proportion of the national income used for investment (including depreciation) by about half in 1948 as compared with 1938. The Working Parties which reported on some seventeen British industries just after the war concluded broadly that competition would spread new techniques once they were launched, but that definite machinery was needed to launch them; or rather to bridge the gap between the research laboratory and the factory bench. Their recommendations took effect in the Industrial Organisation and Development Act of 1947, and the establishment of Development Councils under it. The function of these councils, as illustrated by the most outstanding of them, the Cotton Board, is precisely to change the social norms—the culture—of their industries; that is, to launch new ways of doing things, not only on the technical but often also on the human relations side.

The most remarkable study in industrial relations in Britain in recent years bears the title of, precisely, *The Changing Culture of a Factory*. It shows how a push from outside the normal competitive working of the product and labour markets was needed to make even a firm where the most advanced established practice in labour relations was a matter of routine—a 'representative' firm in the sense defined above—profit by further knowledge about human relations which had long been available. The long battle of the I.L.O. to raise the norms of industrial relations, or David Lilienthal's account of how the Tennessee Valley Authority had not so much to develop the valley as to help valley people develop it for themselves, are other illustrations of the same point. R. S. Edwards shows, from the experience of the cooperative research associations in British industry, how hard it may be in competitive industries to find firms willing to take the first step. His study also brings out the importance of threshold costs. Other studies have shown how 'levels of expectation' establish themselves among groups of workers, and lead to different standards of output under apparently similar conditions; and also how difficult it is to break away from these standards once they are formed. And we shall touch again below on the similar way in which new standards are built up.

Competition is only partly successful either in bringing new social structures into existence or in smoothly and painlessly disposing of, or drastically re-shaping, those now superfluous. Institutions for the supply of certain classes of capital, for instance. The London capital market, though (in some parts of it at least) a text-book example of efficient competition, has never succeeded in creating adequate institutions to serve the small firm. Or, simply, new firms. The life of the new entrant into small business has for generations been nasty, brutish, and short. Of 12,348 new names in a list of trades in the business directories of six major towns in 1928–30, 2,760

remained over the same shop door in 1939. Most of the other 78%
went out in their first three or four years. This massacre of the
innocents could certainly have been reduced by better advisory
facilities, linked perhaps to more adequate capital supplies. But
competition threw up no mechanism for these purposes, though
trade associations and, after the war, the Government made at least
a few beginnings.

So also institutions such as the Development Councils or the
Anglo-American Council on Productivity did not emerge from
competition. The vast but short-lived change in the structure of
industry needed during the war was of a kind which, by common
consent of even the enemies of planning, no competitive market
could have carried through as smoothly or quickly as State direction. A wide range of new industries, experience since 1937 has shown,
can operate economically in what were then the depressed areas of
Britain. But those with experience of these areas also agree that far
fewer plants in these industries would have sprung up there than
have actually done so, even in 1945–8 when these were the only
areas in the country with labour to spare, had the Government not
given an initial push, including special aid towards meeting the high
costs of a new plant in its first year or two. The difficulty of starting
a new, and in the long run perfectly economic, business in an under-
developed land, where services have to be created and workers
trained, has been a text-book example for generations, and has been
strikingly illustrated (groundnuts!) in British schemes for colonial
development since the Second World War.

Changes in the structure of the labour force often also need
special help. The Webbs two generations ago were pointing out the
contrast in the middle of the nineteenth century between the fates
of the handloom weavers and of the hand bootmakers when their
industries were mechanised. The demobilisation of the army of handloom weavers was left to competition. As it turned out, they competed but did not demobilise. They hung on to the bitter end on
falling and eventually starvation wages. For not enough of them
saw, as individuals, good enough reason at any given moment to
move out into another trade. It would have required an overall
policy and some collective action to get enough of them out for the
rest to prosper. The bootmakers' case pointed the moral: for there,
when machine competition began, the trade unions overrode competition and enforced a clean cut. Wages were maintained, or raised,
for those who stayed in the hand trade. Those not skilful enough
for the very high-grade work, which alone remained profitable when
done by hand, were pushed firmly out to work the new machines—

to their own and their colleagues' very considerable benefit. Unfortunately, the lessons of history are not always learnt. The history of the handloom weavers was repeated in that of the miners, cotton operatives, or farm workers in the years of long-drawn-out decline, from 1924 to 1939, when wages in these trades were at or under 50s. a week for a skilled adult man.

The problem in an industry faced with redundancy is to eliminate not only workers but firms. From this point of view the history in the depression years of coal and cotton stands in gloomy contrast to that of flour-milling and shipbuilding. In the former industries the closing of surplus pits or mills was left largely, and at times wholly, to the forces of competition. In flour-milling and shipbuilding by contrast, it was vigorously pressed by strong trade associations. The flour-milling plan provided also for the displacement of workers; they were helped, financially and otherwise, to find work in other trades, or were retired on a decent pension. Coal and cotton, as a result, have remained problem industries even into the post-war years. But flour-milling and shipbuilding have known few problems, apart from those arising directly out of the war. In shipbuilding, wartime expansion followed by post-war contraction caused for a time a mild problem of unemployment. In flour-milling, the problem has rather been one of excessive prosperity.

Paul Douglas's study, quoted earlier, brings out that one reason why prices and profits may diverge markedly from competitive norms is, precisely, that labour forces or plant capacity may not grow or contract fast enough to keep pace with major changes in demand. This may be no great disadvantage if it leads to abnormal profits and high wages in expanding industries. For this provides an inducement to take up new lines and methods and break away from the 'competition of dullards'. But delay in scaling down contracting industries has often very different and more painful results.

A study just after the end of the war by a major engineering firm, with factories in Britain, Canada, and the U.S.A., illustrates the danger that competition may fail to lead to sufficient development of personality. A comparison of productivity on identical work in the firm's British and American factories showed British productivity to be only about 60% of American. It would probably have been higher but for purely wartime disorganisation. Allowing for this, the firm proceeded to analyse the reasons for the difference. Probably a sixth was due to factors outside its control, as, for instance, the availabilities of the right quality of steel in America but not, at that time, in Britain. Another sixth could be attributed to bigger and better machinery in the American plants. The balance,

52

two-thirds, was attributed to the human factor. British workers did as hard a day's work as American; but with their hands, not their heads. American managers were better educated, more dynamic in action, better organisers. In spite of the coexistence for years in the same firm of the two standards of work and, above all, management, the spark had not leapt across the Atlantic. The reports of the industrial teams which visited America in 1949–51 under the sign of the Anglo-American Productivity Council have shown that these findings on British and American personality are not an isolated case.

This discussion of competition and the social framework has been rather weighted on the side of criticism of competition. Let us restore the balance. It is true that desirable changes in social norms and structures and in personality patterns will not necessarily be brought about by competition alone and unaided. For:

(a) competition permits such changes but does not compel them; and

(b) those changes it does bring about, even though justified and desirable in the light of those considerations present to the mind of the people immediately involved, may be undesirable in the long run or from the point of view of people in a wider circle.

But do not conclude at once that competition is a bad mechanism to use for promoting changes in the social framework. For there are also the other considerations with which this discussion began, namely:

(a) that competition is a highly decentralised mechanism which leaves the widest possible freedom to experiment; and

(b) that imposed changes in the social framework tend to meet more resistance than those which people are left free to work out and decide for themselves.

It would seem that:

(1) Where the way ahead is not clear or agreed, competition may be the most effective way of discovering and starting along it.

(2) If, however, the direction and scope of change in the social framework are clear and agreed, it may be more economical to cut through the slow and uncertain process by which economic competition may or may not bring them about, and to enforce them by some other mechanism. Which other mechanism this is to be will depend on the particular circumstances in each case. It will not necessarily be direction.

Confusion is often caused, at times when the social framework is changing rapidly, because prices and production patterns are manifestly not conforming to competitive standards—neither to the standards set by the old social framework nor to those emerging from the new—and yet incomes and worker and consumer satisfaction may be increasing. Such a situation must be judged in terms of three levels of development:

(1) Prices and production patterns conform to the competitive standards set by the older, now superseded, social framework.

(2) The social framework has been changed so as to set new and higher standards, but prices and production do not yet fully conform to these standards.

(3) Prices and production conform to the new standards.

Welfare in situation (3) will certainly be higher than in (1) or (2). But welfare in situation (2) may well be higher than in situation (1).

Situation (2) is, in fact, of the kind which may particularly easily arise in an underdeveloped country, or one which has leeway to make up. Such a country has a known target of technical efficiency to aim at, and it is appropriate that non-competitive mechanisms should be used to reach it. If perhaps on the way the pattern of prices and production departs somewhat from the (new and rising) competitive standard, that is regrettable, but not necessarily a ground for condemning the use of what might be called the planning short cut. In an advanced country, the proportion of genuine innovations will be greater and the case for the free, experimental progress permitted by competition stronger. But even then, progress can as often be measured by the number of firms which have burst ahead into—for the time being—a monopolistic position as by conformity to what may be an old-fashioned competitive norm.

Chapter 5

DIRECTION

THERE is no clear or rigid dividing line between cases where competition is appropriate and those where the right mechanism is direction. It is usually possible to find *some* degree of monopoly, and, therefore, *some* case for direction, even in markets which are predominantly competitive. No distribution of incomes will ever seem wholly fair to all concerned. 'Group solidarity' is a very wide term, and one which covers many by no means respectable relationships. It is obviously not correct, for example, to say that every form of behaviour which offends the village gossips should be stopped. But it is not easy to say just where the boundary lies between this and the other community solidarities which need to be upheld. 'Basic services' can also be stretched a very long way. In the days of sweet rationing, a large part of public opinion stretched it to include gob-stoppers.

In any case, direction can often be substituted for competition without any particular gain or loss, even in cases for which competition is a fully effective form of control. Many purposes can be as well attained—so far, at least, as the action immediately in question is concerned, disregarding remoter consequences which will be considered below—by issuing an order, as by leaving people to make their own choice.

Between direction and competition there thus lies a no-man's-land. To see who is to occupy this, it is necessary to examine in more detail what the mechanisms alternative to competition, and in the first place direction, can do. Economic direction may take many forms and operate on any scale. But to find what it can and cannot do, it is convenient to concentrate on its most massive, extensive, and, often also, detailed use in modern times by the State in peace or war: what is usually known as government economic planning.

The central government, local government, and public corporations are responsible in Britain today for about half of all investment in fixed capital (Table 1). They spend in their own establishments well over half the money available for civil and military research. They trade overseas. In the home market their purchases of goods and services for current use have amounted in recent years

.TABLE 1. Public authorities' share in investment, U.K. 1951

			Gross fixed capital formation[1] £ million
Central Government			
Trading	51		
Other	107	158	
Local Government			
Trading	40		
Housing	284		
Other	115	439	
Public Corporations		370	
TOTAL PUBLIC			967
Companies		700	
Private persons and non-corporate enterprises		195	
TOTAL PRIVATE			895
TOTAL			1,862

National Income and Expenditure, 1946–51, Central Statistical Office.
[1] This excludes, in addition to stocks and enterprises' working capital, the very important category of household durables. See Chapter 9, Table 1.

to 18–20% of the gross product of British trade and industry (Table 2), and to 20–22% of the combined total of public and private purchases for current consumption. The proportion naturally varies (Table 2) from sector to sector. It is as little as 1% in the food, drink, and tobacco industries. It is on the contrary over two-thirds in the sector which includes education, health, and public administration and defence. In addition to their own direct activities, public authorities maintain widespread controls, and exert extensive influence, over non-governmental economic action. They control borrowing and investment through taxation, statutory control of capital issues, their influence on the banks' credit policy, and building licensing. They subsidise research in the universities and industrial research associations. They ration consumption and raw materials, redistribute incomes through taxation, impose standards of production —of pure food, for example, or under utility schemes—and fix prices or retailers' margins. They fix certain wages, control the engagement of labour, and promote or impose arbitration in industrial disputes. They license exports and imports, impose import duties,

TABLE 2. Public authorities' share in current expenditure on goods and services, U.K., 1948

£ million

	Total sales, including sales to other industries and trades	Sales to final buyers					Total
		Persons and private non-profit-making bodies	Public authorities	Exports	Fixed capital formation	Stocks	
Agriculture, forestry, fishing	956	405	19	10	—	32	466
Mining and quarrying	520	85	7	35	4	−3	128
Food, drink, tobacco	1,590	1,339	20	90	—	60	1,509
Other manufacturing	5,136	1,375	335	1,252	773	389	4,124
Building and contracting	1,110	260	85	—	517	30	892
Electricity, gas, water	430	195	15	5	36	2	253
Transport, distribution, other production and trade	3,983	2,379	205	445	69	—	3,098
Public administration and defence; public health and educational services; ownership of dwellings; domestic service to households; services to private non-profit-making bodies	1,436	449	987	—	—	—	1,436
Imports	2,196	590	122	58	35	−20	785
Adjustment for sales by final buyers	—	−30	—	31	−20	—	−19
TOTAL—GOODS AND SERVICES AT FACTOR COST (net of taxes and subsidies)	17,357	7,047	1,795	1,926	1,414	490	12,672

National Income and Expenditure, 1946-51, Central Statistical Office.

57

TABLE 3. Employment in certain public services, Great
Britain, April 1951

Civil Service, non-industrial	679,300
Local government service, excluding trading services, schools, fire service, police, etc.	648,200

From *Monthly Digest*, Central Statistical Office; and Census of 1951.

and apply exchange control. They consult through a network of
committees with private agencies in every field, including not only
business and trade unions but voluntary associations—the Churches,
the universities, arts organisations, social-service agencies—of
every sort and kind.

For all these purposes they employ (Table 3) a million and a
quarter Civil Servants and local government officers, not counting
those engaged in trading services, schools, hospitals, or the Armed
Forces or police. This is between 5 and 6% of the whole working
population.

The curve of State intervention rises and falls. It has risen high
since the Second World War, with the establishment of the new
model Welfare State. But it is, above all, the planning of the war,
from 1939 to 1945, that provides a wealth of evidence on the scope
and limits of State direction; for in the war years direction was
carried to a point unequalled before or since. Just on half the population of working age in 1944 was in the forces or on direct government work in manufacturing industry. Of the rest, all but the elderly
and mothers with young children were subject to conscription; and
even outside the munitions sector, production and consumption
were planned and regulated in detail. This vast and complicated
effort of organisation revealed the limits of direction as if under a
microscope. It happened also that during the war there were drawn
into the Civil Service a number of men trained in social, and particularly economic, theory. These men, having held high positions
in the machinery of State direction, returned to academic life and
had time and opportunity to work out their conclusions.

The case for State direction for the purposes of war and the
Welfare State, is today not seriously disputed in general, though
there may be arguments over this item or that. The Welfare State
has arisen precisely because economic competition is not always an
effective social control. Sometimes it does not exist; there is monopoly. Often it fails to provide for remote or diffused effects or for
changes in the social framework. The State, though not the appro-

58

priate agency to deal with all the cases where competition fails, is appropriate in many.

The difficulties which lead to State direction in wartime are different, but classifiable under the same headings. The conduct of a war is, to the ordinary citizen, a *remote* activity. Only the Government has or can have the knowledge to decide the best strategic plans. Short of government action, there is often nothing to bring home to the citizen even his personal duty in the war.

Total war also involves *changes in the social framework* of a kind which the economic market is unlikely to carry out, or to carry out well. The citizens must put up with a tenth of the motoring, a third of the hardware and furnishings, half the eggs and fruit, and two-thirds of the sugar, meat, and clothing they enjoyed in happier days. Vast numbers must change their jobs and place of work. Large sums must be invested in buildings and machines whose long-term value is problematic. This must be done at top speed, since time is the scarcest commodity in wartime. It is doubtful whether the market could in any case produce the necessary changes within the time available. It would be necessary to allow wages and profits in the war sector to rise far above those in others, and this at a time when the total amount of consumable goods was being severely cut. The result would be great windfall gains to many who found it easy—perhaps because they were in the right occupations already—to switch to war production, or whose normal consumption habits fitted the wartime pattern; but very severe hardships for those who, because of age or health or specialised skill, or because their services even in wartime were needed in the civilian sector, found it hard to take advantage of the new opportunities.

War also necessarily creates *monopoly*. A condition of free entry, and therefore of effective competition, is that there should be a free exit for the inefficient firm. But in war the demand for goods and services of all kinds is, in the interests of bare survival, unlimited. It presses right up to the margin of such production as is physically possible. In these circumstances, even the inefficient firm (or worker) can rely, in an open market, on covering its costs.

Yet there is unanimity among those who have written on this recent experience, whether of war or the Welfare State, that State direction, however necessary, is in many ways an unsatisfactory method of control. The area of the nation's life which can usefully be controlled by the Welfare State is limited, and wartime planning, essential as it was, worked very crudely.

'These inevitable limitations in the planning process in wartime,' writes a former chief statistician of the Ministry of Aircraft Production,

59

'resulted in waste of resources. This waste did not in general take the form of the unemployment of resources, and it was, therefore, in the main not obvious to the public. . . . It led to the Services being provided with inferior aircraft, to aircraft being produced for which there was some vital component missing, or to excess components or spares being produced which merely accumulated in Service Department stores. . . . The sceptics in M.A.P. asserted, and there is little doubt that many of the firms agreed with them, that aircraft were produced in spite of, and not as a result of, M.A.P.'s planning activities.' (Ely Devons, in *Transactions of the Manchester Statistical Society*, 1947.)

In the field of the Welfare State, the most striking fact is the change in the tone of discussion since the first post-war years, when experience of peacetime State planning was limited. The first annual government *Economic Survey*, that for 1947, noted certainly that State control was less easy in peacetime, because the proportion of work done directly on Government account was much smaller. It also observed that:

'Under democracy, the execution of the economic plan must be much more a matter for cooperation between the Government, industry, and the people, than of rigid application by the State of controls and compulsions.'

It went on, however, to add in the next breath that:

'The Government must lay down the economic tasks for the nation: it must say which things are the most important and what the objectives of policy should be . . .'

It must have the decisive influence. It was already in a position to plan for a year or two ahead. The data on which longer term plans could be based were under active preparation.

This confident declaration was unfortunately timed. The most dramatic breakdown of planning since the war was the failure of the Ministry of Fuel and Power, in the winter of 1946–7, to adjust allocations of coal to supplies. Stocks fell so low that, in the cold weather of February 1947, a large part of British industry in the Midlands and South had to be closed down by government order. Two million workers were thrown out of work, and, in the widespread shut-down of plants, the presses printing the *Economic Survey*'s declaration of faith in planning were brought to a standstill. The lesson, reinforced by much other experience, was not lost. Till a new danger of war arose, the tendency was to set closer and closer limits to actual direction by the State. Later *Economic Surveys* give the impression, not of the Government dominating the scene, but of a situation in which the Government is only one, though a major, participant. 'Which things are most important', and what is to be done about them, are determined as much by consumer preferences or trade union policy or the international situation as by the State, whose role is to adjust to the often unpredictable behaviour of others rather than to lay down hard and fast lines into the future. The State figures as concerned in detail with only a rather small range of issues. Even for these, the tendency has been to use what has come to be known as 'voluntarism'—a combination, to be discussed in the next chapter, of competition with consultation—and to keep direction in the background. Most studies of State economic direction, even those (with the notable exception of Dr. Balogh's) specifically of the political Left, have concurred in this.

THE LIMITS OF DIRECTION. (A) CASES TO WHICH DIRECTION IS INAPPLICABLE

On the face of it, the fact that the results of direction have so often been unsatisfying might spring from either of two causes. First, it is obvious that direction, whether by the State or otherwise, is not the automatically indicated mechanism for dealing with *all* the cases where competition breaks down. A direction can profitably be issued only where the directing authority already knows, or can through the machinery of direction discover, what needs to be done. There are quite a number of cases where 'remote' or 'diffused' factors have to be taken into account, or changes in the social framework brought about, and competition unaided is likely to prove more or less inadequate; but where there is no reason to suppose that any authority has the knowledge which would permit an effective direction to be issued. Examples are:

(1) Where it is wished to promote and encourage new developments more than would be the case under competition, but there have not yet been enough new initiatives to point the way for a direction : a typical state of affairs in, for instance, a new field of fundamental scientific research.

(2) Where the direction of advance can be forecast; that is, only a foreseeable change in social norms and structures, in personality and the physical and biological environment is required. But where also there are many independent evaluations of what changes are needed, and these have not yet been combined into a consistent and unified policy on which a direction could be based. Where, that is, many of the factors in establishing policy are 'remote or diffused' from the point of view of any one person or group involved.

(3) Where no change in the social framework is needed, but some

of the factors involved in operations within it appear 'remote' or 'diffused' to the executive responsible for issuing a direction. That is, the full implications of his decision for the whole time and area over which it will be in force are not clear to him, and cannot be made clear by use of the machinery of direction alone. They must be clarified by further initiatives, judgements, and advice—that is to say, by more acts of will of a kind difficult to compel—from persons other than the executive himself. They cannot be settled merely by, for instance, ordering the collection of more factual information.

Direction, in short, is likely to prove useful only where it is already known what changes in the social structure are required, and by what means these changes, or routine activities within a given social structure, are to be carried out. This finding, obvious and common sense though it be, has certainly been neglected both in industrial management and in economic direction by the State. In industry, for instance, attempts are often made to apply direction before policy has been made clear to all concerned and agreed with at least the majority of them. Industrial sociology supplies a mass of evidence of the active and still more the passive resistance which individuals and groups at all levels, from the small working group up to the firm, the industry, and the profession, put up against these premature attempts to direct them, and of the loss of production and welfare to which this often leads. It seems probable that many policies of the Welfare State would also have proved more successful had they been based on recognition that resistances of this sort are likely to arise. Sociologists, for instance, point out how the building and management of housing estates by local authorities creates a 'bureaucratic environment', in which people are apathetic and un-interested in building their local community; an atmosphere which might have been avoided had use been made of tenants' cooperatives rather than of municipal enterprise. Others have raised similar questions about the National Health Service. Would health centres, for instance, be more successful in positively improving health, as apart from merely healing disease, if they were run not, as under the Health Service, *for* the people, but, as in the original experimental Health Centre at Peckham, *by* those whom they serve?

There is no doubt, then, that direction has often been applied in cases where on the face of it there was no reason to expect it to succeed. But this will certainly not account for the defects of direction which became apparent during the war. For the war was a time when, by common consent of the vast majority of the people, the whole of the nation's life was subordinated to one agreed policy, that of winning the war. Policy was clear, and so in large measure were the means of carrying it out. For the war was won—and necessarily so, seeing its fairly short duration—by the development and more intensive application of techniques already well advanced before it. From the Spitfire to radar and the atom bomb, the scientific and engineering side of the war effort was a matter of applying previous fundamental knowledge rather than of laying new foundations. And wartime social policy reflected ideas and trends which had grown up over two generations, and had arrived by 1939 at the edge of their final break-through to nation-wide acceptance, and did, in fact, achieve such a break-through between 1942 and 1948.

THE LIMITS OF DIRECTION. (B) THE TIME FACTOR

If direction, in these conditions, proved to have limits, there must have been some further reasons for this. These reasons can be summed up as the time factor. In the last resort, the limits of direction are set by the capacity of the directors to grasp and sort out the issues involved, quickly enough to keep pace with the events: that is, by the amount of work they can handle in a day. This is partly a matter of will. If State direction, as actually tried in recent years, has been crude and sometimes ineffective, this might have been because the Ministers and Civil Servants were able to do more but failed to do it. But this cannot be seriously maintained in the actual conditions of Britain since 1939, or 1945. Of the five leading members of the Labour Government of 1945–51—they had of course already been working at full stretch through the war years—one collapsed from overwork and had to leave politics, a second died, also largely from overwork, and a third near the end was seriously ill. A fourth was awarded an unexpected holiday for giving away the Budget. Only one of the five served through to the end, apparently intact. If this were merely the record of one group of five men, none of them young, the high rate of illness might be taken as a coincidence. But, in an editorial revealingly headed 'The Price of Administration', *Public Administration*, the Journal of the Institute of Public Administration takes occasion from the premature death of the Deputy Chairman of the National Coal Board to point out that the record of senior Civil Servants, though less well known to the public, has been the same. It cannot be said that those responsible for State direction have spared themselves. Nor can it be said that, as a group, they lacked either intellectual brilliance or administrative ability. If this is true of peacetime it was still truer of the war years, when goodwill reached a peak, and the State machinery, political and administrative, contained a far higher proportion of the nation's best brains than can ordinarily be spared from other occupations. If there were defects in the directors' work, it was because they faced a task too big for them.

Management consists of four functions: planning (or initiation), organisation, motivation (the question of inducements to work), and control, which provides the data from which a further round of planning can begin. The factors limiting the operations which any one man or group can effectively direct can be considered under these four heads.

(a) The time taken to plan

The limits of direction depend in the first place on the amount of attention which needs to be given to planning. It is fairly straightforward to run even a large organisation once its work has been reduced to routine, but far less so when gaps have still to be filled and new departures initiated. This has been a powerful limiting factor in the case of both war planning and the Welfare State. It was only towards the end of the war, when the planning machine had been fully constructed and the battlefields were dominated by the United Nations, who could therefore plan ahead for longer periods, that many of the detailed inadequacies of the early days— difficulty, for instance, in getting out cost accounts in time to control production effectively—were overcome. In the case of the Welfare State, the increase in the amount of work passing over Ministers' and senior Civil Servants' desks has been due even more to the increase in the number of things about which the Government is expected to think, plan, and give a lead than to the growth of the services which it actually operates.

The political struggle of the last two generations has been to establish the principle of public accountability; the rule that the State, as the most comprehensive organ of society, has a right and duty to inspect every field of social action and insist that the agencies active there (or which should be active) do their work. Sometimes the appropriate agency is the State itself. Full employment policy, for instance, will not go very far without the help of the Budget, public investments, or State control of foreign trade. So also in 1945 it was widely agreed, not only on the Left, that the State was justified in taking over the coal-mines. There was a technical case for re-grouping coal-mines on lines which cut across existing ownerships. There was the bad tradition of human relations. And there was the difficulty of dealing with either problem quickly without a radical change of organisation. But for the most part public accountability involves at most State initiation, not operation. The State does not determine wages, except in a rather limited sector where trade union organisation is weak. But Ministers spend a great deal of time thinking about wages policy, and issuing guidance to the public. The Government does not run the universities or, for the most part, scientific research; but it thinks about and has policies on both. It does not actually operate the factories which have relieved unemployment in the Development Areas, and need not even have built the trading estates or provided the local administration which has brought them there. But that does not prevent it from having a location of industry policy and inducing other agencies to fall in with it.

Even in those fields where the Government has long played a major part in operating services, the planning function has emerged in the last few years on a scale not attempted before. In terms of numbers, the staffs concerned with the problems of full employment and inflation are not so very much greater than before the war. But the Government's preoccupation with this field, in fact and as a matter of declared principle, is immensely greater. Ministries today form and enforce a national policy in town and country planning, education, and health, to an extent unknown before the war.

The hall-mark of the Welfare State is, in fact, not that the State does everything but that it thinks about everything. Its business, in the words of one famous statement on economic ethics, is to direct, watch, stimulate, and restrain, and only incidentally to operate. This leads to the paradox that the more of a Welfare State a State becomes—the more it accepts this general responsibility for planning ahead—the fewer the services it can afford to operate itself. For the Minister's day continues to contain only twenty-four hours, and the more he spends on operating problems the less he has for thinking ahead. The less, in particular, he has for thinking about the problems of change in the social framework, since for these experience provides the least guide, and reflection and preparation need to be longest.

Whether, when it comes to the point, the pressure of overwork will lead Ministers to concentrate on day-to-day work and let the future look after itself, or to drive forward with new plans and forget administrative detail, will depend on the circumstances of the time. There is probably a tendency to the former course; for day-to-day work can be done even when tired, whereas to open new fields calls for preference for a fresh brain. But this tendency can be overridden by the pressure of circumstances. In the war the need for change in the social framework, and generally for new policies, was

5 65

immediate and overwhelming. The changes in civilian society after 1944 were the upshot of sixty years' propaganda and debate, which not only clarified the issues but created a powerful public opinion in all parties in favour of change. The difficulty of thinking ahead under pressure has been more clearly shown since 1948, when the war and immediate post-war impulses were exhausted. Long-term issues, not having been sufficiently thought about through the preceding years, promptly dropped out of sight.

The politician, under the British constitution, has always an avenue of escape; sooner or later he will go into Opposition, and have time to think. The effect is, however, that long periods of responsibility without thought are balanced by others of thought without responsibility; and neither of these is as satisfactory as time to think while in power. This escape is in any case not available to the Civil Servant. Nor, when a similar problem of overwork arises in business, is it available to the manager, or the member of the Board of a public corporation.

(b) *The complications of organisation and motivation*

The second limiting factor in State, or any other, direction, is the time taken to sort out the complex problems of organisation and motivation in a large group. This depends to some extent on whether an organisation illustrates what has been called varietal or repetitive extension; whether, like the Post Office, it has many branches doing the same thing or, like the C.W.S. or Lever Brothers, operates undertakings of several kinds at once. The State's activities are of course particularly varied. But experience shows that the time taken to sort out relations in even a repetitive organisation, if it is on the scale of the Army or the National Coal Board, is not small.

The Ministry of Aircraft Production during the war controlled at the peak about one and three-quarter million workers in upwards of 20,000 firms engaged on its contracts, in addition to its own staff of about 21,500. It took, typically, up to a month to send out, collect, and tabulate a request for information on firms' labour requirements, and about as long to collect the quarterly production figures. It might take anything up to two further months to thrash out between departments, on the basis of these figures, the man-power allocations for the next period. There was a further loss of time inasmuch as work in a department tended to slow up when a new allocation was due; it being obviously pointless to plan ahead when the whole basis of the plans was uncertain. Similar experience can be quoted from administration since the war. The time taken to approve location of industry proposals dropped from weeks to days in 1948, when it was made the personal responsibility (in normal cases) of the Regional Controller of the Board of Trade, instead of having to be cleared through a regional committee representing several government departments. Mr. D. N. Chester quotes as typical a case where the approval of a large local authority's proposal for a nursery school dragged on for just over two years, of which eighteen months were after the scheme had been approved in its main outlines.

This loss of time would not matter in a static world, where changes were rare and could be considered at leisure. In the actual conditions of wartime planning, it commonly meant that decisions relevant to one period, and set of circumstances, were not made till it was almost time for the next.

(c) *The resulting loss of control*

When administrators are overloaded with planning, and with complex organisational problems, there follows a loss of precise control, the fourth element in management; and this has been another limiting factor in State management. Decisions have to be handed over to sub-committees with imperfect knowledge of what is going on outside their own field. They can be made only at intervals, because of the time each takes; and during the intervals the directives issued last time may become obsolete. Decisions have to be made on fewer and fewer data, a less and less complete picture of the factors being considered. Instead of a precise knowledge of each firm's capacity, it is necessary to use a crude production index. At one point in the war the Ministry of Aircraft Production could no longer keep track of the production of even major components, and could follow little more than the numbers of complete airframes and engines. It becomes necessary to work only with a few big firms, leaving small firms to depend on them for sub-contracts. Allocation of labour can take only partial account of people's skills and desires: conscription does rough justice, but at a cost to personal relations and family life illustrated by the increase of divorces from 8,400 in 1938 to 54,700 in 1947. Rationing and utility schemes keep the people fed and clothed, but at the cost of limiting new varieties, and changes of taste, out of which better standards of living could be shaped for the future. Much control must normally be based on the 'feel' of the situation, which has been called earlier 'non-logical' thinking. As the pressure of overwork grows it becomes less and less easy for the administrator to have this feel for anything beyond the situation, and the group of people, in and around his own headquarters.

ECONOMIC CONTROL

This loss of control can be summed up in terms of costs in a neat formula developed by Mr. P. W. S. Andrews. Costs, he suggests, may be divided into 'technical' and 'managerial'. Technical costs are those which arise from the use of men, machines, and materials in the most economic possible way, given the existing state of technical knowledge. Managerial costs may be divided into direct costs, such as the salary of the managing director, and indirect, which include all other costs whatsoever—except technical costs as just defined—incurred by the firm. Indirect managerial costs are thus a measure of the uneconomic use of a firm's resources.

Direct managerial costs are high, and have risen greatly in the last two generations with the rise of scientific management. 9·9% of the personnel of American manufacturing industry were administrative in 1899, 22·2% in 1947. They do not, however, increase with the size of firm: indeed, on American experience, they may fall by about a third or a half, in proportion to total sales or employment, between firms with under $1 million assets and those with over $500 million.

But it is the indirect costs that are relevant here; for whereas direct management costs represent the price of control, indirect costs measure the effectiveness with which control is maintained. They seem, on business experience, to fall at first as a firm grows larger, until it ceases to be possible for the firm's senior managers to keep in personal touch with everyone and everything in the firm. This limit may not be reached until employment rises to six hundred, eight hundred, or even a thousand. It may, in a more variegated trade, be reached much lower. In any case, once it is passed, indirect managerial costs begin to rise. The rise, like the fall, is not smooth. It is necessary to think in terms of levels of management, with one structure suitable perhaps for firms employing up to a hundred, another for those in the range of from ninety to five hundred, a third for those from four hundred to one thousand two hundred, a fourth from one thousand to five thousand. On each level, costs tend to be stable. But from level to level, once the critical point is past, there is a rise. It is not a great rise, and becomes slower as size increases. Once a concern is large, it loses relatively little by growing still larger.

But the State is not merely a large firm, as size goes among firms employing three-quarters of a million in its Civil Service. It also acts, in the way just described for the Ministry of Aircraft Production, as a general staff, supervising activities over a still wider area: directly in the case of the forces, public corporations, ordnance factories, or Government contractors; less directly in the case of the

68

universities, or of the labour market or other non-governmental activities which it influences or partially controls. It would naturally be expected, when management operates on so vast a scale, that even a slow rate of increase of indirect managerial costs would accumulate to quite a substantial figure.

Furthermore, when Mr. Andrews speaks of rising indirect managerial costs in large private firms, he is certainly not suggesting that these firms are run solely by direction. Competition and consultation will usually play a large part in them. There will be consultation about policy, and the competitive market will set standards of performance. In public administration also, consultation (public opinion) inside and outside the public service plays a big part. And warfare is a peculiarly exacting form of competition. Nevertheless, for the reasons given earlier, State and especially wartime administration does call for an unusually high proportion of direction to the other two mechanisms. In the circumstances, one would expect the rise in indirect managerial costs to be exceptionally high.

And so, especially in wartime, it is. Whatever the precise measure of loss of control, it is a fact that in State management, as practised during and just after the war, control was lost and, indeed, had to be. Wartime planning, says Professor Devons, from his experience of aircraft production, had to be rough and ready to work at all. In the eloquent words of Professor Robbins:

'Our theories of State action usually imply, not merely infinite wisdom on the part of administrators, but also infinite time in which to use it. It is not until you have sat in the smoke-filled committee rooms working against time to get snap decisions from Ministers who, through no fault of their own, are otherwise preoccupied, that you realise sufficiently the limitations of these assumptions . . .' (*The Economic Problem in Peace and War*, p. 23).

The first duty of the State planner, says Sir Oliver Franks, is to nail the flag to the mast and not to the fence. War-planning worked at all (to paraphrase Mr. Wilson) only because the Prime Minister wielded the axe of decision with the inspiration of genius rather than the justification of facts. Discretion forbids quoting similar comments from post-war planners still in the Service.

How far the loss of precision matters will depend on the extent to which people are willing to put up with being pushed around, for the sake of the benefits State planning may bring. They will put up with a great deal if they are convinced that their personal interests are best served by subordinating their immediate wishes to some activity which only the State, however crude its methods, can carry on; such as a war, or the rapid structural changes required in an underdeveloped society. But the turn of the tide against State management in Britain, which can be dated from 1947, was due largely to the discovery that in present British circumstances people insist on a high degree of precision in the satisfaction of their day-to-day desires, even in such conditions of crisis and reconstruction as have prevailed since the war.

(d) Can the limits of direction be broken by improving its machinery?

It is possible, up to a point, to avoid the choice between sacrificing the future, delaying decisions, and working to rough-and-ready standards by improving the machinery of management. In the case of the State there has been much room for this. The Select Committee on Estimates observed in 1947 that the habit of systematic, skilled review of administrative practice by organisation and methods teams from the Treasury, or in individual departments, had only very recently taken hold at even the lower levels of the Civil Service. The idea of applying it to the work of the Permanent Secretary himself was barely beginning to be mooted. There is a technique of administrative accountancy, or efficiency audit, working with documents and interviews and statistics, parallel to that of the cost accountant who works with many figures. Organisation and methods studies based on it have secured some remarkable results, notably on the side of human relations. One example was the re-shaping of the groups handling claims for insurance benefits, in the Ministry of National Insurance, into what have sometimes been called 'rational' units; groups small enough for personal knowledge and friendship, having their own well-rounded task—or rather series of tasks, allowing change of jobs and a variety of work—and their largely self-chosen leadership. But these are no more than a beginning. Cost accounting, another study by the Select Committee showed, has till recently been very little developed in Government departments; one exception, the system in use in the Medical Branch of the War Office, had been installed by Florence Nightingale and found no imitators. The initial constitution of the National Coal Board, again, with only two non-departmental members and five with departmental duties, conflicted with business experience not only here but in America. The ideal in so large an organisation, experience suggests, is a general management group of perhaps four or five managers with few or no departmental duties. These will act (perhaps in association with some departmental managers) as the general executive committee of the organisation. They will belong to, provide most of the initiative of, but also be supervised by, the board of directors, or 'trusteeship management'. Much vigorous controversy was required before, after two years' experience, a general management group on these lines was set up.

But reorganisation and simplification can usually proceed only slowly, to avoid disorganising work in progress; also, at present, because of a scarcity of the experts who could carry it out. Reorganisation which solves problems by increasing the number of advisers, investigators, and planners is liable to defeat its own object by increasing the complexity of the management machine. This can be seen at work in the recent history of the Civil Service. The time is not long past when an Assistant Secretary could be (as he commonly still is) in close touch with the details of his field of work, and yet was also a power in the land, not far removed from senior Ministers. He is buried today beneath three tiers of Ministers (not counting the Prime Minister himself, or Parliamentary Under-Secretaries), and three senior grades in the Civil Service. It is also true that higher management and the research and advisory work connected with it are highly skilled operations, and the number of men who can be spared for them from other occupations is small. Wartime aircraft production, it has been said, could have been planned to the last screw and rivet by employing several hundred specialist aircraft engineers on this alone. There would, however, have been no engineers over to build the aircraft. Mr. Henry Smith points out, at a more humdrum level, that retail price control in wartime could for the same reason be operated so as to prevent gross exploitation of consumers, but not (even with the help of much consultation with the trade) so as to discriminate in detail between firms providing different forms and amounts of service and to force the least efficient of each type out of business. It would also be wrong to assume that because defects exist, government administration in the past must have been grossly unscientific. It is nearer the truth to say, with Mr. Wilson, that 'the most vigorous and sustained attempt was made to run the war as scientifically as possible'.

(e) Conclusion. An effective State must limit its commitments

The conclusion to all this discussion of the time factor—and remember that there are also the other limits to the use of direction referred to above at p. 61—is not that State direction in economic matters is in any way superfluous or undesirable. On the contrary; it is generally agreed that State direction is superior to smaller-scale direction, or to competition, for a very wide range of economic purposes. In judging the precision with which State direction does in fact carry out the tasks assigned to it, it is fair to remember that

71

these are often the tasks about which a precise judgement is difficult or impossible; those where there is no standard of comparison (monopoly), where results accrue a generation or more in the future, or are diffused over the whole nation or even the world; and those which involve introducing new social structures or standards of action. In its more routine tasks, offering more precise standards of judgement—the postal services, for instance, or the nationalised railways—there are in general no certain grounds for believing that State direction of economic affairs achieves less precise or satisfactory results than could have been achieved in any other way.

But it remains the lesson of experience that, other things being equal, the greater the number of decisions to be handled by any system of direction the higher will be the 'indirect managerial costs' of handling them; the slower, the more spasmodic, the harder to achieve, and the less precise the decisions reached will be. It is probably true over a very wide range of services that State economic direction (and remember that we are considering State direction only as the most far-reaching and extensive form of direction in general) can control *this* service or *that* service or *the other* service as efficiently as could be done with any other sanction or mechanism. But if State direction were used for *all three*, the pressure on administrators would be such that none of them would be operated as speedily or as precisely as citizens or consumers desire. There are some things which economic competition cannot do well, whereas government economic direction (or 'planning') can do them well. There are certainly many other things which, *taken individually*, could be done equally well by either. But, allowing for all possibilities of delegation and 'scientific management', the *total* number of things which can be done well by State direction is limited.

If, therefore, the State is to play the part mapped out for it in achieving objectives not immediately pressing on or apparent to the ordinary citizen, or in promoting change in the social framework, or in managing monopolies, *and also* is to maintain the precision of control which is, in fact, expected from it in a country like Britain in peacetime, it must limit its commitments.

Its prime duty in the economic field has in recent years been defined, and correctly so, as that of enforcing public accountability; supervising, encouraging, checking, initiating, but not necessarily operating services itself. In addition, it has actively to operate services in which economic competition is permanently ineffective: beginning with the classic trio of defence, law and order, and foreign affairs. It will find it advisable, if it is to discharge its function of general supervision, to operate a number of other services distributed among the fields in which it may need to intervene. Intervention, should it become necessary, is best based on first-hand experience. But, having done all this, the State will not on recent experience in Britain have time for much more. If it goes further it will find itself attempting to do in a rough-and-ready fashion what economic competition can do more precisely; and it will also do in an unnecessarily rough-and-ready fashion even those things which it should itself be able to do precisely and well. One of the neglected truths in discussions of planning in recent years is that the case for limiting the field of State management rests, not on the dangers of a strong State, but precisely on the need to allow the State to do with greater power those things which no other agency can do so well.

The lesson that, though State direction is often more effective than competition in dealing with remote and diffused issues and with structural change, it is less capable than competition of reducing to order the vast mass of routine transactions in a modern economy, has been learnt in this country chiefly from the war economy. The most dramatic illustration of it in modern history is, however, the experience of the U.S.S.R. after the First World War. Attempts were made, in the first flush of the revolution, to impose universal State direction. The result was chaos. In 1921, under the New Economic Policy, economic competition was accordingly brought back into play. Within the limits of the existing social structure, and for the purposes set by it, precision of control was restored. The State's hands were freed to concentrate on control at key points, including precisely the question of changing the social structure. Planners were presented with an orderly map of transactions, in relation to which future policy—whether or not it involved a change in the map, or the structural conditions underlying it—could be rationally discussed. Later, the improved technique of planning made it possible to extend the area of State direction without abandoning precise control—at any rate without any greater departure from it than the people would accept as the price of desired changes in the social framework, or than a totalitarian government could compel them to put up with. But frequent, and often (as over the collectivisation of agriculture in the early 'thirties) devastating, excesses of State action kept the limits of direction in mind, and the lesson of 1921 was not again forgotten. The tendency has indeed been for Soviet policy to run to excess, if not in one direction then in the other. It is noteworthy that the U.S.S.R. abandoned consumer rationing completely at the end of 1947, when Russian

73

incomes were less than a third of those in Britain and (especially allowing for differences in the two countries' tax systems) may well have been more unequally divided.

APPLICATION OF THE SAME LESSON TO OTHER FIELDS

The State presents the general problems of direction on the largest scale of which there is experience in Britain. But the principles involved in smaller scale direction, and its limiting factors, are the same. There is no simple formula for transferring the lessons of State management to the industry or firm; it is necessary on each occasion to look at each limiting factor. But a rough comparison of size (Table 4) will at least start the argument going. The national

TABLE 4. Number of Industries and Government Departments employing given numbers of Workers

Number employed ('000's)	Number of industries or departments	
	Industries 1948	Departments 1950
0–4	0	6
5–10	5	9
11–50	67	13
51–250	58	1
250+	19	0
Total	149	29

Employment in certain large unified concerns, 1949

National Coal Board	800,000
Civil Service (non-industrial)	706,000
British Railways (1948)	578,000
Army	394,000
R.A.F.	205,000
Lever Brothers and Unilever	193,000
British Electricity Authority	154,000
London Transport	101,000
I.C.I. (United Kingdom only)	100,000
C.W.S.	60,000
L.C.C.	59,000

Sources: Industries and Government Departments, *Annual Abstract 1936–49* (omitting such headings as 'other manufacturers' or 'other departments'). 'Large concerns'; same, and Milward (ed.), *Large-Scale Organisation, 1950.*

Government, as an employer, is of about the same size as the eight or nine other largest industries or professions, with employments ranging from just under half a million to just over a million—or to a million and a half, if the food and non-food sections of retailing are counted as one trade. Two of these other trades are, like the State, run as units: namely coal and railways, or one should perhaps say the British Transport Commission in all its ramifications. The others are building, farming, general engineering, local government, hotels and restaurants, and the teaching and medical professions. Government departments, on the other hand, are markedly below the size of typical industries, and smaller even than many individual large firms.

A comparison on this basis, of course, can refer only to problems of coordination within departments or industries. It ignores the fact that a government department may be merely the apex of a pyramid of organisation whose base reaches far into the rest of society. The number of workers dependent on the Ministry of Supply, at the peak of the war, was about the same as that quoted above for the Ministry of Aircraft Production. The War Office controls some four hundred thousand men over and above the thirty-odd thousand in the department itself. But the comparison is not wholly unfair, for business also has its outside contracts. The contracts issued by the great assembly industries, such as motors or building, or the National Coal Board with its monopoly of demand for all coal-mining requirements, or by a big retail firm such as Marks and Spencer, have a key importance for the whole chain of productive processes which lie behind them. It has, in fact, long been a good ground for complaint against the building trade, and to a less extent the British motor trade, that this power was not used to rationalise production; and a ground for congratulation to Marks and Spencer, or to the American motor trade, that in their case this power has been used very effectively indeed.

Chapter 6

CONSULTATION AS A FORM
OF CONTROL

THERE is nothing new about consultation as a means of economic control. A common delusion about the nineteenth century is that, since there was then in Britain a prejudice against direction and more particularly State direction, the economic system was abandoned to the sole and by no means tender mercies of competition. In actual fact consultation, formal and still more informal, played a very great part. The City of London, in its palmy days, had few formal rules; but Heaven help the man who transgressed the informal, customary code of the banking world on the Stock Exchange. His credit would melt away, sources of confidential information would dry up, and, if he failed to take the informal advice quietly dropped in his ear by more experienced friends, his business would soon be at an end. The process of price formation and marketing, as Mr. Andrews has pointed out—that is in business in general, not only in the financial world—could never have worked as smoothly as it did had it not been for the educational process, the host of informal understandings, which helped business men to see what their long-term interests in a competitive world required. The 'prevalence of long views', as described in Chapter 2, is the product of discussion and consultation as well as of the experience of profit and loss.

But there is a very real sense in which the present generation might be called the Age of Consultation, or, at least, the beginning of such an age. For consultation, and especially formal consultation, has come to play a much bigger part in economic affairs than it did. This is indeed what might be expected in the light of past experience. The nineteenth century, down to the 1880's, was the great age of competition. The two generations from 1880 to 1945–50 provided a growing body of evidence, partly summed up in Chapter 5, on the scope and limits of direction. It is natural that attention should be turned today to what consultation in its turn can do to solve those problems of economic control with which neither competition nor direction has proved able to cope. The problems in question were outlined early in the last chapter. They arise where remote and diffused causes and effects have to be taken into account or changes in the social framework made, and where competition is therefore inadequate; but where direction also fails, because those who have authority to direct have no clear or agreed policy to guide them, and neither have nor—by using the machinery of direction alone—can get a clear and agreed picture of the means of execution to be used.

THE RISE OF CONSULTATION

(a) Inside firms

Consultation within the firm was much experimented with in the 'twenties and 'thirties. It grew swiftly under the pressure of the war years. An all-out war effort was needed. There was universal goodwill towards it. And the methods of government direction were rough and ready, leaving much room for detailed local discussion and improvement. In these conditions joint production committees and similar forms of consultation spread rapidly, especially in the munition trades. They tended to fade away for a time in the year or two of uncertainty after the war, but revived again from about 1947. Their results are difficult to check, as they are generally diffused over the whole of a firm's operations. 'We installed a works council', is one very typical American comment, 'and in the same month replaced our old boiler . . . Output went up and stayed up. But how much of the improvement was due to either I am not prepared to say.' A survey by the American Management Association suggests that when business men say that joint consultation helps production it is more often because they think it should than because they know it does. Detailed studies of small groups show, however, that remarkable increases in both output and personal welfare can be obtained through consultation. The broader results are summed up by a firm with a generation's experience (the Renold and Coventry Chain Co.) as the growth of mutual respect between managers and workers; of constitutional practice, the rule of law, public opinion sanctioning and supporting a code of discipline; responsible men elected as workers' leaders, and a general feeling of stability and security; and a strong incentive to management to clarify its own organisation and consultative procedures as well as those linking management to the rank and file.

The latter point arises particularly out of the difficulties of middle management. Joint consultation has done as much as any factor in recent years to draw attention to the often unsatisfactory status and responsibilities of foremen and supervisors. There have been many firms where works councils or joint production committees linked

77

top management and workers, but left supervisors to the mercies of inadequate managerial channels of communication. It has been highly embarrassing, in such cases, for supervisors to know less about a firm's position or top-management decisions than shop stewards or works council representatives under them.

(b) Government and Industry—Voluntarism

Consultation has also become widespread and has proved its value at higher levels. As the limitations of State direction became apparent, and especially the fact that it is the State's function to plan and initiate rather than to operate, the Government has made more and more use of 'voluntarism' as a means of maintaining control in areas where competition also breaks down. Voluntarism in this case centres round two institutions. There is first a maze of joint committees linking the Government to trade associations and trade unions, some at the highest national level, as with the National Joint Advisory Council on labour questions or the National Joint Council on Production, but most of them specialised by trade, subject, or region. Secondly, each industry is now within the field of some department, which serves as its point of contact with the Government. The aim in either case is, by bringing together government departments and representative trade organisations, to reach agreement on policy and so either obviate the need for measures of direction, or create a favourable public opinion in their support.

Voluntarism is not some chance growth or timid approach to control by a government which objects to State action. It grew out of a mass of experience with war and post-war controls, under—at least in the first years—governments very strongly favourable to both State direction and State operation. It would have been possible after the war, on the one hand to maintain State direction by statutory rules and orders, and on the other to replace the system of munition contracts, on which the effectiveness of the Government's executive action during the war largely rested, by a device officially approved by the leaders of the Labour Government; that is to say, the nationalisation of wholesaling, which would have made the Government a main contractor for civilian goods as well as munitions. But, in fact, wholesaling was not nationalised, control by orders has been kept as far as possible in the background and voluntarism has been seen as presenting the greatest hope of reconciling the various interests in national policy.

For this there would seem to be three reasons, even apart, that is, from the ups and downs of politics. It has been seen, first, that the State must limit its operative functions if it is to do with precision what it does attempt. Secondly, there has been the evolution illustrated in the last chapter from successive *Economic Surveys*, from seeing the State as determining all main objectives to seeing it as merely one participant whose views must be reconciled with others no less important. This has led to the idea that the clash of views between, say, a firm looking for a site and the Board of Trade with its government location policy may be not merely an unpleasant necessity but a highly constructive activity. The firm represents the consumer's interest in minimum costs, the Board that of the local community in full and satisfactory employment, and of both the local and the national community in avoiding wasteful expenditure on roads or houses. The problem is not to decide whether the interests represented by the firm shall override those represented by the Board (or vice versa) but—and this is precisely what the objective of British location policy has been—to consult together so as to satisfy both at once. Thirdly, on the principle that a car can be driven faster because it has brakes, it seems that more can be left to voluntarism once the principle of the Welfare State is accepted. To say that the State will intervene by law and orders in any field where consultation goes seriously astray is today no idle threat— under governments of any complexion. Public opinion, including that of the business community, accepts this as natural in a way not found before the war. Since, therefore, State direction *can* be firmer and more far-reaching when that seems necessary, it can afford to keep more in the background in ordinary day-to-day administration.

(c) Consultation at the industry or profession level

The same technique has been applied to the management of individual industries and industry-sized firms. Lever Brothers, for example, retain in their central organisation only three main controls: over large-scale capital expenditure, annual budget, and the appointment of key personnel. Otherwise the formulation of policy and provision of central technical services proceeds on an advisory basis. General Motors is another illustration of the same tendency, and Ford's went over to a similar system as quickly as possible after the death of Henry Ford I, whose rule was autocratic to the end. In the last twenty years of his reign, Ford sales had dropped from 40% to 15% of all car sales in the American market, and General Motors, which relies greatly on consultative procedures in management, had been the chief beneficiary. The British Iron and Steel Federation, after its reorganisation in the 'thirties, became not merely an outstandingly successful example of the 'voluntarist' technique, but a particularly vigorous public defender of it. It supplies central services, formulates policy, and reconciles the views of the industry and the Government. It was responsible, among other things, for the industry's development plan of 1945, which was officially adopted by the Government. Member firms, however, retain their independence over against the Federation, and the Federation itself insists that this is a main condition of its usefulness. It must be able to sell its services to the industry on their merits, and to speak to the Government as their representative, not as dominant over them.

A combination of voluntarism as a tool of the Government and of the technique of the Iron and Steel Federation is found in the Development Councils set up under the Industrial Organisation and Development Act of 1947. Members of these are appointed by the Ministry concerned with the industry in question, in equal numbers from the management and the workers' side of the industry, with an independent chairman and other independent members to represent the public and consumer interests. A council is set up on the authority of the Government, but after consultation with persons engaged in the industry. It may be given three compulsory powers: to register firms, require information from them, and raise a levy for the purposes of the Act. Otherwise, however, it acts, like the Iron and Steel Federation, as a purely consultative body, supplying services, acting as a centre for discussion of policy and for contact with the Government, but with no power to compel.

Most of the few councils set up at the time of writing are still finding their feet. One, however, the Cotton Board, dates in another form from 1940, and has a remarkable record in the post-war reconstruction of the industry. Cotton is on the face of it a depressed and depressing industry. There is a marked contrast between its failure to recapture lost markets abroad since the war and the success of many other trades in not merely regaining old markets but breaking into new. But this impression can easily obscure the fact that the industry has made far more progress since 1945 than at that time seemed likely. The credit for this belongs first and foremost to the Board.

It was due very largely to the Board's work on recruitment that the industry's labour force in 1951 was one-third higher than was believed possible in 1945, when a working party reported on the future of cotton, and that the $9\frac{1}{2}\%$ of school leavers in the North-West entering cotton in 1945 became $16\frac{1}{2}\%$ in 1949. The Board has played its part in the slow but steady progress of labour redeployment. It helped to bring rather over half the industry's spindles into groups, for purposes of modernisation and subsidy under the Cotton Spinning (Re-equipment Subsidy) Act of 1948, by the end of 1949.

Its general effect in livening up discussion in the industry is illustrated by the fact that two hundred and fifty managers and trade unionists attended its Annual Conference in May 1947, but 1,300 in October 1949. It has reconciled the views of Government and Industry effectively enough to retain the confidence of both Lancashire and Whitehall.

All this has been done by persuasion and education; partly by direct propaganda, but largely by finding the progressively minded firm here and there which would undertake an experiment under commercial conditions, and by basing propaganda on the results. The Board has worked throughout on the basis that education is most successful where those undergoing it are convinced (and with much justification) that they are doing it all themselves.

(d) Consultation and regional planning

The most famous single example of voluntarism, applied in this case to the planning of a region, is probably the Tennessee Valley Authority. The T.V.A. owed its initial influence to its executive functions in flood control, power generation, and the improvement of navigation. But its charter directs it to attend not only to these things but to the general development of its region. For this purpose it has no compulsory powers, and it has further preferred, where possible, to cause local agencies to provide services rather than to provide them itself—a parallel to the policy pursued in Britain by the pre-war Commissioners for the Special Areas. It has improved farming methods, not by opening its own demonstration farms but by finding the individual in each community who would experiment under ordinary commercial conditions on his own farm. It has developed river ports, not under its own powers, but by interesting local communities and enterprises, even though this might entail some delay. Instead of itself developing farm machinery of special types required in the area, it has preferred to bring together manufacturers and users to work out plans to their common advantage. Its aims and achievement have been summed up in two comments: by a local newspaper, that it had 'given the people of the Valley a new vision of their own powers', and by its Chairman, that in his opinion these 'human methods are also'—to judge from the authority's experience—'efficient methods'.

(e) International consultative mechanisms. The world of science

On the international plane, the International Labour Organisation has for thirty years done admirable work in raising working conditions throughout the world by creating agreed standards, educating

6   81

public opinion, and, in particular, governments, trade unions, and employers' associations, and leaving it to the pressure of opinion to carry these standards into effect. And probably the most effective application of voluntarism in any sphere is that which is found in the world of science. Proposals for nationally planned science have been made from time to time, notably towards the end of the war. They have, however, in general been discredited, not least by recent Soviet examples of the degradation of the standards of science to which direction, and especially political direction, can lead. Direction has its place in scientific as in other institutions, and the area over which this should extend—the importance of teamwork or of collaborations between teams—has been and is growing. But as means of overall control, the scientific world prefers a combination of competition between individuals and institutions, as giving the maximum scope for discovery and growth, and consultation. The exchange of information, the process by which educated public opinion enforces high standards of teaching and research is, in fact, more highly developed in the world of science than in any other field of society. Direction may be the quickest way (as happened with work on the first atom bomb) to force the pace of a scientific development whose general principles are clearly understood. But consultation plus competition is better for guiding the first green shoots of discovery without distorting or ignoring them. It has produced the scientific advances of the past; and scientists have yet to be satisfied that another method will do better in future.

THE LIMITS OF CONSULTATION

The value of consultation as a method of control is then proved and recognised. It is something more than the mere multiplication of talking-shops. It has, however, like the other mechanisms of control, its limits. Consultation is accused of involving a massive waste of time in committee work, or of tying up action in a maze of precedents and red tape. Development councils, even the Cotton Board, reach results rather slowly, and have been variously accused of weakness ('lack of teeth'), of preparing the ground for an undesirable extension of State direction, and of allying managers and workers in conspiracy against the public. A British government which refused to use taxes to control inflation and deflation, and relied solely on agreement with the T.U.C. and British Employers' Confederation, would, it may be agreed—judging by recent experience—be living in a fool's paradise; though so also, it is only fair to add, would be one which relied only on taxes and ignored consultation and agreement.

It is universally accepted that consultation will work well only if there are strong sanctions in the background; if public opinion is active, markets are sensitive, the State is ready to step in, and the alternative mechanisms of competition and management are also in full use. There are then limits to consultation: what sets them?

(a) *The time factor*

The limits of direction are set by a number of factors—the need for planning and precise control, and to solve the complex problems of organisation and motivation—which can be reduced to the common denominator of *time*. Given time, all things are possible; but time, in practical affairs, is always limited. This is also, and to an even greater extent, the first limiting factor on consultation; precisely because consultation involves taking all opinions into account, and preferably waiting until the differences then revealed can be resolved. A good system of consultation within a firm may well take three, five, or ten years before representatives are trained, confidence is established, and procedure is put in working order. Even given such a system, the discussion of major issues of policy may drag out over months or even years. The Cotton Board started with great advantages. It had a long pre-war history, in the depression years, which convinced the industry of the need for some body of the kind. For several years the Board served as a wartime control agency, making itself familiar to the industry in an atmosphere of common effort and general goodwill. It has enjoyed personal leadership from a Chairman whose many years as Secretary of the Manchester Chambers of Commerce gave him a unique knowledge and skill in the matters with which the Board deals. Nevertheless, from the time the Board went over to questions of post-war policy, round 1943, it took three or four years' hard work before results began to flow. The big jump in juvenile recruitment was in 1946. The great success of the Board's conferences dates from 1948–9. Consultation is immensely time-consuming by comparison both with direction and with competition.

(b) *Ignorance about how to make consultation work*

The second limit to consultation is lack of knowledge of how it should be run. In the case of direction also there has been plenty of room for improvement in the techniques used. But there is probably more room for improvement in the techniques of consultation than of direction, because so much of the movement for consultation is new. The move for scientific direction, in the State or in the firm, dates from the 1870's and 1880's, and was coming in strongly around

1914. That for consultation dates from the 1920's and 1930's, and its great successes came in and after the Second World War.

(i) *The need for a consultant*. There are three main conditions for successful consultation. The first is the presence of a *consultant*, using that word in its medical sense. Study after study in recent years has shown the importance of some individual, or group, within a consultative system, not committed to any one party within it, but serving as an adviser, capable of precipitating people's thoughts and helping them to work through their problems. This is a role exactly like that of the psychiatric consultant, and one which needs like his to be rather carefully defined. When medical psychologists from the Tavistock Institute organised a study of the Glacier Metal Company they defined their research role precisely as they would have done in relation to a patient in the consulting-room. The Cotton Board and T.V.A. have been helped to achieve a consultant's role by their official status; though fully committed to the interests of Lancashire or the Tennessee Valley, the fact that they are government bodies has given them a useful detachment over against local interests. However it may be defined, and whoever may perform it—individual, organisation, or department, as, for instance, a personnel department —this role appears essential, and the successful leaders of consultation in recent years have all been skilled in playing it. The role of departments like the Board of Trade, as a point of contact between Government and industry, can be seen largely in this light. The role of departments like the Ministry of Labour or of local government is at least as much to focus and precipitate the ideas of people in local government and industry as to make regulations or enforce the law. It is, in fact, probably true that the need for a permanent role of this sort is more clearly and explicitly recognised in government than in industry. Among firms, there are as yet rather few which see the need for a permanent consultant—or at least an individual with a consultant role—on their own staff. Such a role is, of course, often implicitly present in the shape of an unrecognised craft skill on the part of managers, and the role of the *occasional* outside consultant is coming to be more clearly seen.

(ii) *The need for comprehensive coverage*. The second condition of success concerns comprehensiveness, or unity of vision. People find it easier to see a part in relation to the whole. It is therefore easier to hold their interest and secure intelligent discussion if a system of consultation can be made to cover the whole of a well-rounded set of problems.

This implies in the first place unity of the area of consultation. The workshop representative, in a firm's consultative scheme, should represent one of Sir Charles Renold's 'rational units', a group of men with a common task and interest. A development council—and this has in practice caused much trouble—must cover firms and unions which feel a genuine common interest. A regional organisation like the T.V.A. must cover a well-defined region.

A second requirement is complete coverage of the subjects arising in the area of consultation. A consultative system should be free to discuss, and accustomed to discuss, all matters of importance to its members arising within its area. There does not seem to have been much difficulty about this in the relations between government and industry. There has been a good deal, over the issue of managerial prerogatives, in the relation between management and workers within firms. The discussion also must be connected, so as to allow the relation between part and whole to be seen. A unified report on the whole of a firm's activities, or a town-planning exhibition in which the problems and policies of a city can be seen all of a piece, are several times more valuable than the same information delivered in fragments.

This unified consideration of all the problems arising in a certain time or area can be useful not only in clarifying discussion but in improving the relations between those who take part in it and those to whom they report back. If, for example, a single works council handles both questions of wages and working conditions and those usually assigned to a separate joint production committee or works council, and if its members are also shop stewards, the prestige and contacts which members derive from each of their two roles will help them out in the other. The inevitable lull from time to time in works council business need not lead to a drop in the prestige of council members; for they will still be active in their role as shop stewards, and enjoy the standing which that gives them.

Comprehensiveness also implies complete coverage of all persons in the area of consultation. All groups and levels must be brought in; and consultation must be many-sided, and should for safety flow through several channels. At least one firm has formally adopted the traditional Quaker rule that, as a safeguard for full consultation, major decisions must be unanimous; and many consultative systems have an informal convention to the same effect.

The need for comprehensiveness is more generally understood today than that for a consultant. The impression is still, however, of a rather ragged level of actual achievement. What, in fact, *is* the right group of people to draw into consultation on any given question? What constitutes a satisfactory unit for business relations? More and more attention has been given to this question in recent studies of industrial relations. That is precisely because rather few firms or industries—for this question arises at all levels from the small working group up to the industry or profession—have yet set their house in order in this respect. Again, a study in 1950 showed a general feeling in industry that, in consultation within a firm, no questions should be barred. But a minority still objected even to this principle; and of 439 firms reporting the actual subjects of discussion in their joint committees, one-third reported no discussions on the firm's general position and policy, and four-fifths had none on profits and the balance-sheet. Other recent studies show that even firms with first-rate records in industrial relations may need to be reminded of the need not only for free discussion but also for keeping discussion well in focus—not merely a matter of isolated items on the agenda. The relations between works councils and wage-negotiating machinery are still a matter of debate. Consultation between management and the rank and file is far more adequate than it was. But the National Institute of Industrial Psychology finds that consultation between foremen and technical staff—not so much between foremen and personnel staff—is inadequate. It is 'the exception rather than the rule' for foremen to be used as a channel of communication between management and trade unions. Though 490 out of 703 firms claimed that consultation between foremen and higher management was standard practice, the Institute felt that this gave far too favourable a picture of the actual effectiveness of consultation at this level.

(iii) *The need for continuity, cumulation, and clarity. Constitutional procedure and written documents.* The third and last group of conditions for successful consultation concerns *continuity and cumulation of experience.* This follows from the importance of the time element in consultation. Just because this type of procedure takes so long, it is essential that the ground gained in the past be not lost. Continuity and accumulation of experience rest on *constitutional procedure and written documents.* Here also the impression is of a rather ragged degree of achievement. That regular meetings, agenda, procedure, membership, or arrangements for reporting back help the work of a committee is obvious enough. There has, it is true, been a strong reaction in recent years against suggestions of standardised procedures for consultation. It is insisted that if the representation of different groups in a firm, say, is adequate, it does not matter if it is precisely equal. There is no point in elaborate arrangements for works council members to report back a certain type of question, if, in fact, the managing director and the convenor of shop stewards are the only men in the works with the personality to get a point of that sort across. But though mathematical formulas and rule-of-thumb methods are rejected, the value of constitutional procedure in helping people to know where they are, speeding up work, and preventing petty politics, is not disputed.

What is much less generally grasped is the need to clarify roles and relationships, including channels and occasions of communication, and the difficulty of doing it. Many big concerns, public and private, have, it is true, manuals of procedure. But the reports of the Anglo-American Council on Productivity bring out that real clarity under these heads is more commonly attained in the United States than here, and is a main factor in the higher outputs attained in American industry. The National Institute of Industrial Psychology found that of the firms visited in its study, one in twelve showed a 'marked lack of definition' in its organisation structure, and only one in four could be said to have a structure which was logical and clear. The Tavistock Institute's study of the Glacier Metal Company gives a number of illustrations of the confusion which may in particular be caused by failing to distinguish between two or more roles filled by the same person or group. The highest management committee of that firm could be regarded as either a meeting of the general manager's subordinates, or the executive committee of the board of directors, or a cut-down version of the board itself. The general manager himself was also managing director of the firm and chairman of the board. Failure to clarify these relationships, the study shows, led to uncertainty, lack of confidence, and reluctance to consult unreservedly among members of the top management. This, the authors of the study point out, happened not in a firm whose organisation was by current standards confused but in one where prolonged and successful efforts to clarify it had already been made.

So also the concept of a common law, known to all and enforced by due process, is gaining ground in British firms. But the 1950 study just mentioned showed that half of all firms reporting gave their employees no more than a verbal explanation of conditions of employment at the time of engagement, and that the rule-books handed out by others read more like the commination service than an industrial charter. The authors felt strongly enough about this to recommend that here, alone of all the questions they covered, the law should step in and compel.

CONCLUSION

Lack of knowledge of how to make the best of consultation is, of course, a passing fault. But the long time required for consultation is a permanent characteristic. It means that consultation must always be inferior as a means of social control to both competition and direction, in all cases where the two latter mechanisms can operate with full efficiency. It comes into its own only in the narrow range of cases where neither of the other mechanisms is at its best. But, narrow though it may be, this range has proved wide and important enough to justify the rapidly increasing use made of consultation in recent years. It includes—to repeat and expand a little on the list given in Chapter 5—the following cases:

(1) *Consultation in the world of scientific research, or for promoting new enterprise*

Initiatives or enterprises of a new kind—a change in the social framework—are needed in a certain field. Competition permits but does not compel these. It is wished to guide and encourage them more than would be the case under competition; but the direction of advance is not yet clear enough to allow an order to be issued. Consultation—among scientists, for instance, or between them and those who finance them or whose needs they serve—provides the missing link.

(2) *Consultation for the purpose of agreeing on policy*

Many interests may be concerned in establishing the policy of some enterprise within an existing social framework, and in modifying it as the occasion may require. To impose a policy without full consideration of all these interests, and, if possible, their consent, would provoke resistance and might frustrate the policy imposed. In principle (unlike case 1), what needs to be done *can* be worked out from knowledge already available. But this knowledge is scattered among various people, to each of whom *some* factors in the case are 'remote' or 'diffused'; none of them is in a position to issue a direction. Just because there are 'remote' or 'diffused' factors in the case, competition cannot be relied on to produce the required result. Consultation among the interested parties is the answer.

(3) *Consultation within an executive chain, or joint consultation within the framework of an agreed policy*

Policy is clear, there is no question of any change in the social framework; but the knowledge needed to carry it out is scattered among various people, as in case 2. Competition is unlikely to produce the right solution, and the responsible executive or group is not in a position to issue a direction. Consultation among the executives concerned is again the answer.

Chapter 7

THE NEED FOR A PERIODIC AND
SYSTEMATIC OVERHAUL OF
CONTROL MECHANISMS

THE last chapter completes the review of the economic sanction as combined with various mechanisms of control in the field of production. On the one hand appears competition, exerting a control precise, highly differentiated, self-registering and self-enforcing, and capable of coordinating very large numbers of transactions at once. It is at its best when a certain framework of personality patterns, social norms, and social structure is given, and in dealing with transactions whose main significance is immediately apparent and important to those taking part in them. Even in these cases, it breaks down at times, though the area of monopoly, that is of marked departure from the standard of 'full' competition, is smaller than many writers of the last generation supposed. For promoting changes in the social framework, or dealing with remote and diffused issues, economic competition is effective up to a point; indeed, for many purposes more effective than any other combination, particularly through its decentralised character, and the scope for initiative which it therefore leaves to individuals and groups. But its performance for these purposes is much more erratic than where the transactions in question have a more routine and obvious character.

On the other hand appear two mechanisms, consultation and direction, which are strong where competition is weak, and weak where it is strong. They are often effective in sorting out problems of change in the social framework, or remote and diffused effects; provided, at any rate, that competition has first cleared the ground by leaving room for initiative and experiment. But they fail if they are expected to produce precise coordination of a really large number of transactions from any one centre, within a given and short time.

Here, obviously, is ground for a division of labour. The *general run of routine transactions* can be left to be worked out by economic competition. Economic competition will also provide the groundwork, the orderly presentation of facts, and the experimental data needed for decisions in what are usually (war apart) the exceptional cases of *decisions with remote or diffused causes or effects* and of *change in the social framework.* Direction and consultation will be brought to bear chiefly on these exceptional though vital decisions. They will explore remote implications, and what Katona calls 'genuine' decisions, which involve setting and seeing problems in a new light. They will be organised in small packets, dealing each with a limited range of problems; the State, for example, limiting itself to general supervision and the essential minimum of intervention, and not attempting to undertake wide operational functions as well. They will have also to provide for the limited number of cases of routine, immediately significant *transactions in which competition is significantly less than 'full'*.

As between direction and consultation:

(1) Direction will be appropriate where policy and the means of carrying it out are already clear; for instance, in developing an under-developed country, to the extent that there is agreement on its development and that this implies not inventing new techniques but taking over techniques applied elsewhere.

(2) Consultation will be appropriate:

(*a*) For encouraging, guiding, and securing agreement on innovations or new enterprises (changes in the social framework) as to which policy is not yet clear.

(*b*) For reaching agreement on policy, or the way to carry agreed policy out, where some of the factors in the case appear 'remote or diffused' to those immediately responsible for taking executive decisions.

The general effect will be a groundwork of competition, with direction and consultation brought in for clarification at key points. Provided that the number of remote and diffused, or structural, cases does not account for a very high proportion of all transactions, a system on these lines may be expected, with even the existing knowledge of how to make the best of each sanction or control mechanism, to achieve a fairly precise degree of control of economic affairs. The chief cases in which this condition is at present unlikely to be fulfilled are war and the raising of backward countries (which may, like Britain, be 'advanced' relative to others still more backward) to the standards already established by their more advanced brethren.

This is easy to see in principle. Essentially the same conclusion has been reached about it in recent years on the one hand by economists, trying to define the scope and limits of the economic market, and on the other by writers on management, trying to define, notably with the aid of the 'exception principle', what can and cannot usefully be done by higher managements in perpetual danger of being swamped with routine work. But the boundary between cases of routine administration and of change in the social framework, or between 'remote' and 'immediate' cases, or cases of full and not quite so full competition, is not rigidly fixed. Knowledge of the various techniques of control changes; so, from time to time, do the circumstances to which they are applied. There is always room for discussion, and often a case for change. From this has arisen in recent years the idea that organisation and methods—market practice, industrial structure, consultative techniques—should be submitted to periodic and systematic reviews. In Great Britain such reviews have taken notably—though not solely—three forms:

(a) The institution of a Monopolies and Restrictive Practices Commission, to review economic market practice.

(b) Regular reviews of management structure in government offices and private business; primarily, that is, reviews of direction and consultation.

(c) Special types of review for certain cases excluded, because they involve restraints of trade approved by statute, from the scope of the Monopolies Commission, but involving something more than a mere review of management procedure: the nationalised industries, the labour market, and a miscellaneous selection of government-regulated fields such as that of the Agricultural Marketing Acts.

THE MONOPOLIES AND RESTRICTIVE PRACTICES COMMISSION

The Monopolies Commission (to cut a long title short) was set up under the Monopolies and Restrictive Practices Act of 1948. It consists of ten members, most of them part-time, and its jurisdiction extends to cases where a third or more of the supply of any class of goods or services in Britain, or of exports from Britain, is under a single control. An exception is made in favour of controls authorised by statute, other than the Patent Acts; this, as just stated, excludes among other cases the nationalised industries and restraints of trade authorised by the Trade Union Acts or other labour legislation. The Commission controls its own procedure, though it may be given directions on this by the Board of Trade. It has power to require witnesses to attend, to produce all necessary accounts, papers, and estimates, and to give evidence on oath. It is bound to hear, if necessary orally, any individual or group with a substantial interest in a case before it.

It does not, however, have power to take up a case on its own. It has to wait for the Board of Trade to call on it for a report on a specified trade or question. The Board may ask for a purely factual study, or for recommendations on policy. In the latter case the Board is normally bound to lay the report before Parliament. If it is shown that restrictive practices exist, or in any case if the House of Commons so resolves not less than three months after a report has been laid, an enforcement order can be issued. This may make it illegal to carry out any existing trade agreement, or require that an agreement be wound up. It may ban discrimination in favour of particular customers or suppliers, withholding of supplies from particular buyers, or tying clauses, such as those common in the shoe-machinery industry, under which a customer who takes goods of one class is bound to take also goods of another. The decision to make an order, like the decision to take up a case, is not the responsibility of the Commission. The order is issued by the government department responsible for the sector of trade or industry in question, and this department is also responsible for following up to see that it is obeyed. The Commission may follow up a case only at the request of the Board of Trade, and only in cases where no enforcement order has been issued. The penalty for failure to obey an order is £100 fine, three months' imprisonment, or both.

To the beginning of 1954 the Board of Trade had invited the Commission to report on sixteen trades, and reports were issued. Many other suggestions of trades to investigate came in from various sources, principally from business men. The Board's policy has, however, been not to take up complaints as they come in, but to select cases in the first years so as to secure a wide cover of restrictive practices, and so create precedents on which general rulings can eventually be based.

The two countries with the most extensive experience in this field are Germany and America, and of these the American experience has been less interrupted by wars and revolutions. American writers, though vigorously critical of the anti-trust laws, are most of them strongly agreed that their objectives are 'socially desirable, economically sound, and capable of practical attainment'.[1] But experience in administering these laws points to some five lessons; and it is worth considering how the constitution of the Monopolies Commission appears in the light of these.

The first is that the front line of any action to police the market

[1] *Temporary National Economic Committee Report No. 38.* ('Construction and Enforcement of the Federal Anti-Trust Laws'), 1940, p. 100.

should be an administrative, not a legal, procedure. An illustration would be the fair-trade practice procedure of the United States Federal Trade Commission. This begins with a request from the industry. After informal preliminaries a conference is held with all interested parties, and suggestions noted. The Commission, on the basis of the conference, drafts rules, and after a further public hearing these are promulgated. They fall usually under two heads, one covering practices which appear definitely illegal under the anti-trust or other laws, and the other recommendations on such matters as the collection of statistics or an industry's central services. This procedure has been applied successfully to a large number of trades, from radio and rubber tyres to baby chicks and (shades of *The Loved One!*) the concrete burial-vault manufacturing industry. It has its dangers. The Commission could collaborate too closely with an industry, tolerating and covering undesirable practices instead of suppressing them. But its advantages are immense. It goes forward with the goodwill of the industry as well as of the Commission. It forestalls breaches of the law instead of punishing them, and shows business men precisely where they stand. It is flexible enough to take account of what one author calls the 'evasive actualities' of business: changing trade practices, and the fact that a mere flat ban on restraint of trade would be unrealistic. For the reasons shown in previous chapters, certain restraints—certain measures of direction —are everywhere required. It represents, in short, not an attempt to put down a few clearly definable crimes, but recognition that the problem is actually the more positive one of working out, to quote the same author, the 'technology of industrial order'.

To this first requirement the Monopolies Commission measures up well. The procedure for selecting cases, and for enforcement, is essentially administrative, not legal. The Commission is, in effect, the market-practice research division of the Board of Trade, and its published reports show that it interprets its task as covering the whole investigation of the 'technology of industrial order' in the fields referred to it. Its main weakness, so far as this heading is concerned, lies at the stage of following a case up. Effective adminis-tration would require, in a field such as this where circumstances change continually, that the files of each case be kept open for a possible revision. Not only has the Commission too little staff for this, it has also no power to do it except on the specific direction of the Board of Trade; and not even then in the more serious cases in which an enforcement order is made.

The second finding of American experience is that it is dangerous to pick cases on the basis of isolated complaints alone. These can be useful; but they should be woven into a grand strategy—a comprehensive attack capable of yielding principles for general application. This is precisely what the Commission and the Board of Trade are doing.

Thirdly, however, the law, though not the front line, is important as a reserve. Legal procedure is cumbersome in American experience, may exclude relevant evidence, is slow—cases are quoted of up to twenty years' litigation—and immensely expensive. The average cost of an American anti-trust case before the war was (allowing for the change in prices) about equal to the entire budget of the Monopolies Commission for 1951. Precedents, which in other legal fields build up into a system of case law, are here difficult to apply, because once again of the changing circumstances of business. Fifteen volumes of Supreme Court decisions, it has been said, accumulated over the first fifty years of the anti-trust laws without producing clarity. The law also provides for no administrative follow-up once a case is decided. But with all these disadvantages the law can do certain things which no other agency can attempt. Clear, legally binding directions as to what is and is not permitted are a safeguard against easy-going administration. A spectacular law case is an excellent way of making an example. The law, if its penalties are heavy enough, can take the profit out of undesirable practices. Business men are on the whole law-abiding. They may argue with an administrator, but will be reluctant to face a positively illegal act; especially under a procedure such as has been canvassed in the United States ('open covenants openly arrived at'), whereby trade associations would be expected to hold their minutes and records open for inspection, and members would sign an annual affidavit that no illegal matter had been either formally or informally discussed.

Here, so far, British legislation lags behind. The control exercised by the common law has been relaxed in the last generation, and the statute law has not filled the gap. Further statutory codification will no doubt have to wait until there are case histories to codify. This is not, of course, necessarily a disadvantage. There is a good deal to be said for letting data accumulate before jumping to conclusions; but it must be admitted that the British law on this subject has some way to go to catch up with the American. Penalties under the Act are also at present negligible in relation to the interests at stake.

American experience has been, fourthly, that large staffs are needed if either a legal or, still more, an administrative procedure on the lines just suggested is to be operated so as to penetrate the entire economy. Just before the war, when the combined staff of the two main American anti-trust agencies was just under a thousand, it was estimated that perhaps four times as many were needed to make the anti-trust laws fully effective. The combined budget at that date had risen from $1-1¼ million in the 'twenties to $2-2¼ million in the 'thirties, and to $3½ million for 1940 and 1941. For 1947 it was $5 million. The United States is a big country, but even allowing for this, there is a considerable discrepancy between these figures and the 61 staff (including only seven administrative grade Civil Servants and one accountant) employed by the Monopolies Commission in the spring of 1951. The Commission's budget for 1950–1 was £80,000, and its staff had risen to 85.

Lastly, American experience indicates that there is often a case not merely for regulating practice as between firms but for breaking firms up. Recognising fully that concentration is often needed for efficiency, that the break-up always means some short-term disorganisation, and that the separated parts will not act with full independence till the initial personal links disappear, American authors still insist that there are cases where breaking up a big concern is worth while. The classic case was that of Standard Oil, broken up in 1911 into some thirty-four constituent units, many of which in due course became fully independent and competitive. There are at present no powers in the British law to permit similar action here.

The essential fact about the Monopolies Commission, as things now stand, is its newness. It represents the first attempt in recent generations at a general review of the practice of the market in Britain. In view of this, its small present scale of operation and the fact that the problems of stream-lining the law and of breaking up overgrown firms have not yet been fully faced are not so very important. Much more important is the fact that the Commission has been started on the right—administrative rather than legal—lines, and that it is working under the sort of comprehensive strategy which this initial stage obviously requires.

THE ORGANISED REVIEW OF MANAGEMENT PRACTICE

The organised review of management practice in this country is, like the Monopolies Commission's systematic review of the market, brand new. Organised thought of any sort about management dates largely from within the last generation. The technicians were forming their associations from the end of the eighteenth century onwards. The engineers, chemists, architects, and stockbrokers have associations dating from before 1850; the accountants, actuaries, secretaries, patent agents, mine managers (with a technical rather than a managerial bias), and merchant navy officers from 1848 to around the turn of the twentieth century. Only in the generation before the First World War did interest in management as such begin to spread among accountants and engineers, and at first this interest was mainly in such topics as cost accounts and work measurement. Management associations and institutions began to appear in quantity about the time of the First World War: the Institute of Personnel Management in 1913, the Office Management Association, Industrial Health Research Board, Industrial Welfare Society, Institute of Public Administration, National Institute of Industrial Psychology, and Institute of Industrial Administration (now merged with the British Institute of Management) in a succession from then until 1922. The Works Management Association, the Purchasing Officers' Association, and the final conversion of the accountants' organisations to an interest in the human side of management date only from the 'thirties. Many of these bodies—the I.P.A., for example, or the I.P.M.—were then still struggling. Not till 1934 did they come together in the Confederation of Management Associations, to develop professional standards and, in particular, organise a joint syllabus for management training. Through all these years from 1913 onwards it is fair to say that the theory and professional organisation of management was being elaborated, but that there was no introduction of scientific management on any mass scale. The final breakthrough came only in and after the Second World War, with the foundation of the British Institute of Management and the Staff College at Henley, and the landmark in management education represented by the Urwick Report on Education for Management.

Against this background, it is not surprising that the idea of systematic and organised reviews of management practice has only recently taken hold. In the public service, proposals for such reviews run back at least to 1914, and were strongly pressed by the Haldane Committee on the Machinery of Government in 1918 and by the Royal Commission on the Civil Service in 1931. From these mountainous labours there emerged, however, only a rather ridiculous mouse. The Treasury acquired from 1919 onwards a few investigating officers who were specialists in office machines, to encourage their use in government departments. After the outbreak of the Second World War a number of outsiders were added to these; by 1940 there were in all twenty-two, six permanent and sixteen newly recruited. In 1941 an outside adviser and from 1942 onwards a panel of business men reviewed the position, and from then on rapid progress was made. Staffs were increased and the scope of their work widened. By 1947, nineteen of the hundred departments, including most of the larger offices, had their own organisation and methods

branches, and the rest—indeed, these also for special purposes—
were served by a staff of some fifty at the Treasury. In all, to use the
precise arithmetic of the Civil Service, some 224½ persons were then
employed on organisation and methods. The use made of organisation and methods was still in many departments limited; in particular, review was usually kept to the lower levels of the official
hierarchy. But a small section in the Treasury, concerned with the
higher level machinery of government, was at that date being brought
into the organisation and methods division. Organisation and
methods—though the Select Committee on Estimates still found
reasons for impatience, and staff of the right quality were hard to
recruit—was thus, at last, fully established.

A systematic review of a rather different type was set on foot by
the Local Government Manpower Committee, which did invaluable
work in 1949–51 in streamlining the controls of central over local
government, and relations within local government itself. The Committee recommended a continuing study worked out in cooperation
between central departments and the local authority associations. A
number of local authorities, led notably by the City of Coventry,
have also taken up straightforward organisation and methods work.

In business, organisation and methods work is likewise new. This
is indeed true even in America. When a selection of thirty-one large
American corporations was studied in 1941, it turned out that only
'at least four' had recently set up staff agencies for this purpose.
'Owing no doubt to their comparatively recent origin', the report
goes on, 'none of the agencies observed has as yet fully achieved its
logical ultimate place in the organisation'.[1] A British study just after
the war showed that similar staff agencies are spreading here. They
seem often to be more high-powered than in the Civil Service, in the
sense of including more senior staff and having a more clear-cut
conception of efficiency to give these leverage. But, like Civil Service
Organisation and Methods, they tend to be confined mainly to the
lower levels of management.

THE EXCLUDED CATEGORIES

In the excluded categories, finally—the cases of government-regulated bodies operating in the market—there are again beginnings,
but as yet no general or settled policy. In some cases there have been
extensive and thorough occasional reviews, as, for instance, by the
Lucas Committee on the Agricultural Marketing Acts, but with no
provision for regular periodic studies. In another major sector, that

[1] Holden, Fish, and Smith, *Top Management Organisation & Control*, 1941,
p. 79.

of the nationalised industries, the idea of regular reviews has in the last few years taken shape. The need to review these industries' largely novel and experimental organisation has been generally understood, at least since the war. The idea of an internal 'efficiency audit', on organisation and methods lines—though not of a similar audit by a supervising body from outside—has found a good deal of favour. For an outside review, similar to that conducted in the field of private industry by the Monopolies Commission, it has often been proposed that a select committee of Parliament would be appropriate. The experience of the Select Committee on Estimates has shown how effectively such a committee can throw up information; and, being staffed by back-benchers, it is less sensitive than an investigating Minister to the need to justify (or as the case may be to blacken) past or present government policy. Another solution might be based on experience with the B.B.C. The B.B.C. operates under a charter, which has from time to time to be renewed; and on the occasion of each renewal there is a fundamental and general review of its purpose and structure. These reviews seem to strike a happy medium between the need for public control and the danger of keeping the Corporation in a state of permanent dissection. In 1950 an undertaking was given in the House of Commons on behalf of the then (Labour) Government that similar reviews would be extended to other nationalised industries.

In the labour market, the question has arisen in the last few years of a regular review of collective bargains in order to bring them into line with the needs of the national economy as a whole. The solution so far adopted has been to leave the Industrial Disputes Tribunal (formerly the National Arbitration Tribunal) to build up a body of case law from disputes brought before it. The Tribunal has no settled rules, and no power of compulsion. The need to appear before it, however, and to argue out a case in public, has a considerable influence on employers' and workers' organisations. There has, in fact, grown up a body of jurisprudence which the Tribunal applies, and to which parties to disputes (not always very clearly or consciously) adjust their claims. The T.U.C., meantime, though again with no compulsory powers, has from time to time reviewed the structure of the trade union movement. Its recommendations have had a marked effect in reducing the number of unions and improving their conditions.

CONCLUSION

The cases quoted are not the only ones in which systematic and periodic reviews of controls and sanctions are needed, and, indeed, are practised. In the field of local government, for example, there is already provision for regular reviews of one aspect of political competition, namely district council areas, and much attention has been given recently to the need for reviews of the way in which public opinion about local government is formed, and of the channels—especially the consultative channels—through which it impinges on councillors and officers. The conception of a systematic review of international trade policies was written into the abortive Charter of the International Trade Organisation, and into the Geneva Agreements on Tariffs and Trade. The International Labour Organisation has a regular procedure for checking the application of its conventions. But enough has been said to bring out the two essential facts: first that the need for such reviews is now widely accepted, and secondly that the actual provision of them is as yet in its early stages. It may well be that at this point, when the first tentative experiments are over, but machinery has nowhere received its final shape, the most useful step would be a comprehensive review of reviews: to note where there are still gaps, show where one reviewing agency can learn from another, and where perhaps there is a need for the various agencies to keep more closely in line.

Part III

DECISIONS ABOUT OBJECTIVES

Chapter 8

CONSUMPTION AND SAVINGS

PART II was concerned with the effectiveness of the economic sanction, operating through various mechanisms, in getting decisions about what is to be produced and distributed carried out, *assuming that these decisions have already been made.* This assumption has now to be turned the other way round. Suppose that problems of monopoly, or of 'remote and diffused' factors, or of changes in the social framework, so far as they affect the *execution* of these decisions, have been solved. Suppose, in short, that consumers face a set of prices, and possibilities of production, which will accurately reflect their preferences once they have been shown what these are. How effective then is the economic sanction, operating through one or another mechanism, in guiding and controlling these more basic decisions themselves—decisions about consumption and savings, investment, or international and inter-regional economic relations?

WHAT IS THE PATTERN OF EXPENDITURE IN BRITAIN?

To begin, then, with consumption and saving. Significant features of the pattern of consumption and saving in Britain and Western Europe are summed up below in Tables 1-7. As incomes rise, the proportion spent on basic necessities falls, in some cases indeed ('inferior' goods such as potatoes or margarine) so sharply that even the absolute amount of consumption drops. There is a particularly marked shift towards services, such as travel, education, and domestic service. The free margin, over and above what has to be spent on basic needs, is now high in Britain even in the working class. It was reckoned as only 5% of an average working-class income in 1904, in the enquiry which for a generation was the basis of the official cost of living index. In the new cost of living enquiry in 1937-8, it came out at 30%, for families with the main earner alive and in full employment. It may well be 35-40% now. Four-fifths of all consumption, in spite of the great increase in taxation in recent years, still passes through household budgets; for, though governments in socialist and non-socialist countries alike take about two-fifths of net national incomes in taxation, nearly half this amount comes back to

103

TABLE 1

Working and middle-class consumption, Great Britain, 1938

Income, 1938 / Income required to give same purchasing power, after tax, 1949–50	Expenditure per head (£)			Per cent of all expenditure		
	Working class below £250¹ below £470	Middle Class — Lower £250–499 £470–1,224	Middle Class — Upper £500 or over £1,225 or over			
Food, drink, tobacco						
Food	24	39	64	52	39	19
Alcohol	4	9	38			
Tobacco	3	5	17			
Houseroom and heat						
Rent and rates	7	18	51	25	27	15
Fuel and light	4	8	5			
Furniture	2	8	21			
Hardware	1	2	9			
Household consumables	1	2	2			
Clothing						
Footwear	1	2	11	9	8	16
Men's clothes	2	4	16			
Women's and children's clothing	2	6	65			
Services						
Travel, car	2	8	93	12	23	41
Post, telephone	less than ½	1	5			
Entertainment	1	2	5			
Other services	4	18	125			
Miscellaneous goods						
Other goods	1	4	58	2	4	10
TOTAL	60	140	595	100	100	100
At 1949 prices, approx.:	109	259	1,270			

From Seers, *Changes in the Cost of Living and Distribution of Income since 1938*, and *Bulletin of Institute of Statistics*, June 1950.

¹ But including manual wage-earners with incomes above these levels.

Note: The 'upper middle class' is a very miscellaneous group. Of the total income of this class, after direct tax, in 1938, the percentage received by those with incomes of:

```
£500–  999 was 41
£1,000–1,999  ,,  26
£2,000–9,999  ,,  25
£10,000 and over   8
```

TABLE 2

Value, *not* recorded in national income statistics, of the annual "income"
assumed to be derived from the use of consumers' durable goods

	National income per worker ($ at prices of 1925–34) per annum	Annual Value of stream of services from consumers' durable goods as per cent of annual total of rents of dwellings
Sweden 1870	368	10
,, 1930	818	41
U.K. 1939	1,429	—
,, 1947	1,383	—
U.S.A. 1909	1,386	50
,, 1929	1,904	72

Based on Clark, *Conditions of Economic Progress*, 1951.

TABLE 3

Percentage of total expenditure available for items other than food,
housing, electricity, fuel and light, Great Britain

Working class	1904	5
	1937–8	30
Lower middle class	1937–8	45–50
Upper middle class	1937–8	
Spending up to £836 p.a.		51–6
All		64

From Bowley, *Review of Economic Studies*, June, 1941; Massey, *Journal of the Royal Statistical Society*, 1942, and Table I.

households through social security benefits or other income transfers. Governments in Western Europe finance from a third to a half of all investment in their countries, but—war apart—undertake only a fifth of all consumption.

Very broadly—*very* broadly—net savings, after deducting depreciation, tend to run around 10% of a country's national income per annum. But there are great variations around this trend. In 1949, for example, net saving accounted for 7% of the net national income of Belgium, but 26% of that of Norway and Finland. Though

TABLE 4

Expenditure of public authorities as per cent of net national income, 1885–1949. Government and personal consumption in 1937–49

| | As per cent of national income | | | | | | | Government consumption as % of total consumption | | Government investment as % of total (gross) investment | |
| | Expenditure of public authorities | | | | | Government consumption | | | | 1948 | |
	1885–90	1913	1929	1937	1949	1936–8	1949	1936–8	1949	Investment undertaken by public authorities or enterprises	Investment (including last column) financed by public authorities or enterprises
Belgium	—	6	16	18	41	16	17	18	19	31	35
France	12	14	26	22	44	14	15	14	17	32	55
Holland	—	8	15	—	36	13	18	14	20	19	32
Sweden	8	9	13	14	35	11	16	12	18	33	—
Switzerland	—	7	10	13	—	—	—	—	—	25	33
U.K.	8	12	24	24	43	15	20	16	22	36	42

In all cases figures are for the years named or the nearest available year. From the *Economic Survey of Europe for 1949*, and Clark, *Economic Journal*, 1945.

TABLE 5

Savings and taxes, working and middle-class families, Great Britain, 1949

	Working class (70% of families)		Middle class (30%)	
	per family	Total	per family	Total
Spent per annum on:	(£)	(£ million)	(£)	(£ million)
Savings	6	60	34	150
Direct taxes	20	200	250	1,100
As % of total expenditure of each class:				
Savings	1½		3	
Direct taxes	4½		23	

From *The Home Market*, 1950. 'Working class' includes all families whose head earns less than £400 p.a.

TABLE 6

Net savings, per cent of net national income

	Per cent of net national income					Per cent of commodities available for home use	
	1860–9	1870–9	1900–10	1925–30	1934–7	1938	1949
France		6	9	11		12	11
U.K.	17		12	8	7	8	11
U.S.A.			14	11	5		
Russia		3 (1890–1900)	8	8	14		
Switzerland			10	13		15 (1939)	26 (1948)
Norway						8	
Netherlands							19
Germany			19	8	12	17	15 (Western zones)
Japan				20	22		23

From Clark, *Conditions of Economic Progress*, 1951, *United Nations, Economic Survey for Europe*, 1949, and *Economic Survey for Asia*, 1949.

TABLE 7

Estimated net investment and net output in industry per person engaged.
Dollars in 1938 prices

Country	Net investment in fixed capital per head of population		Net value of industrial output per head		Net investment per person engaged in industry	
	1948	1949	1948	1949	1948	1949
U.S.A.	—	—	2,000	—	190	—
Norway	50	59	780	810	150	160
Sweden	44	36	1,080	1,090	170	130
France	22	24	590	640	100	100
Netherlands	22	31	620	650	60	100
U.K.	40	41	920	980	50	60
Finland	26	—	340	—	30	—
Italy	7	9	420	440	20	30
Belgium	19	21	—	—	20	—
Hungary	6	12	320	—	20	—
Poland	6	9	500	620	20	30

Note: 'Industry' comprises manufacturing, mining, gas, water and electricity supply, and handicrafts.

savings tend to be higher where incomes are high, this does not necessarily apply (Table 6) where the comparison is between people at different times and places (at different stages of the trade cycle, for instance), or in different social groups. The purposes for which consumption is postponed also vary greatly from country to country. Thus in 1949 some 30% of Finland's, and 22% of Great Britain's, gross investment was in housing, but only 10% of Italy's; and whereas net investment per head of the population, in dollars, was higher in Britain than in Sweden, and no less than 70% higher than in France, *industrial* investment in Britain was only about half as high as in these countries.

National income accounts, on which Tables 1–7 are chiefly based, do not record all items of consumption. They exclude, for instance, unpaid domestic work at home. For Sweden in the 'twenties this was reckoned, counting only housewives' work actually in the home, to add 20–25% to the national income. This figure would be much higher if it included the work of other members of the family, and the mass of unpaid leisure activities, whether classified as social service or religion or politics or entertainment and sport, carried on

CONSUMPTION AND SAVINGS

outside the home. This of course represents chiefly an addition to the lower and more numerous incomes. There is, on the other hand, an excluded item which benefits chiefly the well-to-do. Nearly a half of all durable goods sold in Britain, apart from building work, are bought by private households. Depreciation on these is roughly taken care of in the national income accounts, but not the net value, after deducting depreciation, of the annual stream of services they yield to their owners—what would correspond, were this industrial or commercial capital, to rent, interest and profit. On American and Swedish data it looks as if the income from this source might be valued for Britain today, taking all classes together, at about half the figure for rents shown in Table 1, or, say, about 5% of all consumers' expenditure (Table 2). It would be higher in proportion to rents in a richer economy, as in the United States, much lower in a backward country.

HOW ARE CONSUMPTION PATTERNS DETERMINED?

Patterns of expenditure in Britain develop most immediately out of the influence exerted on individual consumers, or consuming units—principally households—by the competitive market. Changes in prices and incomes lead in the competitive market to substantial and predictable changes in consumption, on which a good deal of statistical work has been done. One of the earliest and most useful generalisations of economic statistics, Engels' law, describes how the pattern of consumption tends to change as incomes rise (see again Table 1). Engels' law has been refined in recent years, notably by showing that for a single household—as apart from big aggregates—the relationship it describes is better expressed as a curve than as a straight line. It has also been enlarged by Colin Clark and others to show on a world scale how consumers' expenditure tends to shift, as wealth increases, from food to manufactures and then from manufactures to services. And others again have studied the way in which savings behave as incomes change.

For Great Britain, a quantity of recent work on how consumption patterns alter with changes in incomes and prices is summed up and completed in a massive series of studies issued by the Department of Applied Economics at Cambridge. The broad impression of these studies is conveyed by Table 21, and is familiar enough. There are 'superior' and 'inferior' goods, the latter being articles such as margarine, condensed milk, and fish and chips, whose consumption falls off as incomes rise. The demand for such basic commodities as food, drink, tobacco, and fuel and light is, in general,

109

inelastic, so that a rise or fall in incomes or prices leads to a smaller change (either way) in the amount of them bought. It is not surprising that among the exceptions (to take the column showing changes in demand as incomes rise) are wine, coffee, cream, restaurant meals, several kinds of fresh fruit, and the type of fuel suitable for boilers and central heating: for these, demand grows more than in proportion as incomes rise. Table 22 gives a fuller and less familiar impression of how the Cambridge studies have tried to disentangle the intricate relationships between the demands for related commodities. The demand for dried fruit seems to be little affected by its own price; it rises less than in proportion to an increase in consumers' incomes; is greatly influenced by the price of other goods in what might be called the 'dessert' market; and suffers very greatly indeed (other things being equal) in the event of a general price rise in which 'dessert' articles do not share. It is notable how, among the other 'dessert' articles, the demand for dried fruit seems to vary *with* that for bananas but in the opposite direction to that for apples, jam, or chocolate and sugar confectionery. Bananas turn out to be complementary to dried fruit, whereas the three last-mentioned articles are competitive or substitutes.

Studies of this kind can of course be put to many practical uses. The authors of the Cambridge studies point out, for instance, that the failure of the attempt to end sweet rationing in Britain in 1949 and the success of the attempt made in 1951 could both be predicted from their data. In 1949 the attempt to balance supply and demand in a free market could have succeeded only if prices had been allowed to rise about 75%, which politically was out of the question. In 1951, on the other hand, supply and free demand were about equal, and no major price adjustment was required. So also it is important for international trade policy to have at least an approximate idea of the change in demand which will follow a given alteration in incomes or prices in different countries. Sir Donald MacDougall has shown that in the 'thirties a uniform change of 10% in the prices of British relative to American exports could be expected to lead to a change of 15–20% in the volume of demand in the first part of the decade, and 20–25% in the last half. The change in the demand for a single commodity resulting from a change in the price of that commodity alone would be larger still.

But to say that patterns of consumption are mainly worked out in the market does not mean that they depend exclusively, to quote from previous chapters, on 'factors, within a given social framework, whose full significance is present and clear to consumers'. Straightforward decisions based on factors of that kind—the sort of decisions, that is, over which competition is usually an effective force of control—do, in fact, play a very important part. But studies of consumption tend to lay more and more stress on remote or diffused factors, and on the possibility of change in the social framework itself: that is on the factors which may call for intervention through direction or consultation.

The distribution of income and wealth

In the first place, expenditure is obviously limited by the distribution of incomes, which is largely outside individuals' control. 'Income' must be understood rather widely, to allow for expectations as well as current income, and for such 'enabling conditions' as the

TABLE 8

Number of persons living before 1939 in countries having a national income per head of:

Income per head $	No. of persons living in countries at this level ('000,000's)	Typical expectation of life of these people (males only) (years)	Countries
Over 1,250	139	62–5	U.S.A., Canada, New Zealand
900–1,249	72	58–63	U.K., New Zealand, Argentine, Australia
700–899	11	59–66	Holland, Ireland
400–699	241	52–64 (Europe)	Rest of Northern and Central Europe, Uruguay
		36–54	Chile, Brazil
200–400	519	38 (S. America)	Southern and Eastern Europe, U.S.S.R., Middle East, North Africa, South Africa, Japan, Philippines, Hawaii, rest of South and Central America
Under 200	1,113	27 (India)	India, China
	2,095	41 (Formosa)	South-east Asia, rest of Africa

From Clark, *Conditions of Economic Progress*, 1940, and *Statistical Year Book of the United Nations*.

TABLE 9

Rate of increase of national income per head of the working population, per cent, per annum, compound interest

	1850/85–1913	1913–29	1929–37
U.S.A.	1·1	1·8	0·7
Australia	1·0	2·8	0·9
France	1·5	0·6	—
Germany	1·5	0·8	2·8
Sweden	2·3	2·3	2·4
U.K.	1·3	1·0	1·5
Italy	2·4	1·7	—
U.S.S.R.	0·9	0·3	3·0
Japan	2·3	5·2	2·7
India	1·1	nil	—

From Clark, *Conditions of Economic Progress*, 1951. The starting date for each country for the decades to 1913 is the earliest, after 1850, for which Clark gives data.

TABLE 10

Great Britain, households where head receives a given income, per cent of all households, 1949

£1,000 per annum and over	4
£650–1,000	8
£400–650	18
£225–400	62
Below £225	8

From *The Home Market*, 1950.

availability of hire-purchase facilities, or of liquid savings. Data on the size and distribution of incomes and their rate of growth are summed up in Tables 8–15 in the next pages. The most striking impression is of the poverty still characteristic of most of the world. More than half the world's population, in India, China, South-East Asia, and Africa, live on incomes per head less than one-fifth of that for Great Britain. There are, moreover, only limited possibilities, in the short run, of raising incomes. Typical rates of growth of national income per head, in the generations when what are now the advanced nations were pushing forward into the lead, were 1–2½% per annum, compound interest. These are not low rates; they will easily add 50% to national incomes in a generation, or even double them.

CONSUMPTION AND SAVINGS

TABLE 11
Number of incomes above £500 for each income above £5,000[1]

	1900	1925	1939	*Most recent*
U.S.A.	28	35	59	89
Canada	—	—	69	191
Latin America	—	—	—	20 (approx.)
U.K.	20	41	37	65
France	48	—	66	—
Germany	40	62	47	—
Denmark	—	68	87	380
Sweden	25	52	33	251
India	28	17	35	45
Japan	78	51	—	—
Australia	34	—	89	132
New Zealand	—	—	224	—

From Clark, *IX* Congrès International des Sciences Historiques*, 1950, p. 256.
[1] About the same ratio would hold for any tenfold difference in incomes, provided the lower income is within the ordinary range of incomes.

TABLE 12
Great Britain, proportion of income before direct tax retained after tax

Corresponding income ranges

1938 £	1948 £	1938	1948
250–499	500–999	97	85
500–999	1,000–1,999	91	74
1,000 and over	2,000 and over	70	50

£250 was usually taken in 1938 as the dividing line between the working and the lower middle class. The middle-class cost of living index, 1938 =100, was 199 for 1948, and 201 for 1949.

From Cmd. 7.933 and Seers, *Bulletin of the Institute of Statistics*, June 1950.

But neither do they hold out prospects of revolutionary change over short periods. The highest sustained rate of growth on record is the 5% per annum of Japan in the generation down to the slump of 1929–30.

A further impression is of the large remaining inequalities. Some inequalities have diminished greatly. The gap between skilled and

TABLE 13

Great Britain, earnings of farmers and farm workers, pre-war and 1949

(a) *Parity between farm and other incomes*

Attitude surveys show that usually middling farmers, holding 100–150 acres, are assigned by public opinions the social status of an industrial manager. But their incomes were equivalent in:

> 1938 to those of adult male factory workers;
> 1947 ,, foremen or senior clerks;
> 1949 ,, qualified professional men and women in responsible positions, but not the highest paid or policy-making groups.

Adult male farm workers' earnings were equivalent in 1938 to 55–60% of those comparable factory workers; in 1949 to 85–90%.

(b) *Purchasing power of certain classes of income, after direct tax, 1949* (1938 = 100)

Farmers' incomes	191
Others, mainly non-farming:	
(a) Wages	122
(b) Salaries, professional earnings	82–9

TABLE 14

Gap between the earnings of skilled and unskilled workers, 1930–9. Standard deviation of wages from average wage of all workers in each country in a comparable group of occupation, in % of the average wage

Scandinavia, Switzerland, Belgium, France, Australia	14–16
U.K.	18
Spain, Canada	24
Japan, Yugoslavia	40–2

Clark, *Conditions of Economic Progress*, 1951, p. 225.

unskilled workers is typically very wide in undeveloped countries, and diminishes with the advance of education. The gap between the British farmer or farm worker and his opposite number in the towns was wide, but has been largely closed. The gap between rich and poor, even before tax, has diminished in most of the economically advanced countries, and in some others, notably India. Taxation has reduced it still further. In Britain, however, it still remains wide, both absolutely and compared to Scandinavia, Australasia, or North America. The British middle-class family is still reckoned to enjoy after tax 3½ times the income of an average family in the working

TABLE 15

Incomes required to give a family with two children the same standard
of living as a family with none. Great Britain, 1948

	When the family's earned income is:	The family with two children already receives benefits to the value of:	But needs a further payment to cover the full cost of two children of:
	£	£	£
Semi-skilled worker	297	39	52
Foreman or clerk	500	65	75
Professional grade	1,000	80	163

Based on Vol. V of the *Papers of the Royal Commission on the Population*. The
estimates of additional needs for families with £500–1,000 a year are on the assumption that the proportion of the cost of two children to the basic salary, net of direct
tax, is the same at these levels as at £300 a year. The benefits already received and
allowed for here include family allowance, income tax deduction, and school meals,
milk, and an adjustment on account of rationing.

TABLE 16

Income in worst slump year, 1929, average of 1929 and 1937 as percentage

	1929	Average of 1929 and 1937
U.S.A.	57	59
Australia	77	74
France	93	—
Germany	84	75
Sweden	96	88
U.K.	82	76
Italy	88	—
U.S.S.R.	92	80
Japan	101	95

of class. Another inequality which still remains substantial in Britain
is that (Table 15) between families with and without children. There
is still a very marked 'poverty cycle', whereby a child is born into
relative poverty, grows into relative affluence in early manhood, drops
back again after marrying, while the children are young, then returns
to prosperity for a time after the children in their turn have grown

TABLE 17

Personal consumption in Great Britain, 1938 prices, 1938 and 1943

	£ million		
	1938	1943	1943 as % of 1938
Rent, etc.	491	498	101
Food	1,297	1,056	81
Clothing, household goods	734	354	48
Miscellaneous goods and services	660	460	70
Private motoring	127	8	6
Alcohol, entertainment, reading	590	629	107
Postage, telephone, rail, bus, and business motoring	192	223	117
Income in kind of armed forces	17	135	795
Personal expenditure abroad	34	73	214
	4,339	3,623	84
Of which, spent by foreigners in U.K.	43	48	—

From *Statistical Abstract*.

TABLE 18

Real income per head, U.S.S.R. $, prices of 1925–34

	1913	1928	1934	1938
Consumption	107	107	68	95
Total production	130	120	98	136

Clark, *IXe Congrès International des Sciences Historiques*, 1950, p. 254.

up and are earning, only to drop back finally into relative poverty in retirement. But the most striking inequality of all is that between the advanced and backward nations. The average income per head in India, Pakistan, and Ceylon is about one-eighth of that in Britain. Allowing for differences in purchasing power, the real ratio may be five or six to one. This may be compared with the ratio between the upper middle class and the general run of the working class in

116

TABLE 19

Distribution of capital, Great Britain, 1946-7

Percentage of persons aged 25 or over having holdings of at least:	Per cent of all persons	Per cent of all capital held by persons with this or larger holdings
Amount		
£		
100,000	0·05– 0·06	14–18
25,000	0·4	33–37
10,000	1·1 – 1·2	49–54
5,000	2·5 – 2·8	60–66
1,000	11·2 –11·8	83–86
100	38·1 –40·4	95–96
0	100	100

Estimated by K. Longmore in *Bulletin of the Institute of Statistics*, 1951.

TABLE 20

Capital per head of the working population, 1928–39 (dollars, prices of 1925–34), excluding land

U.K., 1932–4	6,660	
Holland, 1939	6,320	
U.S.A., 1939	5,820	
Canada, 1929	5,500	Clark, *Conditions of*
Norway, 1939	2,732	*Economic Progress,*
Japan, 1930	2,380	1951 edn., p. 486 ff.
Hungary, 1928	1,088	
Italy, 1928	890	
Egypt, 1937	450	

Britain, which even before tax is probably not more than four or five to one. There is some reason to believe that the gap between the advanced and backward countries has actually increased since 1939.

The distribution of wealth, in the sense of capital, also affects consumption inasmuch as wealth can be drawn on temporarily, or entirely consumed, to supplement current income. It remains far more unequal in Britain than the distribution of incomes. The richest 2½–3% of all households in 1948 received 30% of the national income after tax, but in 1946-7 the richest 2½–3% of adults over twenty-five owned no less than 60–65% of the national property. There is also very great inequality between nations (Tables 19 and 20).

117

TABLE 21a.   The demand for food, drink, tobacco, and fuel in the
United Kingdom, 1920–39

An increase of 10% in the price of the article in question led, other things
being equal, to an increase or decrease in demand of:—

Decrease	15–20%	Dried beans, peas, etc. Apples (home)	} Elastic demand
	10–15%	Mutton and lamb Canned meat (imported) Condensed milk Potatoes (imported) Canned and bottled vegetables	
	5–10%	Flour Cakes and biscuits Beef and veal (imported) Mutton and lamb (imported) Pork Bacon and ham Fresh fish Cream Lard Potatoes (home) Apples (imported) Oranges Bananas Other fresh fruit and nuts Chocolate and sugar confectionery Beer Spirits Wine (imported) Coal Electricity	} Inelastic demand
	0– 5%	Cereals (other) Beef and veal (home) Eggs Fresh milk Butter Margarine Root vegetables, tomatoes, etc. Canned and bottled fruit Dried fruit Sugar Tea ALL FOOD Wine (British) Tobacco	
Increase	0– 5%	Cheese Cocoa	

TABLE 21b. The demand for food, drink, tobacco, and fuel in the United Kingdom, 1920–39. *An increase of 10% in consumers' incomes led, other things being equal, to an increase or decrease in demand of:*

Decrease	5–10%	Condensed milk	⎫
	0– 5%	Flour	
		Margarine	
		Lard	
		Cocoa	
		Fish and chips	
		Beer	
Increase	0– 5%	Cereals (other)	
		Beef and veal (home and imported)	
		Canned meat (imported)	
		Sausages, etc.	
		Butter	
		Cheese	
		Suet, etc.	Inelastic demand
		Potatoes (home and imported)	
		Dried beans, peas, etc.	
		Sugar	
		Tea	
		Jam, marmalade	
		Chocolate and sugar confectionery	
		Tobacco	
		Coal, Gas and Electricity	
	5–10%	Cakes and biscuits	
		Mutton and lamb (home)	
		Mutton and lamb (imported)	
		Pork, bacon and ham	
		Eggs	
		Fresh fish	
		Fresh milk	
		Root vegetables, tomatoes, etc.	
		Canned and bottled vegetables	
		Oranges and bananas	
		Dried fruit	
		ALL FOOD	
		Spirits	⎭
	10–15%	Apples (home)	⎫
		Apples (imported)	
		Canned and bottled fruit	
		Coffee, etc.	
		Wine (imported)	
	15–20%	Cream	Elastic demand
		Other fresh fruit and nuts	
		Wine (British)	
		Coke	
	20–25%	Meals away from home	⎭

Adapted from Stone, *Measurement of Consumers' Behaviour in the U.K. in 1920–38,* 1954, Table 106.

TABLE 22

United Kingdom, 1920–38.   The demand for dried fruit

A 10% rise in	Is associated with a change in the demand for dried fruit of
	%
Consumers' incomes	+ 7·5 (±1·3)
Price of dried fruit	− 2·6 (±3·6)
Price of bananas	−12·2 (±2·7)
Price of jam	+23·4 (±5·7)
Price of chocolate and sugar confectionery	+17·6 (±5·6)
Price of apples	+ 7·2 (±2·2)
Price of all other articles	−33·3 (±9·3)

From Stone, *ibid.*

Stability of incomes and expectations

The second background determinant of consumers' behaviour, largely outside consumers' own control, is stability of income and expectations. A big rise or fall of income, or a change in family size, will involve a family in reorganising its whole field of expenditure; and such decisions are not easily or quickly taken. This is all the truer where a fall in income is involved, since a family will generally have standing commitments, structural elements in its expenditure pattern, which are hard to get rid of. Examples might be an insurance policy or the rent of a house. These factors make changes in the pattern of expenditure irreversible in time. There will, for instance, be a tendency for a family's savings to be a constant percentage of its income so long as incomes are rising, provided at least that it keeps its same relative social status; but let incomes fall, and in the effort to maintain existing consumption standards, the savings percentage will be cut down. Conversely, unstable expectations may deter a family from entering into permanent commitments, such as owning its own house; even though some such commitments—to a certain neighbourhood for example—may be desirable for a stable and satisfying social life. Tables 16–18 illustrate various forms of instability: those due to the trade cycle, to war, and to the catastrophe of farm collectivisation in the U.S.S.R. To these must be added the effects of seasonal and casual employment. There are also many data available on consumer behaviour in times of inflation. The effect which individual market decisions, in their turn, have on

120

the general stability of income will be shown in more detail in the next chapter. Consumption and savings decisions play a less dynamic part in this than decisions on investment, which the next chapter will discuss.

Basic elements in expenditure

The standing commitments, or basic elements, in expenditure patterns are important even apart from the problem of stability. They are more likely than casual or habitual expenditures to be planned. But they have far-reaching 'remote' or 'diffused' effects on the whole pattern of a family's life, and these may well be less adequately allowed for, in spite of planning, than decisions whose effects are narrower and more immediate. A simple illustration from the pre-war depression is the case of unemployed families moved from a slum area in Stockton-on-Tees to a new housing estate. The new surroundings were healthier and more attractive. Rents, however, were higher, and in the new, more spick-and-span social environment families were unwilling to cut down on household incidentals. They therefore allowed for the rise in rents mainly by cutting down on food, with the result that their standardised death-rate rose 46% above what it had been before. The effects of alcoholism would be another example; and much subtler chains of cause and effect can also be traced.

Group standards

The fourth, and in many ways the most important, background determinant beyond individuals' control is group standards, the existence of social solidarity: the fact that people's consumption decisions are not independent but interdependent. People belong to social groups, in the family and neighbourhood or at work. These groups, to a great extent, prescribe both reputable aims and reputable means of achieving them. These standards grow out of the decisions of individual consuming units, which are thus interdependent; what people buy depends very largely on what the neighbours buy. A family will try to keep to a minimum the number of occasions when it comes in contact with 'superior' goods; finds, that is, members of its own social group engaged in activities, or employing means, which attract more social approval than those it uses itself. It will try to keep up with the Joneses. Thus television aerials tend to sprout, not uniformly over an area, but in clumps as neighbours catch the infection from one another. And the proportion of its income a family saves depends, not on its absolute income, but on its position in the income distribution of its particular social group.

121

A family half-way down the income distribution of the white population of New York saves only about the same proportion as one half-way down the distribution of the coloured population, though its income is half as high again. This relation between place in the income distribution and percentage of income saved seems to be quite general, and to account for the broad tendency for net savings, over long periods, to average around 10% of national incomes.

Group pressures may influence patterns of consumer behaviour negatively as well as positively. Families on new estates, for instance, may feel the need to live up to the standards suggested by the high technical quality of the estate's equipment, but may lack the means or social skill necessary for this. They accordingly tend to withdraw from social contacts, so producing the well-known phenomenon of social 'deadness'; once at least the initial period of settlement, with its obvious and easy tasks of moving furniture and complaining of inadequate bus services, is over. The final state of apathy has been called one of 'social poverty'.

(e) *The framework of society. The Just Price.*

Ultimately, the way people react to any of these factors—'immediate' or 'remote or diffused'—in their decisions on consumption and saving depends on the social framework itself; the personality patterns, institutional structure, and norms of belief and practice characteristic of each community. The norms of consumption and saving in Britain—people's ideas about what ought to be saved or spent, as apart from what actually is—were neither very well developed nor very explicit in the early days of modern industry. But as the generations have gone on they have crystallised and converged on a modern version of the mediæval doctrine of the Just Price. The mediaeval doctrine arose, as has the modern debate over competition, direction, and consultation, out of the need to review and correct the working of a competitive market. It is not surprising that it concerned itself with the same points and can be stated in similar terms. As mediaeval theologians saw it, and as we tend again to do today, consumption patterns ought not simply to be left to develop under the influence of a competitive market. The competitive pattern ought on the contrary to be modified to ensure:—

(1) Attention to 'remote and diffused' factors.

(a) The distribution of incomes must be such as, first, to make pay equal to the value of each class of work to society. For this ensures the continuity of production by rewarding work in proportion to its social utility, and by delivering the means of further work into producers' hands in proportion to their ability to satisfy consumers' needs. This much can normally be ensured by competition. But—and here competition tends to break down—pay should also take account of human needs. These needs are limited, and no one has an unlimited claim on the world's resources. But within the limits appropriate to each case people have a strict right to satisfy their needs. They have a right to a *minimum* income, and a duty not to exceed a *maximum* of expenditure. Surplus income, above this minimum, must be given or invested or taxed away. 'Surplus' must be strictly interpreted, and 'needs' assessed by reference to the most economic means of providing for them.

(*b*) Stability and the time factor must also be allowed for. Human personality and patterns of expenditure mature through time, and where values and needs have to be assessed this should be done on a long-term basis. Prices, for instance, should not be allowed to reflect purely temporary scarcities. Provision must be made for the future; this calls in particular for attention to the accumulation and distribution of property. And unstable incomes and expenditure patterns have the dangers and disadvantages outlined just above.

(*c*) Social solidarity, again, must be allowed for, in addition to individual needs. The circle of solidarity—the people of whose needs policy must take account—includes in the first place neighbours and members of the same family and working group. But it extends as far as actual social relationships reach, and in these days is therefore world-wide.

(*d*) And 'basic services' must have their share of attention. Aquinas' *Prince*, to take a mediaeval example, contains as pretty a statement as will be found anywhere of the general objectives of town and country planning, their importance, and the need for the State to help in achieving them.

(2) Attention ought also to be paid to the relation of consumption patterns to change in the social framework: in personality and social norm and structure. Some patterns of consumption arise out of and help to build up satisfactory personality patterns. Others do not. Particular patterns contribute to and are caused by particular types of social structure. It is probably at this point that the greatest divergence between mediaeval and modern thinking appears. Mediaeval opinion regarded a rather rigidly structured class society

as desirable; modern opinion favours high social mobility and a tendency towards a classless society. But the two ages at least agree that, whichever pattern be desirable, the social structure is important in discussing and controlling consumption. And they also agree that the effect of consumers' decisions in changing personality, institutions, and social norms, and the effect on consumption of changes in these things—in the class structure, for instance—is unlikely to be satisfactory if worked out through competition alone. Competition, as usual, opens the road to change, and facilitates people's acceptance of it. But it does not enforce it, or necessarily select changes desirable on diffused or less immediate grounds.

PROBLEMS OF CONSUMPTION AS INDICATED BY THE THEORY OF THE JUST PRICE

(a) The distribution of incomes and wealth

Let us pause for a moment and compare actual British consumption and saving with the theory of the just price. This is a useful means of checking the success of current policy in this field, and noting the importance of the problems remaining in it. Do wages and profits actually correspond (heading 1 (a)) to the value of work done? In most Western countries the answer is 'yes'; but only roughly so. The problem of equal pay for equal work for women, for example, is far from being solved in most countries. Or are satisfactory floor and ceiling limits built into expenditure patterns? In Britain, in particular, much progress has been made in achieving satisfactory *minimum* incomes. In the city of York, in 1936, 31% of all working-class families were, by Rowntree's standards, in gross poverty. In 1950 the proportion was 2¾%, and this was then reduced further by a rise in old age pensions. But the 'poverty cycle', the relative poverty of the aged or of families with children, remains.

Redistributive taxation has aimed at imposing a proper *maximum* of expenditure, and transferring the surplus of the well-to-do to those less well off. But it can be shown that there is still much wasteful and unnecessary expenditure in a country like Britain. Some of it represents plain luxury and extravagance, in the ordinary meaning of these words, in the high income groups. Upper middle-class incomes (after tax), 3½ times as high as working class, leave plenty of room for splashing, at least in childless families; even apart from any question of spending capital. There is also waste in the fringe of 'problem' families in all classes. But this refers to luxury or waste defined as it commonly is by the average man, namely luxury or waste by the standards of the average household. These standards themselves, judged by circumstances in the world as a whole, are not beyond criticism. There is a surprisingly large amount of fat to be melted off the general mass of solid working and lower middle-class families. The wastage here may well be far greater, in total, than in the small marginal 'luxury' or 'problem' groups which waste on a more conspicuous scale. The best-known surveys of recent years, those by Rowntree and Lavers, give the impression that the chief spending outlets of the British masses are pubs, pools, and prostitutes. This is not the whole of the truth, but neither is it entirely remote from it. The average expenditure of a British household on drink, tobacco, and gambling in 1953 was about £160–170. A certain spareness and asceticism, the craftsman's elimination of superfluities—the achievement in short of a certain 'style'—is part of the good life, and it would hardly be claimed that the British consumer has attained it. It is a good exercise to imagine British spending habits as seen, for example, through the eyes of a Japanese.

(b) *Stability and the time factor*

Nor, again (heading 1 (b)), has everything possible been done to stabilise incomes and patterns of expenditure. Much has certainly been done to this end by full employment policy, control of the location of industry, or social insurance. It is today recognised that consumers commonly prefer stable prices and rationing if, as in the war, free choice would mean violent fluctuations in supplies, prices, and the relative shares of scarce goods obtained by rich and poor or by those with fixed or flexible incomes. But many problems remain, clustering especially round the question of a stable association between the worker and his job. The idea of a guaranteed annual wage is catching on, but spreads only slowly. There is still (Chapter 3) a rather rapid turnover—almost certainly an unnecessarily rapid turnover—in the composition of working groups, of firms' labour forces, and of neighbourhoods. The significance of this can be seen by contrasting town and country life. There is some evidence that the pattern of consumption in farming areas, income for income, tends to be more satisfactory than that in the towns. This came out very strongly, for example, in the years of wartime evacuation from the bigger cities; the standards of farm labourers' families proved to be in general far superior to those of families of similar income and status in the towns. If so, this must be attributed at least in part to the rather high stability of rural neighbourhoods and working groups.

Or (still under heading 1 (b)) what of the 'ethical imperative' on provision for the future? It is known within broad limits what is likely to be saved under competitive conditions, and what forces operate to bring this saving about. But only recently—notably in relation to the problems of underdeveloped areas—has there begun to be much really fundamental discussion of the rate of saving desirable when the possibility of non-competitive mechanisms of saving is brought into account as well. *Who* is to save? Is the right policy that so graphically though unkindly described by Dr. Balogh, of saturating maharajahs and millionaires with brandy and concubines until some surplus runs over into investment for the greater provision of concubines and brandy in future? Or is saving, in a world where maharajahs and millionaires no longer command the respect they once did, to be by or for the account of the small man? If so, how does one get him to save? Does one start by altering tax allowances, or with a youth movement, a Marriage Guidance Council, a Women's Institute, or perhaps co-partnership in industry? In what form is he to hold his savings? (This will be touched on again in the next chapter.) Or ought the main source of savings to be the Budget? And in any case, whoever does the saving, how much saving ought they to do?

(c) Social solidarity

The circle of solidarity in Britain (heading 1 (*c*)) has been extended in the last two generations to include the whole of the national community. It is taken for granted that for many purposes—social insurance, for instance, or the pooling of surplus incomes—the whole population of Britain will stand in together. Inequality of opportunity still exists; but it has to be defended, and equality is accepted as the norm. But here again only part of the ground has been covered. The case is only now beginning to be accepted for extending the circle still wider, indeed to the whole world. There is equality of opportunity in the British medical profession, or in mining, only for those who are born with a British passport: and preferably one issued in the United Kingdom. It can be roughly estimated that, were income redistributed between the richer and poorer countries on the same basis on which it is redistributed between the middle and working class in Britain, this country would have to find £1,500,000,000 a year for underdeveloped areas. United Nations experts, more modestly, have suggested that about 8½% of the national income a year (say, in round figures £1,000,000,000) might be a fair contribution. But the actual percentage of the national income annually invested overseas has equalled even this lower figure only in the great days of City overseas finance, just before the First

World War. Since the Second World War this figure has never been even remotely approached.

(d) Basic elements in consumption

Propaganda for the Welfare State during the last seventy years has been largely built up on the idea that, as R. H. Tawney put it:

> 'By concentrating surplus resources, directing them to objects of primary importance, and applying them, as in the case of the services of health, housing, and education, under expert advice and in accordance with a specialised technique, it makes possible the attainment of results which no body of individuals . . . could achieve for themselves by their isolated action.' (*Equality*, 1938 ed., p. 164.)

It has, in fact, been one of the main tasks of the Welfare State to ensure that the basic elements in consumption (heading 1 (d) above) are available freely and cheaply enough to provide a satisfactory basis for patterns of consumption as a whole. The degree of success achieved in the cases of health and education will be discussed below in Chapter 11. There is still, as will be seen, room for improvement under these heads, particularly in education. And the same can be said of housing and town planning. There were 9,000,000 houses and flats in Great Britain in 1920, and between that date and 1954 some 6½ million more were built or adapted; including in this figure temporary housing and conversions after 1945, but not between 1920 and 1939. This amount of building very nearly kept pace with the quantitative increase in demand, with a small allowance for the replacement of slum and war-damaged dwellings. But the bulk of the problem of slum replacement, as it grew up before 1920, still remained to be solved; and the problem of generalising satisfactory standards of town planning began to be tackled on a really comprehensive scale only after the Town and Country Planning Act of 1947. The question of how much and what kind of house ownership is desirable—individual or cooperative ownership, for instance—is still unsettled. So are the principles of rent control. Among other unsettled questions about the ownership and use of major consumers' durable goods—those whose acquisition causes a major and permanent change in a family's pattern of expenditure—might be picked out that of the place of the car in family and social life, and the significance of this for tax, town planning, and transport policy.

(e) Consumption and the social framework

Finally, the relation between consumption patterns and the social framework—heading (2) of the just price list—still presents a number of unsolved problems. It has always been obvious that people's family, local community, class, and occupational group influence their expectations and so determine what constitutes a satisfactory standard of consumption for them. Patterns of consumption in their turn—clothing, for example, or different types of schooling—help to mark or blur, strengthen or rub out, the distinctions between classes or other social groups. The right policy in a particular case may be to alter the class or occupational or family structure so as to make possible a more satisfactory standard of consumption, rather than to try to adapt the standard of consumption to the social structure. In the last generation this usually meant altering the class structure so as to level off standards of consumption, and offer a higher standard to classes less favoured within the existing structure. This process is far from complete. But because it has already gone so far, the question more often arises now than in the last generation of what its effective limits are. What are the minimum advantages of status and normal expectations, and of patterns of life and expenditure based on them, needed to enable teachers, managers, doctors, or for that matter skilled craftsmen, to do efficiently the work society expects of them?

And what sorts of personality are being developed by consumption as practised today? The Aunt Sally of an earlier age was the economic man, a ruthless individualist whose experience as a consumer as well as a producer was supposed to train him to disregard the wider social consequences of his acts. He was supposed to disregard among others those which have led to the, in many ways, disorganised or ill-organised society of the modern big city. For that reason, he figures in studies such as Lewis Mumford's *Culture of Cities* as megalopolitan man. On either count, he might be called underdirected man; man left too much to his own devices. Laboratory specimens of underdirected man (as of any other pure type of man) have never been easy to find; yet there was much truth in the charge that the spirit he embodied was characteristic of the early industrial age. Reaction against that spirit has now gone far, and, as in the case of the social structure, the question has arisen of its proper limits. Of the average consumer's income in cash and kind in 1938, net of both direct and indirect taxes, about 13% came to him from the State; and 7% of this was in the form of payments and allowances of which the consumer had the spending himself. Only 6% of his realised income, therefore, was spent for him out of his control. In 1949, on the other hand, $26\frac{1}{2}$% of his net realised income came from the State, and 18% came in subsidies or services in kind and was thus spent out of his control. Is the underdirected consumer in danger of becoming overdirected? Or is he, perhaps, under the impact of modern ideas of social solidarity, and of high-pressure advertising and rising margins for 'free' or luxury consumption, in danger of becoming too other-directed; too much inclined, as David Riesman's *The Lonely Crowd* suggests, to rely on others' judgement and adopt their standards?

(f) Conclusion

No more can be done here than to ask these questions about the just price and its application. There is no space to answer them; they are brought in simply as pointers to issues which remain to be settled. And they show that at every one of the points where experience suggests that the control of consumption by competition may need to be supplemented with direction or consultation, important issues of policy do, in fact, arise. In the consumption field, the 'ethical imperative' as today understood in Britain is very far as yet from being fully obeyed.

These unsolved problems cannot be ignored. Forces are building up which seem likely to compel attention to them, as the rise of the labour movement compelled attention to those of full employment or social security fifty or sixty years ago. International circumstances, in particular—defence, communism, the demands of the under-developed nations—have forced the idea of a further critique of consumption to the fore. The rise of the under-privileged countries is playing the same part in this generation as that of the under-privileged classes in the last. It has become necessary, for very practical and compelling reasons, to release British resources for these international purposes. And it is necessary to make better use of such income as is left, so that the standard of consumption in Britain may not suffer as a result, and that the British—and generally the Western—pattern of life may have a style attractive to Africa and the East.

MECHANISMS OF CONTROL OF CONSUMPTION AND SAVINGS

What part, then, is to be played by competition, direction, and consultation in the economics of consumption? Competition will obviously not be sufficient by itself, seeing the number of 'remote and diffused' elements in people's decisions about consumption and savings, and the importance of change or stability in the social framework. Direction is, in fact, currently used to supplement competition at most of the points already mentioned. The distribution of income and wealth is controlled by the State, and no longer left to the free play of the market. The law, full employment policy, or price control and rationing, guarantee stability of expectations. A basic, structural element in expenditure patterns such as housing is carefully watched and controlled by the Government and local authorities. So, though the control is less effective, is the equally structural factor of savings. If necessary, savings are supplemented or offset with Budget surpluses or deficits. Types of expenditure grossly offensive to group standards—public drunkenness, for instance—are punished by law. The social framework itself is altered by compulsion to attend school, and submit to the resulting change in personality pattern; by the compulsory regrouping of communities through town and country planning, and through the progressive inculcation of new standards of conduct by the law.

How far should this use of direction go? Should it extend into the field which *can* be covered by individual choice and competition? How much, in short, can consumption and savings decisions usefully be planned? Seeing what has been said in Part II about the limitations of direction, this question can be restated in another form. Granted that direction can maintain precise control over only (compared to competition) a small number of variables, can desirable standards of consumption be expressed in terms of human needs standards: few, simple and clear-cut enough for direction to enforce efficiently?

Human needs standards which on the face of them meet this condition can be and have been drawn up. Nutritional experts describe the calories, vitamins, and minerals needed to secure a standard of nutrition such that no further improvement would add anything significant to health or well-being. Housing experts define the number of square feet of living space required by a typical family, and the services and amenities to go with it. More general 'minimum needs' standards have been prepared, as for instance the Rowntree Minimum; and rough attempts have been made at a comprehensive classification into 'basic', 'comfort', and 'luxury' goods. The possibility of a standard of full social health, similar to the nutritionists' standard of full physical health, has been pressed, notably by the medical group which established the Pioneer Health Centre at Peckham, and social research has advanced some way towards it.

But such standards do not carry any ethically compelling force in themselves. Even if variations in taste and patterns of living from one family or group to another be disregarded, human needs standards measure only one of the complex of factors summed up above as the 'ethical imperative', and relevant to decisions on consumption. It is relevant to know, for example, that if an adult man doing medium-heavy work has less than three thousand calories a day his health will suffer to a specified extent. It is in clarifying such consequences that the value of human needs standards lies. But no ethical law declares that each man, everywhere, shall have three thousand calories. There are other claims on income. Man does not live by bread alone; and it is necessary to provide for maintaining or increasing production in future. Over by far the greater part of the world, and in the world as a whole, when these other claims are allowed for, resources are too limited and other demands too pressing for the full number of calories to be supplied.

A human needs standard may indeed carry a good deal of weight in decisions about how to spend, or to supplement, incomes at or about bare subsistence level, for at that level the bare satisfaction of needs—especially physical needs—bulks large. Even at that level it neither is nor should be the sole determining factor. Cobbett, a big man and a big eater if ever there was one, on one occasion sacrificed his last farthing not for a herring but for pen and ink. Was he wrong? Do we necessarily condemn those more normal souls who feel that, if life is hopeless, so much the more reason for a cinema or a pint? But in any case, such ethically compelling force as a human needs standard may possess evaporates once the bare subsistence is secure, and in Britain this is the case for the vast majority of the people. The rise in the free margin on even working-class incomes was noted above. This margin is calculated after deducting the cost of 'basic' goods such as food. But even 'basic' expenditure in a country like Britain contains a considerable 'luxury' element. In 1943, when expenditure on food was cut to 80% of pre-war, it seemed to most people that a very creditable standard of austerity had been attained. So it had; if it were assumed that the pre-war tastes and food habits of the British people were sacrosanct. Consistently with these, it was impossible to cut deeper and still maintain a full standard of nutrition. But in 1940, when the submarine campaign looked threatening and it seemed as if the choice might be between changing habits and starvation, a committee of scientists was appointed to discover a diet which could be mainly grown in Britain, but would still maintain full health and working efficiency. The diet they arrived at would not have been appetising; it would have consisted of potatoes, oatmeal, bread, and milk. But it would not merely have solved the problem of war transport and, since 1945, of the balance of payments; it would also have cost about half what was actually spent on food even during the war, and, taste apart, would have been no less nutritious. If 'basic' means basic, this is what a basic diet is. The actual diet of the British people represents a (perfectly legitimate) decision to use surplus income to buy tastier food rather than more clothes, holidays, or washing machines.

In any case, whether at the subsistence or at higher levels, it is neither possible nor desirable to determine consumption patterns by simple standards which ignore variations from one individual or family to another. Marghanita Laski, writing in *Vogue* on the Intellectual Budget, observes that intellectuals spend rather little on underwear and rent, but a great deal on Picassos and rum. Fact or not, this expresses the truth that there are many and varied patterns of consumption, none of them necessarily better than the rest. As between the lady who shudders at Picasso and wears wool next her skin and the female intellectual passionately devoted to strange pictures, but unwilling to buy wool to save her life, who is to say which, in the light of eternity, lives better? It is possible to say of some forms of expenditure, as, for instance, on alcohol, that they are either immoral in themselves or liable to lead to immorality. But of the vast majority of expenditure patterns one can say only that they are different; not that one is worth more than the next.

If one is worth no more than the next, it might be argued that no reason remains against overriding individual variations, and standardising consumption sufficiently to make direction of consumption possible. But the evidence that people, or families, get great satisfaction from choosing their own pattern of consumption is too strong to be seriously challenged. And variety is the spice of life, not only in this short-term sense, but because—one of the standard arguments for competition, as has been seen—from variety of choice spring the mutations on which future progress depends. 'Variety', Keynes wrote,

> 'preserves the traditions which embody the most secure and successful choices of former generations; it colours the present with the diversification of its fancy; and, being the handmaid of experiment as well as of tradition and fancy, it is the most powerful instrument to better the future.' (*General Theory of Employment, Interest, and Money*, 1936, p. 380.)

Intellectuals, to quote Marghanita Laski again, do not go to fashionable holiday resorts; but those they do go to very quickly become fashionable afterwards. The truth that the quality goods of today create the mass-production standards of tomorrow has been recognised, in particular, as one of the main difficulties encountered by the war and post-war schemes for utility footwear, clothing, and furniture.

In short, to answer the question with which this section began, it is neither desirable nor even practicable—in Western political conditions and in peacetime—to standardise consumption to the point where it could be effectively controlled by direction. There is a strong case for retaining free individual choice as a main element in the shaping of consumption patterns. And from this follows a case for retaining competition. For a situation in which many, infinitely varied, decisions and patterns of decision have to be kept in orderly coordination, but with full scope left for individual choice, is precisely that with which competition is well fitted to deal.

THE ROLE OF CONSULTATION

Is it then correct to say that the right policy is to use direction to control the background determinants—the stability and distribution of incomes, the structure of social groups, and such structural factors as housing—which are of a kind with which competition can deal only rather ineffectively, and for the rest to let the untutored housewife go her own way in a free competitive market? Social surveys do not suggest that a policy of this kind would be adequate. The no-man's-land between competition and direction is wide, and if the role of direction is limited in the way suggested there will remain a number of problems to which direction is not to be extended and with which competition is nevertheless unable to deal. Competition has to be supplemented with education—consultation —as well as with direction.

It is useful first of all to guide and promote the emergence of new, experimental standards. This, as in the field of scientific research, is a case where competition is inadequate, but consultation will usually be a far more effective way of supplementing it than direction.

Secondly, individual consumers and families have to be helped to reach the right decisions within the existing framework of habit and custom, in cases involving factors 'remote or diffused' from the point of view not only of the individual consumer but from that of any possible directing authority. No higher authority, in these cases, has the knowledge to issue a direction allowing fully and in detail for all the 'remote or diffused' factors involved in each consumer's decision. Given the necessary and useful diversity of individual and households' consumption patterns, it is in effect impossible for any higher authority to produce standards tailor-made to individual families' requirements. The aim must be to go through, family by family, respecting and, indeed, encouraging individual variations, but cutting out waste and helping each family to devise higher standards for itself. And this can be done, though not by direction.

133

For the evidence is not, indeed, that direction plus competition will do the trick but that they will go much of the way, and consultation, or education, will fill the remaining gap. Competition may be used to give families a wide measure of initiative. Then direction can ensure them fair and stable incomes, satisfactory housing, and protection against gross violation of their community's standards, or temptation to violate them. It can place them in communities and working or family groups cohesive enough to be able to establish and enforce standards. It can thus put them compulsorily on the road to acquiring a personality pattern suited to the problems of current life. Then a situation has been created in which education, or consultation, can secure a quick, wide, and deep enough response to do the rest.

For this it is, of course, necessary to have the means of education. General education already plays a large part here. This includes not only that given in the schools but also the work of such bodies as Women's Institutes or community associations, and particularly of those, like the marriage guidance movement or certain youth movements, which catch people at a particularly formative period in their lives. There are also many possibilities of specifically consumer education. Advertising, though generally a useful aid to consumer choice, has abuses which need to be regulated. They are already regulated by the law—as, for instance, under the Pharmacy and Medicines Act of 1941—and by the industry itself; the Advertising Association has a code of practice considerably in advance of the law. It may well be, however, that in both these directions more could be done. Many proposals have been made for voluntary or compulsory marking of goods, particularly those, such as furniture, not easy for the average consumer to judge at first sight, so as to indicate standards of performance. Food standards have long had to be indicated in this way, though the control has not always been satisfactory. The most ambitious attempt to indicate to consumers the standards of performance of other goods, that made under the wartime utility schemes, proved to be workable only under wartime conditions. In peacetime, standards had to be widened to the point where, as an official report concluded, 'the control no longer gives assurance of value for money'. For it did not prove possible, with the method of grading adopted, *both* to require manufacturers to conform to clear-cut standards *and* to allow them enough freedom of design to be consistent with a satisfactory range of consumer choice. More success seems to have been attained since then by the quality-testing scheme of the Furniture Development Council, set up under the Industrial Organisation and Development Act of 1947.

A suggestion often put forward has been the creation of consumer research and advice centres on lines already well developed, as a form of consumers' cooperation, in the United States. American buyers' guides give reliable and remarkably outspoken advice on a wide range of consumer goods and services. A service of this sort naturally reaches only the more active minority of consumers. But it is these, on the whole, who create standards for the future; and buyers' guides can serve a particularly valuable purpose as a basis for the work of such groups as Women's Institutes or community associations. The cost of establishing such a centre in Britain would not necessarily be high. A recent survey suggests that a staff of about eighty and a budget of £125,000 a year might be enough. It would also be necessary to alter the law of libel to give the centre reasonable freedom of comment; though this requirement has been at least partly met by the Defamation (Amendment) Act of 1952.

The trade union movement, management associations, and bodies like the Industrial Co-partnership Association have played an important part in consumer education, particularly as regards savings; and the National Savings Movement has also played its part here. The lack of clear and agreed views about how much can usefully be saved, and by whom, has been a difficulty here. Nevertheless, there have been times when the efforts of these bodies had a marked effect in inducing people and corporations to hold back either their existing spending or their claims to spend more. This was particularly the case when, from 1948 to 1951, unions and management collaborated with the Government in a policy of restraining wage claims and dividend increases.

Experience in that case was perhaps the best illustration in recent years of the difficulties of education and consultation in matters of this kind. Checking what actually happened against the conditions for successful consultation as outlined in Chapter 6, one might tabulate as follows:

(1) Discussion in 1948–51 was too often at the purely political or wage-bargaining level, with no sufficient effort to find a 'consultant' who would precipitate the points of common agreement in matters of consumption and saving, and related matters of production: to reveal what has sometimes been called the 'law of the situation'. The Anglo-American Productivity Council set out to do this, but was primarily concerned with production, not consumption. And in the first years at least, its influence reached, even indirectly, only a narrow range of people. Research by social scientists might have filled the gap, but was used to only a slight extent.

(2) There was rarely (see p. 89) 'complete coverage of the subjects arising in the area of consultation'. There were not many cases where, for example, firms and unions negotiated with the books open, all the cards on the table, and all relevant factors brought together and clearly summed up.

(3) There was 'complete coverage of all persons in the area of consultation', in the sense, for example, that in national discussions between the Government, the British Employers' Confederation, and the T.U.C. the great majority of the relevant groups were directly or indirectly represented. Since the nation as a whole is (p. 85) a 'natural' unity, it could also be said that the principle of unity of the area of consultation was observed. But it was observed at what, from most people's point of view, was a high and remote level. The discussion tended to stay at the national level, and not to be brought down into the smaller 'natural units' of the firm and the working group. And, from the point of view of some special group or interest —middle management, for example—representation, often indirect, at the national level, useful as it may be in itself, is no substitute for representation at the point where day-to-day decisions are taken. Discussion, in fact, was not carried down into small enough units, and not enough care was taken to secure full participation of all concerned at the local level.

(4) Only gradually, through the work of the National Arbitration Tribunal and its successor the Industrial Disputes Tribunal, or through similar judgements at lower levels, has a code of 'case law' been building up, as a result of debate and consultation, to take account of all the factors relevant to consumption and savings decisions. And, as was emphasised in Chapter 6, the build-up of this industrial 'common law', in this as in other matters, has been hampered by widespread failure to see the need for codification and for clear-cut definition of roles and channels of communication.

It is not surprising, in these circumstances, that the efforts made in 1948–51 to educate the ordinary run of managers and trade unionists in matters of savings and consumption were only partly successful, and tended after 1951 to break down. They achieved a certain success in educating those, both managers and trade union leaders, immediately concerned in them. If they failed to build up quickly a body of case law on consumption and savings decisions, this was, at least in part, because no very clear ideas on these subjects existed in Britain at the start, and it would have been unreasonable to expect them to emerge very soon. But the fact that the discussion was not carried down into each small group concerned, and that often all the cards were not on the table, represented an avoidable failure.

The conditions for the successful education of small groups, whether at work or in the local community, have been extensively studied in recent years. One which is particularly relevant here was made by Kurt Lewin and his colleagues during the war, on how to alter the buying and cooking habits of housewives. The essence of effective education, it was found, lay in using group discussion rather than an individual approach: getting a group interested and actively involved in a given housekeeping problem, as one important and worth bothering about; bringing home to them that 'people like themselves' could solve and had solved that problem; and only then introducing expert advice on how they themselves might go about it. The final step was for each group as a whole to make up its mind about what its members should do. In groups of housewives approached in this way, about one-third actually tried new foods and cookery methods, compared with only 3% of those who listened to an ordinary demonstration-lecture.

Chapter 9

PROVISION FOR THE FUTURE (I)

I. INVESTMENT

HOW much is, or should be, saved was considered in the last chapter. What sort of investment it is to be used for is a matter for this chapter and the two which follow. The pattern of investment in Britain in recent years has continually changed. But figures for 1950, summed up in Tables 1–6, will do as an example. Probably 25–30% of the gross national expenditure at market prices in that year was on durable goods, though figures for one major category, maintenance work on plant, ships, and vehicles, are not available. A surprisingly high proportion of this was contributed by consumers' direct purchases of durable goods, including furniture, furnishings, and cars and cycles. This, as was shown above, is a typical feature of an advanced economy. About two-fifths of all new investment goods in the business and government sectors (excluding additions to stocks and work in progress) went directly into production and distribution. One-third—the high proportion is worth noting—went into public utilities and communications, and a quarter into government building and the social services, including housing. As regards international comparisons, the proportions for transport and communications were (Table 3) about the same for most West European countries. There was, however, a very sharp contrast in policies for industrial investment and housing. Britain came rather low in the scale for investment in manufacturing industry, but far and away at the top for housing. There were also big differences in the proportion of all new business and government investment to the national income. The chief contrast in 1949 was between the Iron Curtain countries of Eastern Europe, which invested relatively little, and Western Europe. On the Western European scale, Britain showed a lower rate of investment than Norway, Finland, or Holland, but higher, though usually not much higher, than the rest. Purchases of durable goods (and especially buildings) fluctuate much more than those of perishables or semi-durables, and this is illustrated for the United States in Table 5. The source of funds for investment in Britain, finally, is shown in Table 6. Omitting depreciation allowances (nine-tenths of them on business

138

account), about half of all saving in 1950 was by households, a fifth
by businesses, and a third by public authorities.

HOW DOES THE MARKET DETERMINE THE FLOW OF SAVINGS AND INVESTMENT, AND TO WHAT PURPOSE?

Here as before, what part is to be played in social control respectively by direction, consultation, and competition on the market?
It can be seen from Table 2 that three-quarters of all investment
goods in the business and government sector are bought by enterprises which have to balance their budget in the market, that is, by
reference to economic competition. This is true even where, as with
the nationalised public utility industries, their aim is to balance it
with maximum sales at a fixed profit rather than by maximising profit
without qualification. Probably two-thirds of the savings recorded

TABLE 1

Investment of all types in Great Britain, 1950, by categories of
investment (£ millions)

			Per cent of gross national expenditure at market prices
New investment goods purchased:			
Business and Government Sector			
Ships, aircraft, public service (road) and railway vehicles	239		
Plant, machinery, cars for business and official use	641		
Buildings and works	697		
Additions to stocks and work in progress	115		
		1,692	12½
Household Sector			
Household durables	567		
Others (say)	80–90		
		650	5
Overseas Sector			
Net investment overseas		229	2
		2,571	19½
Repair and maintenance			
Buildings and works		585	4½
Other		?	?

From Cmd. 8203.

139

TABLE 2

New investment goods purchased, business and government sector, by industry or department (£ million) (excluding additions to stocks and work in progress) 1950

Production and distribution		Per cent of total in this category
Agriculture, forestry, fishing	78	
Mining (coal)	28	
Manufacturing	405	
Miscellaneous, including services, distribution, and some non-productive	170	
	681	43
Public utilities and transport		
Gas, water, electricity	177	
Transport, post, telecommunications	317	
	494	31
Public and social services		
Police, fire, central, and local government	21	
Health, sewerage, etc.	29	
Education, B.B.C.	52	
Housing	300	
	402	26
	1,577	100

From Cmd. 8203.

in Table 6 are made with at least some reference to the market; this includes consumers' purchases of durable goods, savings out of business and personal incomes, and public authorities' decisions to raise capital for trading services. The market takes, therefore, a large place in the foreground of savings and investment decisions. There are, also, as with consumption, background factors which it only in part determines, and by which it is influenced in its turn; we shall come on to these. But let us leave the focus for the moment in the foreground. Given such background factors as the level and stability of demand, the distribution of income and wealth, and the social framework and its pressures on those who make investment decisions, how does the market—economic competition—influence the individual saver or investor in deciding upon his course of action?

TABLE 3

Business and government investment (excluding depreciation and additions to stocks and work in progress) in transport and communications, and housing, per cent of all such investment, 1949

	Industry	Housing	Transport and communications
U.K.	26	26	21
Belgium (1948)	20	11	24
Hungary	24	4	29
Italy	28	5	16
Norway	32	6	40
Holland	40	12	21
Sweden	56	—	—
France	62	4	26

From *Economic Survey of Europe*, 1949.

TABLE 4

Business and government investment (excluding depreciation and additions to stocks and work in progress) per cent of commodities (not services) available for home use, 1949

U.K.	16	Yugoslavia, Sweden, France	13
Czechoslovakia	5	Denmark	14
Poland	7	Germany (Western)	15
Germany (Soviet Zone)	9	Holland	17
Hungary, Italy	10	Finland (1948)	19
Austria, Belgium	11	Norway	24

From *Economic Survey of Europe*, 1949.

TABLE 5

Cyclical fluctuation of investment, deviation from long-term trend, expenditure in U.S.A., 1929–33

Household Sector	Per cent
Perishables	− 2·1
Semi-perishables	− 7·2
Services	− 9·9
Durables	−16·9
Business Sector	
Producer durables (excluding depreciation)	−25·5
Construction (excluding depreciation)	−69·5

From Kuznts, *National Income*, 1946. For British figures see Beveridge, *Full Employment in a Free Society*.

TABLE 6
Source of funds for new investment, U.K., 1950 (£ millions)

Personal Saving			
Purchases of durable goods, household sector, approximately	650		
Gross saving	332		
Addition to tax reserves	26		
	——	1,008	32
Business Saving			
Addition to company reserves	364		
Addition to tax reserves	92		
	——	456	14
Public Savings			
Public authorities' net surplus		611	19
Depreciation—business and public		1,124	36
Less overlap between public and business or household sectors		−43	−1
		3,156	100

From Cmd. 8203.

(a) The limited scope for varying the rate of interest

The traditional answer was, through the rate of interest. Interest is the price at which loanable funds change hands. It seemed a reasonable deduction, therefore, that if, say, business men's desire to invest fell off, so also would the demand for and price of loanable funds. This would on the one hand encourage businesses to invest more, on the other induce savers to save less. Thus the balance would be restored. But this does not work out in practice. The rate of interest can in practice fluctuate only within rather narrow limits. The lower limit is set by the fact that in the last resort people will prefer to hold cash or buy 'lock-up' goods rather than lend money without interest; for even the securest of loans involves at least some inconvenience and risk. £100 nominal of $2\frac{1}{2}\%$ Consols were worth £96 in 1946, £58 (and depreciated pounds at that) in 1952. It is no reflection on the honesty of British governments to describe this as a risky investment. The rate of interest *can* nevertheless be forced down to somewhere not far from zero by increasing the amount of cash in the hands of potential lenders. This can be done either by running a Budget deficit, financed from newly created money, or by direct action by the Bank of England and the Joint Stock Banks. These buy securities, or increase their advances, out of newly created money, and so increase the amount of cash standing to depositors' credit. The difficulty is, of course, that potential lenders are also potential spenders on goods of all kinds. Once a point is reached where they are reluctant to lend at a lower rate of interest, the increase in cash needed to induce them to do so may be very great. They may well use the extra cash, not for holding or lending, but to buy more goods and so to raise prices and aggravate shortages. They are, indeed, all the more likely to do so the more the prospect of a flood of money, and so of others buying more and inflating prices, comes in sight. For these reasons, the effective lower limit for long-term loans in Britain has since the war been about 3%.

The high limit to interest rates is set by several factors. The traditional practice of the capital market has been to keep interest rates relatively steady, and to vary the volume of lending instead. A more important factor today is probably the existence of a large national debt, of which some £6,000 million, at the time of writing, has to be re-financed from year to year, and much of the rest at fairly short intervals. There is also a large and increasing mass of local authority debt, notably for housing and education, and of loans by the nationalised industries. In 1919–22, housing authorities were forced to finance their programmes with loans at around 6%, not repayable before 1970–80. This involved commitments extending far beyond the period to which high interest rates may have been appropriate, and (this would also be true of high rates on even the short-term debt of the central government) a shift in the distribution of incomes, to the disadvantage of relatively poor municipal householders, or the generality of rate and tax payers, and the advantage of the relatively well-to-do owners of capital. These tendencies are undesirable if capital could be equally well rationed in other ways. The high limit to interest rates which emerges in this way is not clearly defined, but is probably, for government or municipal borrowing, around 5%.

The rate on government loans is not the only one; there are different rates, allowing for differences in risk, ease of disposal (not all securities are equally marketable), and prospects of repayment, for loans of all kinds. But all these are tied together in the market. Investors switch from one type of security to another whenever differentials widen—or contract—more than is justified by differences in the underlying conditions. If one set of rates, and especially one so important as that on public loans, is to be kept within certain limits, all others must be controlled as well. The price of capital as a whole thus tends to be inflexible, and becomes a rather ineffective means of limiting or stimulating demand.

143

What then are the variables which matter—those whose size and range of movement is great enough to be decisive in the capital market?

(b) *The importance of the yield on capital*

The essential point would seem to be the distinction between the rate of interest, which is the rate at which money can be borrowed, and the return, in cash or kind, to be expected by those who actually make an investment; that is the marginal efficiency of capital. The former has relatively little influence, though it is certainly not negligible. The latter has very great influence indeed.

In the case of *household* savings and investments, for example, there is little reason to think that the rate of interest obtainable on small savings, or at any rate the customary changes in it, counts for much. The intake of Savings Certificates does not increase immensely when the rate of interest goes up by a half of one per cent. But the real return from investment in consumers' durable goods does certainly count a great deal. The valuation placed on this return depends, as has been shown, largely on social pressures, that is on public opinion. But the market does supply an efficient means of transmitting these pressures to consumers and enabling them in their turn to react by acquiring the goods they want. The real though non-monetary return from investment in housing—people's desire, or lack of desire, to become owner-occupiers—has likewise great influence on saving. So also has the cash return on small investments in income-earning trades, where the road to this lies open and the yield is substantially above that of normal rates of interest.

The yield on *business* investments depends, so far as the market is concerned, on a group of factors—the demand for the product, related to the cost and rate of obsolescence of capital goods, and to the cost (rate of interest) and availability of finance—whose importance varies from case to case. For one important class of goods, housing and public utilities, the rate of interest and the cost of construction are the main considerations; for demand is steady and predictable, and obsolescence may be covered, as with a standard council house, by a charge of little over 1% per annum. For general business investment, on the other hand, the most doubtful single factor will often be the prospective level of demand. Also, this investment is very largely in plant, machinery, and vehicles, which become obsolete and have to be written off over, commonly, a maximum of five to seven years. The appropriate period may be lower still; as little as two years, even for major items of equipment. 20–50% per annum must be earned to cover this. Moreover, calculations both of demand and of obsolescence are subject to wide margins of error.

A recent case-history of steel divides investment decisions into three classes. There are those arising from the breakdown of machinery, or its arrival at a point where the risk of breakdown and cost of maintenance give it a marked nuisance value. There are cases of minor or relatively minor replacements justified, not by the breakdown of old plant, but by the superiority of the new. There are, thirdly, major schemes of reconstruction or extension. Calculation of earnings will be decisive only in the second group. Changes of the first sort will be made automatically, and those of the third will depend on broad considerations of profitability and obsolescence, which, however, cannot be at all accurately expressed. The cost of capital goods will be a relevant item in such calculations. Variations in the rate of interest will not; for they count for very little over against the major uncertainties about demand and obsolescence. The question whether funds are available (as apart from their cost) will be relevant; but, except for small new firms (to be discussed below), it can be treated as a function of the demand for the product compared with the cost of capital goods. For if demand is such as to justify investment, either this reflects past experience, in which case profits have been earned and can be ploughed back, or a good case can be made to the capital market for a loan.

(c) *The rate of interest is nevertheless not negligible*

To say that the rate of interest is not a major determinant in investment decisions is not of course to say that it is to be neglected. A firm may well see other factors as decisive in timing its investments, and yet think it worth while to save what it can on the cost of finance. In 1946 large old firms were borrowing through the London new issue market at $4\frac{1}{4}\%$, including costs of issue, and small new firms at $8\frac{1}{4}\%$. A schedule of rates charged to American firms for various types of finance, from period loans by banks to hire-purchase and loans on accounts receivable, ranges from 1 or 2% to 19%. The actual choice open to a firm of a given size, in a given place and time, may be small. But it will often be far from unimportant.

(d) *What exactly does the control of savings and investment by economic competition achieve?*

So much for how the capital market works. But to what purpose does it work? As a control over savings and investment, it achieves principally two things. It causes investment, and the means for further saving, to be distributed broadly in proportion to consumers'

10   145

needs as measured by the market. There are no fully satisfactory British figures on this. But in those countries (Table 7) with similar economies for which data can be found, it seems that the payment made for capital, as for labour, corresponds to the value of the marginal product of each. In Australia in 1936–7, for example, a 1% increase in the supply of either labour or capital, the supply of the other remaining constant, added 0·49% to the national product; and the fraction of the national income paid to capital was 0·49, and to labour 0·51.

TABLE 7

Share of labour and capital in total product

	An addition of 1% to either labour or capital (the other remaining constant) increased output by (%)		Labour received, fraction of total product
	Capital	Labour	
U.S.A., 1899–1922	0·25	0·76	0·74
Australia, 1912	0·47	0·52	0·54
,, 1936–7	0·49	0·49	0·51

From Clark, *Conditions of Economic Progress*, 1951 ed., p. 518, quoting Douglas.

The market also, secondly, performs here its usual function of decentralisation. It reduces to order a vast mass of transactions, with a precision impossible under direct planning, and leaves the road open for innumerable detailed and local initiatives.

THE ROLE OF DIRECTION AND CONSULTATION

Especially in the last generation, the capital market has been supplemented, or superseded, by a host of official controls, or semi-official controls by trade associations such as those of the Stock Exchange. The controls over consumption referred to in the last chapter influence the flow of savings. There is also a quantity of further controls concerned specifically with the capital market. In 1950 public authorities raised through their own budgets about a third of the finance available for new investment; made nearly a quarter of all new investment, in non-trading services, with little or no reference to the market; and had direct powers of control over a further quarter in the nationalised or municipal industries, transport services, and public utilities. They have in addition very wide powers of control over the remaining half of new investment. These controls fall into three groups.

The first, control of the capital market, includes the Companies Acts, designed primarily to give security to the investor. They are supplemented for this purpose with the supervision of new issues exercised by the Stock Exchange. Control over the capital market is also exercised under the Borrowing (Control and Guarantees) Act of 1946, under which the Treasury may regulate the sale or placing of shares in the United Kingdom, or by companies registered here, and the borrowing of amounts of over £10,000 in any twelve months, other than ordinary bank loans. In 1952, for instance, the limit 'of regulation was £50,000. Control is exercised by the Treasury on the advice of a Capital Issues Committee appointed by it. The Act allows the Treasury to guarantee loans for industrial reconstruction and development within Great Britain up to £50,000,000 a year; and related powers exist to guarantee loans for export and colonial development, and to make grants for colonial development and welfare.

Secondly, there is general credit and budgetary policy. Some of the controls here are quite general, including the power to run a Budget surplus or deficit, and for the (nationalised) Bank of England to increase or reduce the 'credit base', the volume of cash and deposits with the Bank of England, on which the Joint Stock banks partly decide their credit policy. Others are specific. These include income, profits, and excess profits tax. The three taxes together take at the time of writing 50–65% of profits at the rates earned in 1947-9, the lower figure being that for wholly undistributed and the higher for wholly distributed profits; and 80–95% of earnings above that rate. The depreciation allowances agreed between firms and the Inland Revenue have been varied in recent years so as to encourage or discourage investment. Death duties also play their part here.

Thirdly, building can be controlled under Defence Regulations and the Town and Country Planning Act. In the years just after the war this was the most important control of all; for the policy was, at least till the end of 1951, to create conditions of easy money, in which a very large number of investment projects would come forward, and then to use the building control to select among these more precisely.

All these controls, finally, are supplemented with an elaborate machinery of consultation. Bank lending policy is a matter for consultation between the Treasury, Bank of England, and Joint Stock banks. Investment policy is one of the main subjects of discussion between government and industry, and particularly between the departments concerned with each branch of industry and the firms within their sphere.

The use of this machinery of control and consultation is subject to the same limitations as direction of any other kind; more particularly as it is mainly operated by the State, and forms part of the whole complex of State direction. But it can also, on the other hand, be justified on grounds similar to those raised in previous chapters. There are first of all monopolistic industries and services, such as the nationalised industries, whose investment policy makes some reference to the market, but over which the market does not by itself exercise an adequate control. Secondly, there are, as in other sectors of the economy, remote or diffused influences and effects, unknown to or not seriously considered by those who take individual investment decisions. Though the market achieves in the foreground of saving and investment the socially desirable results just mentioned, it copes less satisfactorily with their remoter results or background determinants. These fall under the four heads already familiar—distribution of income and capital, stability, basic services, and group relations. Competition is also rather ineffective—again as usual—in cases involving a change in the social framework.

(a) The distribution of income and capital

The distribution of income and wealth affects the direction of investment as well as the volume of savings. Table 8 shows, from pre-war data, the typical difference between the 'small man' and the really rich in the way capital assets are held. The small man buys his house and the goods in or around it, including his car. He holds insurance policies, has some cash in the bank or savings bank, may perhaps have placed some money in a mortgage through a local solicitor, and probably holds some Savings Bonds or other Government securities. Having done all this, he has very little left over for 'productive' investment, or for the less obvious forms of municipal or overseas government borrowing. The rich man on the other hand tends to hold the great bulk of his assets in one or another 'productive' form, above all in stocks and shares.

It would be wrong to conclude that since in the past the rich have been the most prone to 'productive' investment, therefore they must remain so in future. The road from the small man to the Stock Exchange can be opened. About a third of the capital of a sample of large British firms turns out to be held in amounts of £500 nominal or less. The American capital market has gone much further than

PROVISION FOR THE FUTURE (1)

TABLE 8

Kinds of property held by persons in Great Britain dying in 1936
*Percentage of total capital held by people with capital holdings of
each size*

	£100–£1,000	£5,000–£10,000	£100,000+
House property and household goods	34·3	17·3	4·7
Insurance policies	12·1	3·8	2·0
Cash and Savings Bank	21·9	8·6	4·7
Mortgages, Bonds, etc.	10·2	10·8	5·0
British Government securities issued since 1914	10·6	15·1	12·2
Trade assets	2·6 ⎫	3·0 ⎫	5·2 ⎫
Land, ground rents, mineral royalties	1·5 ⎬	3·1 ⎬	6·9 ⎬
Stocks, shares, and 'other' British and foreign government and municipal securities	⎰8·6 ⎱ 4·5 ⎭	⎰41·2 ⎱ 35·1 ⎭	⎰69·7 ⎱ 57·6 ⎭
Other	2·3	3·2	1·7
	100·0	100·0	100·0

From Campion, *Public and Private Property in Great Britain*, 1939, p. 104.

the British in making it possible and attractive for ordinary families
to buy shares, if necessary by instalments. Through investment trusts
it is possible for even the smallest of small men to spread his risks.
The money which the small man pays to his insurance company is
often reinvested in industry. So, under certain conditions, might
be what he deposits in his savings bank. Industrial co-partnership
schemes may help him to acquire a stake in the firm for which he
works. Some of these questions will be touched on again below. The
essential point is that, whatever is done about the distribution
of income and capital and the difference it makes to the direction
of investment, there *is* in the first place a difference, and one of
which it is necessary to take account.

(*b*) *The stability of investment*

More important, in recent policy on capital investment, has been
the question of stability. There is no prima facie reason why a free

market in capital should produce a steady and even flow of investment, or—however satisfactory in its broad distribution of investment in relation to consumers' needs—should guarantee in detail the absence of speculation and fraud. As recently as 1928 the preservation of the investor from being 'misled in times of speculative fever by glittering—even tawdry—appearances' (Macmillan Committee, 1931) remained a major problem. It has since been largely solved by two Companies Acts and the control exercised over new issues by the Stock Exchange and, now, the Capital Issues Committee. The question of the steady and even flow of capital remains, however, of very great importance.

It was at this point that the rate of interest, according to older theory, should have played its most useful role. Suppose the national income to be £10,000 million a year, and savers to be saving £2,000 million; but investors wish to invest only £1,000 million. As soon as the prospect of a gap of this sort appeared, the rate of interest would fall. Investors would revise their plans and invest more, at the cheaper rate. Savers would reduce their savings and buy more consumption goods. This might cause temporary dislocation, with short time in engineering and overtime in the manufacture of mink coats; theories of the trade cycle have been built on this. But it has never been shown convincingly that such dislocation need, or would, be great if the rate of interest worked as expected.

If, however, factors other than the rate of interest chiefly determine saving and investment, some other common factor or factors must be found to account for the two coming (if and when they do) into equilibrium. This common factor turns out to be the general level of demand for goods and services. In a free market, the supply of and demand for savings are balanced by changes in the money value of the national income and expenditure, such as at one time to cause unemployment and at another inflation. There is, moreover, no guarantee that, even apart from this instability, the point of balance between savings and investment will correspond to the level of full employment. Very crudely, the process might be supposed to operate something as follows:

YEAR I.	National income (full employment and maximum capacity)	£ 10,000 million
	Savings	2,000 ,,
	Investment	1,000 ,,
	Goods left on the shelf	1,000 ,,

YEAR II. National income (lower because £1,000 million saved in the last period is withdrawn from circulation, and this entails in British experience a drop in incomes of nearly twice this amount)   £ 8,000 million

Savings (lower out of lower incomes)   1,000 ,,

Investment (lower because of gloomy experience and prospects; can be cut in short run below even the level needed to replace existing capacity)   nil

Further goods left on the shelf   1,000 ,,

YEAR III. National income   6,000 ,,

Savings   nil

Investment (depreciation cannot be neglected for ever; end of slump anticipated; new developments not exploited during slump)   1,000 ,,

Goods taken off the shelf   1,000 ,,

YEAR V. National income (back to full employment)   10,000 ,,

Savings   2,000 ,,

Investment (optimism induced by the upswing)   3,000 ,,

Inflationary increase in incomes and prices (no goods off the shelf, as none left to take)   1,000 ,,

YEAR VI National income (same real output as Year V)   12,000 ,,

Savings   3,000 ,,

Investment (labour and material shortages discourage expansion; no longer catching up with investment neglected in slump)   2,000 ,,

Goods left on the shelf   1,000 ,,

Trade-cycle prediction is a tricky proceeding, in which more economic reputations have been lost than in almost any other field. It must therefore be insisted that the above figures bear no resemblance to any actual situation, alive or dead. They are not, however, wildly unrealistic in relation to recent British experience, and do clearly illustrate why State control has seemed necessary in this field.

(c) Basic services

The third heading under which the market fails to give full satisfaction is, as before, that of basic services; the general case of services which yield their benefits or cause losses over a wider circle than that of their immediate customers or operators, or produce results too remote in time to be appreciated by potential investors in a free market. These will include such matters as the geographical distribution of investment (the location of industry), whose aesthetic, social, and economic effects extend far beyond the view of firms and workers immediately concerned; or investment in education or health; or increasing the 'liquidity' of family finances by the accumulation of small savings, with their great 'structural' value for stabilising consumption patterns. They will also include such activities as forestry, river control, and land reclamation; and, under the same heading, housing, not only because of its significance for the structure of consumption and family life, but because a house is a long-lived article which must be adaptable to the conditions of sixty or seventy years hence. A council house is financed over sixty years and may well last eighty or a hundred. At the very least, therefore, it should be of a size and standard which will not seem obsolete thirty or forty years ahead, halfway through its life. Incomes have increased over the last century and a half at a rate which, if it continues over the next thirty or forty years, may raise them by 50 or even 100%. The problem is, therefore, to enable people to pay from current incomes for houses of a standard suitable for families with incomes half or twice as high again; and this lies at the bottom of the difficulty, generally understood in this country since 1918, of obtaining satisfactory working-class houses from the free building market.

(d) Group pressures

Fourthly, investment decisions, like consumption decisions, are subject to group pressures. In deciding, for example, the proportion of profits to plough back, firms typically work to a rule of thumb geared to investors' expectations; a certain minimum dividend plus a more or less fixed percentage of the remaining profits. But these expectations, and so the rules based on them, are interdependent. To a considerable extent, what investors regard as a fair return depends on what other investors are getting, and regard as fair. Within limits, it is possible to alter expectations by changing the weight attached, in firms' councils, to financial claims on the one hand and those of labour, consumers, or the State on the other. This may be done either within the firm or through outside influences, or more commonly and effectively by both together. The same may be done for government borrowing; an excellent example is the general acceptance by investors of the conversion of War Loan from 5% to $3\frac{1}{2}$% in 1932.

(e) Changes in the social framework

The market tends to be specially ineffective in cases involving not merely remote or diffused effects but a change in the framework of society; new techniques, institutions, or patterns of personality. It compels conformity to the best established standards of practice—or at least to prices based on them—but merely permits, or at most encourages, the introduction of new standards. The question whether or not such standards should be introduced needs to be separately and specifically posed and answered. Investment, as a main means of breaking through to new levels of technical efficiency, obviously often implies a question of this kind. To see that this question is, in fact, posed and answered has come in recent years to be recognised as one of the chief responsibilities of the Government.

CHANGES IN THE STRUCTURE OF THE CAPITAL MARKET

One type of change in the social framework which economic competition in the capital market has failed to produce, or, at any rate, to produce fast enough to keep pace with the growth of new problems, and which is particularly relevant here, is change in the structure of the capital market itself. The problems in question focus on the finance of the new small firm. Such firms are often in practice the source, not perhaps so much of new products, but certainly of new competition in established fields. They are, however, in their early stages usually an unattractive proposition to investors. Their resources are limited, and their prospects speculative. The ideal form of finance for them is personal; either the personal savings and ploughed-back profits of the owner and his family, or investment by individuals who know him personally and are prepared to take a chance, not on the firm as such, but on him as its manager.

(a) The decline in the supply of risk capital

The sources of such finance have, however, been dried up in the last generation by taxation. The tax on ploughed-back profits was of the order of 20–25% in the 'twenties and 'thirties. It is now, as has been shown, anything from 50 to 80%, and may be higher in small 'director-controlled' firms in which the Inland Revenue may assess undistributed profits for super-tax as well. Voluntary dividend limitation since the war has kept down the capital value of businesses, and discouraged the type of investor whose main interest is in capital appreciation. Such savings as remain tend to come from the working and middle class, and to flow through such channels as building societies, insurance companies, and investment trusts. Some of these intermediaries will invest only in special fields, while others are reluctant to touch risky or non-marketable investments. Insurance companies, for instance, have in the last generation become willing to buy ordinary industrial shares, as apart from preference shares or debentures, but only if they are easily marketable; which means, in effect, that they buy only the shares of relatively big and established concerns. Technical development, meantime, has increased the amount of capital needed to enter many lines of business. The extent of the drought of capital varies from area to area. Bristol, for example, has recently been quoted as one where capital is not too difficult for the small firm to obtain; Newcastle as one where the difficulties are great. But it would be difficult to quote any area where the supply, given the obstacles just mentioned, is not only satisfactory but likely to remain so. Even where capital flows fairly freely, it tends to take the form of loans, involving fixed-interest commitments which can be disastrous to a firm in the ups and downs of its early days.

The problem here is not merely that too little provision is made for a socially valuable form of investment. It is also that an increasing proportion of savings, particularly those coming from small men, does not normally have access to the most potentially profitable forms of investment. And any encouragement which the high return on this investment might give to saving is prevented.

(b) Possible solutions

The shortage of capital for the new and small firm has been recognised, at least since 1921, and especially since 1931. The report of the Committee on Finance and Industry (Macmillan Committee) in that year commented on it so vigorously that it has since been known as the 'Macmillan Gap'. Various institutional changes between 1931 and 1952 have helped towards filling it. Finance companies such as the United Dominions Trust and Charterhouse Industrial Development Company offer loans to small firms; not usually, however, to the riskier prospects, and the total of such finance is not large. Insurance companies and investment trusts, as just noted, prefer the more marketable shares of established companies. The banks are reluctant to grant long-term loans. Though they do, in effect, do so —many firms have substantial bank credits outstanding from year to year—the total amount of such finance, allowing for the fall in the value of money, seems not to have increased for many years. Trading estates, on the other hand, have multiplied in recent years. By leasing plants and services to small business, they have reduced the needs for firms to raise capital of their own. Hire-purchase finance of plant and equipment has grown much since the war, and could probably with advantage grow further. The Government and, before the war, semi-official and charitable institutions such as the Special Areas Reconstruction Association and the Nuffield Trust have offered special facilities to firms going to Development Areas. The Industrial and Commercial Finance Corporation, set up and financed by the banks in 1945, supplies capital in amounts up to £200,000, and will take up ordinary or preference shares of small firms. It also, however, like most of the other institutions mentioned, is concerned (not surprisingly, seeing its association with the banks) on the whole with the safer propositions.

The most significant change of all in the last generation may well have been the adaptation of the London new issue market to the needs of small firms. This had gone some way by 1939, and has progressed further since. In 1945-7 the average value of each small new issue handled was 30% lower than in 1937, allowing for the fall in the value of money. The costs of issue had also fallen. It is still the case, however, that before a firm can reach the new issue market it must be well established, with a good profit record, and with capital requirements of the order, normally, of £10,000 or more.

These improvements in the capital market have barely (if at all) kept pace with the growth of the problem of the small firm. The problem remains as before: the finance offered is too small, or is offered only to established firms or on fixed-interest terms. There is therefore a case for further action, if necessary from outside the market. Some existing forms of lending, notably hire-purchase finance, might well be extended, and there are at least two new lines to be explored. One is to reduce the pressure of taxation on ploughed-back profits. The other is to follow up an interesting experiment, a local development trust, the Glasgow Industrial Finance Development Company, set up by a group of Scottish investment trusts before the war. The advantage of this local corporation, as of the similar running work of the pre-war regional industrial development councils, was that it provided on the spot the personal supervision of new firms without which investment in their early stages becomes mere speculation. It might be possible to kill two birds with one stone—to break the barriers between working and middle-class savings and high-yielding investment, as well as finding funds for the small industrial firm—by associating such trusts with the local Trustee Savings Banks. Along these lines, the small investor could expect a considerably higher rate of return than the present 2½% of the Savings Banks, under conditions which minimised his risks by spreading investment over a number of small concerns.

155

CONCLUSION

There is today in Britain, not certainly a fully satisfying synthesis between different forms of control in the capital market, but a workable compromise. Government and Stock Exchange controls are effective enough to ensure reasonable honesty, stability, and, in times when the demand for investment further outruns the supply, limitation of the total quantity of investment. It remains to be seen whether they will be equally effective in stimulating investment in times when the supply of savings may tend to exceed the demand: though the means for this—State guarantees of loans, the alteration of depreciation allowances, or a change in income and profits tax so as to exempt an amount equivalent to funds actually spent on capital goods within the year—are fairly powerful. Yet at the same time the market has not been prevented from doing, very largely, its traditional work of distributing capital in accordance with consumers' needs, and of offering openings to the progressive firm. New issues are controlled, but the ploughing back of profits, once the tax-gatherer has been satisfied, is not. New buildings are controlled, but the acquisition of existing buildings remains free.

The present situation is, however, a compromise, not a final solution, for many issues remain unsettled. The finance of the small firm, the access of the small saver to high yielding investment, the redistribution of capital, the many detailed roughnesses and inadequacies of the existing system of controls remain open issues. The problem of the small firm may indeed turn out to be a focal point from which an attack can be launched in several of these directions at once. A scheme on the lines suggested above for making small savings available to small business through local trusts would encourage the accumulation of small property, and so (looking back to the last chapter) to a more equal property distribution and greater ability to ride out the short-run ups and downs of income. It would help to solve the problem of the small new firm. It would also, by linking the supply of saving more immediately to the demand, reduce the area over which planned intervention in investment is necessary, so leaving the control agencies free to devote more time to, and control more precisely, the areas where their intervention is essential. Here, as elsewhere, the function of the market is not to supplant directing agencies, but to relieve them of a mass of detailed operations and leave them the time to do well what they have to do at a few key points.

A scheme on these lines might be encouraged by making available to the local trusts part of the capital taken over by death duties. The yield on this would considerably increase the rate of interest which could be offered to small depositors. This increase could not perhaps be justified on investment grounds alone. It can, however, be justified as helping to build up the buffer of liquid resources, which, as was shown in the last chapter, is one of the most useful basic or structural elements—and for that reason, because of the breadth of its significance, liable to be overlooked by individual consumers—in consumption patterns.

Chapter 10

PROVISION FOR THE FUTURE (II)

II. RESEARCH

RESEARCH today is a major industry in its own right, with a turnover, about 1947–8, of the order of £130,000,000 a year, and employing anything up to forty or fifty thousand graduates and a hundred or a hundred and twenty thousand other staff. The figures today would be considerably higher. Of the known expenditure in the immediate post-war years, rather less than half—£60,000,000 for 1947–8—was for military research.

In the civilian field, for which the available data are summarised in Tables 1–7, the biggest single contribution comes from firms' laboratories. These were spending in 1945–6 about £30,000,000 a year, and increased this, in real terms, by about 50% by 1950–1—an expansion, that is, in staff and floor space, not allowing for increasing costs due to the falling value of money. Other operating agencies for whose research expenditure no figures are available would include, for example, local authorities, with their extensive studies in the field of town and country planning.

Behind the operating agencies stand in the first place consultants. One in eight of big firms with their own laboratories in 1945–6 employed consultants regularly, and a further three in eight occasionally. It is not clear whether this covers also consultant service in management and industrial relations, which has developed very fast since 1939.

Next comes cooperative research. This may take various forms. One favoured in America is the research institute which provides staff facilities, and either undertakes specific projects on behalf of firms, to be carried out by the institute's staff, or (the industrial fellowship laboratories) offers facilities to a scientist appointed and employed by a firm. One or two examples of this exist in Britain, and it is often proposed that there should be more. The favoured form here has been the cooperative research association. These associations emerged at the end of the First World War as one result of the general stimulus of the war to research, which led also to the formation of the Department of Scientific and Industrial Research. They receive a grant from the D.S.I.R., which has certain limited

158

PROVISION FOR THE FUTURE (II)

THE BRITISH RESEARCH EFFORT

TABLE 1. Expenditure on scientific research, per cent of national income, before the Second World War

		£	
U.S.S.R.	1·0	75–125,000,000 p.a.	(1934)
U.S.A.	0·3	75,000,000 ,,	(1935)
U.K.	0·1	7,500,000 ,,	(1934)

From various estimates quoted in Hill, *Cooperative Research in Industry*, 1947, p. 39.

TABLE 2. Research in firms' laboratories, 1930–46

		£
1930	422 firms spent	1,736,000
1938	566 ,, ,,	5,442,000
1945–6	420[1] ,, ,,	21,815,000
1950–1	301 ,, ,,	23,779,000

[1] Estimated to represent about 75% of all research expenditure by British firms.
From *Scientific and Technical Research in British Industry*, F.B.I., 1947, and *Research and Development in British Industry*, F.B.I., 1952.

TABLE 3. Research by cooperative research associations
1921–40. Maximum of 21 associations, with a total income of:

£
1921–33   175,000–235,000 p.a.
1938–40   510,000–550,000 ,,

1949–50. 40 associations with an income of:

£3,259,699, of which £1,099,714 (plus £26,678 special grants) from the Department of Scientific and Industrial Research.

From Edwards, *Cooperative Industrial Research*, 1950, p. 54, and *Report of D.S.I.R. for 1949–50*.

TABLE 4. University research

Salaries of teaching staff and departmental maintenance, all faculties (excluding certain expenditure for Oxford and Cambridge):
1938–9. £3,848,258, of which:

	%
Arts	28
Science, technology, agriculture	46
Medicine	23
Social science	3
	100

1948–9. £9,363,579, of which:
Social science   4

Figures quoted in *P.E.P.*, 'Planning', 321, December 1950.

159

TABLE 5.   Government research, civilian only.   1900–51.   £'000's

	1900	1920	1939	1950–1
Agriculture and fisheries	4	335	1,240	4,250
Industry[1]	36	777	1,713	7,378
Medicine and health	3	129	269	1,862
Overseas	—	16	750	2,261
Grants to learned societies	17	17	14	56
Miscellaneous	2	18	7	19
Total	62	1,291	3,993	16,056

Military research amounted for 1946–7 to around £60 million (Ministry of Supply and Admiralty).
[1] Including D.S.I.R. grants to research associations.
From *Government Scientific Organisation in the Civilian Field*, H.M.S.O., 1951, and *Report from the Select Committee on Estimates on Research and Development*, 1946–7.

TABLE 6.   Action taken under the Development of Inventions Act, 1948

	Inventions submitted to the National Research Development Corporation, 1949–51	Patents granted to or applied for by the Corporation
Government departments	1,196	826
Agricultural Research Council	3	2
Medical Research Council	23	9
Universities	101	42
Industrial research associations	13 ⎫	
Charitable organisations	4 ⎬	18
Private sources	927 ⎪	
Overseas	15 ⎭	
	2,282	897

From June 1949 to June 1951. From reports of the National Research Development Corporation.

powers of control over them. It can, for example, require the research results of one association to be disclosed to others, or can forbid publication of results where disclosure might be contrary to the national interest. It can also of course refuse or withdraw its grant if not satisfied that an association is, in fact, pursuing an adequate research programme. But, in fact, control rests almost entirely in

TABLE 7. Classification of social science research projects

Mainly 'analytic' fields of study	1952–3	
Economics, economic and social history	549	
Politics, international relations	278	
Sociology	121	1,144
Cultural anthropology	106	
Psychology	90	
Mainly 'synthetic' fields		
Geography (social), social surveys, area studies	151	
Education	108	
Industrial relations and management	56	405
Social medicine	50	
Demography	40	
Bibliography	8	

From *National Institute of Economic and Social Research, Register of Research in the Social Sciences*, 1953 ed. The list is incomplete.

the hands of those firms in the industry or industries covered by each association which choose to become subscribing members. Twenty-one associations were formed by 1921. The number remained practically constant till the end of the Second World War, when a new jump occurred; by 1950 there were forty associations, with an annual budget of £3¼ million, one-third of it from the D.S.I.R. The thirty-five associations existing at the end of 1947 had some 14,000 subscribing members. There is some double counting in this, as a firm may operate in more than one industry and belong to more than one association; the true figure may be nearer 10,000. A subscriber may be anything from the National Coal Board, or an industry's trade association subscribing on behalf of all its members' firms, down to a single plant employing a couple of dozen workers or less. Bearing in mind, however, that the total number of individual firms eligible for association membership is not much over 50,000, it is certainly true, as the most complete post-war study of them says, that the associations are 'potentially a major influence in British industry'.

Research associations serve a double purpose. They provide a consultant service, of special value to small firms, and may in theory undertake specific projects on firms' behalf, though they are usually reluctant to do so unless these fit into a wider programme. Their main purpose, however, is to carry on what might be called inter-mediate research; neither on detailed problems, of the sort dealt with by an individual firm, nor yet fundamental, in the sense of the study of the general principles of science carried on in a university. They are concerned, that is, with the general scientific background of the work of a particular industry. This function has not always been clearly understood by subscribing members. The Pottery Working Party, for example, found it necessary even in 1945 to defend the industry's association against those who wished to turn it into a mere enquiry bureau.

There are regional as well as industrial research associations. Before the war certain regional development councils, constituted from local authorities, business men, trade unions, and the regional universities, did valuable work on the location of industry, as for instance in the Second Industrial Survey of South Wales, sponsored by the National Industrial Development Council of Wales and Monmouthshire, or the long series of studies published through the Scottish Development Council. The North-East Development Association and its associated Northern Industrial Group still supply a couple of projects each to the annual Register of Research in the Social Sciences, and the Scottish Council (Development and Industry) has made some interesting studies in the technical field. The Scottish Council's work has been not so much research as liaison between research and its potential users. This is also the aim of the Manchester Joint Research Council, founded in 1944 to promote cross-fertilisation between local industries, some of them research-minded and some, such as cotton at that date, very much the reverse; and, in particular, to forge the link between the research laboratory and the small firm.

At the top of the tree, finally, appear the universities and the government research agencies. University research is not formally coordinated, but is, in fact, regularly reviewed, at least in its broad outlines, by the University Grants Committee, the body through which government grants reach the universities. With the universities should be classed various non-university research institutions. In the social science field, for example, one in eight of the research projects in progress in 1951 were undertaken by these.

The Government's own research organisation in the natural sciences (Chart II) shows much the same division between applied and background (as apart from fundamental) research as that in industry. Its structure on the side of economic and social research is less clear-cut. Here also there are agencies with a wide general remit —the Economic Section of the Cabinet Secretariat, the Central Statistical Office, and, for field studies, the Social Survey of the Central Office of Information. More specific projects are undertaken

CHART II
Government organisation for research in the natural sciences

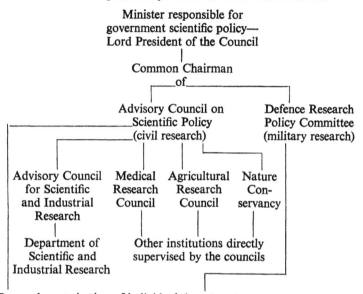

Minister responsible for
government scientific policy—
Lord President of the Council

Common Chairman
of

| Advisory Council on Scientific Policy (civil research) | Defence Research Policy Committee (military research) |

Advisory Council for Scientific and Industrial Research — Medical Research Council — Agricultural Research Council — Nature Conservancy

Department of Scientific and Industrial Research — Other institutions directly supervised by the councils

Research organisation of individual departments

From *Government Scientific Organisation in the Civilian Field*, H.M.S.O., 1951.

by the departments concerned with industry, agriculture, labour, housing and town planning, or the Census. A standing Inter-departmental Committee on Social and Economic Research (the North Committee) 'surveys and advises upon' research in government departments, and reviews the links between government and outside research. Research on human relations may fall into the field, not only of the Inter-departmental Committee, but of the Medical Research Council or D.S.I.R. Colonial research has its own separate machinery of coordination, a Colonial Economic Research Committee and Colonial Social Science Research Council.

The scale of the nation's research effort has, as the tables show, leapt forward since 1939. Allowing for the fall in the value of money, research by firms may well have been quadrupled, university and research association expenditure trebled, and government civil expenditure doubled between 1935–9 and 1950: and it must be remembered that much of the Government's vastly increased military research effort, notably on aircraft and in the atomic field, has value or potential value for civil purposes. In 1947–8 the total national research expenditure, military and civil, may have amounted to 1·1% of the national income at market prices, or 1·2% at factor cost. This is a greater proportion (Table 1) than that recorded for the U.S.A. or U.S.S.R. before the war. As an absolute amount, allowing for the fall in the value of money, as much was probably being spent in this country in 1947–8 as in the U.S.A. or U.S.S.R. in 1935; and by 1950 much more. It can of course be assumed that these countries have also increased their expenditure; but a more up-to-date comparison seems not to be possible.

The balance of the British research effort has been criticised in recent years on two grounds. One is that insufficient attention is paid to social science as apart from technology. It is a fact that the vastly greater part of research expenditure is in the physical and biological fields: 93% of the graduate staff employed by firms in 1945–6 were physicists, chemists, engineers, and metallurgists, and 5% mathematicians and biologists; barely 1% had economic or medical qualifications which might bring them into the social science field. Plans for expansion at that date showed that the gap was likely if anything to widen. The interest of the cooperative research associations is also overwhelmingly in technological research, though slightly less so in recent years. The Electrical Research Association, for example, has recently done interesting work on costs and price structures, and associations in the textile and shoe trades have studied productivity, labour redeployment, and the effect of changing working conditions. The Government's expenditure is also principally in the natural science field.

One reason sometimes alleged by applied research organisations for their reluctance to enter the social science field is that basic concepts and techniques have not yet been sufficiently worked out by the chief fundamental research agencies, the universities. It is therefore disturbing to find the same lack of balance in the universities themselves. The position just before the war is shown in Table 4. Of all ascertainable expenditure on salaries and departmental maintenance in 1938–9, 69% was incurred for science, technology, and medicine, and 3% for social science. Part of the difference can be accounted for by the greater need of the natural sciences for buildings and equipment. But the social sciences also need a great deal of working space and computing and clerical help, and depend on field work, often (as in social surveys) of a very expensive type, far more than the natural sciences. No difference in needs can account for the contrast between the £595,000 available in 1938–9 to the natural sciences for purposes other than the salaries of teaching staff, and the £7,600 available for the same purposes, for economics, economic history, anthropology, industrial relations, social science, social psychology, demography, economic statistics, commerce, sociology, and political science.

This state of affairs was severely commented on by an official committee in 1946 (the Clapham Committee), and as a result the University Grants Committee offered certain earmarked grants to the universities for expansion of the social sciences. By 1951–2 the expansion of social science staffs and expenditure had not merely kept pace with the general growth of university research and teaching but considerably outstripped it. But the percentage of university expenditure devoted to social science was still no more than 5% or 6%. The expansion of social science teaching had, moreover, at least kept pace with the growth in staffs, so that the stimulus of the new finance to research was limited. An unduly high proportion of the new grants seems also to have been captured by the old-established social sciences of economics and politics, though this does not show so much on the side of research as of teaching. Taking the universities and the research institutes together, the number of research projects in what might broadly be called the human relations field was by 1951 equal to that in economics, and much higher than in politics.

The other form of unbalance commonly noted in the British research effort has been between fundamental and applied research, or development. It has been said with justice that Britain equals any other country in the quality and quantity of its fundamental discoveries, but not in its capacity for applying them. It was reckoned in America at the end of the 'twenties that to carry a major laboratory discovery through to the stage of routine commercial production might take up to seven or eight years. By the end of the 'thirties, four or five years may have been nearer the mark, and the war, in Britain as in America, taught many lessons about speeding the process further. It remains, however, a slow and expensive process, and one to which too little British effort has been directed. This tendency to do too little on the side of development studies, applied to particular fields such as industrial relations, is also apparent in the social sciences (Table 7)—though it should be remembered that the classification there is rough and ready, and some 'development' work is concealed under 'fundamental' headings.

One difficulty in this country has been the lack of facilities for developing inventions, especially those from non-commercial sources. To meet this, the Development of Inventions Act of 1948 established a National Research Development Corporation, which acts as a patent pool for government departments and is also required to 'secure, where the public interest so requires, the development and exploitation of . . . any invention . . . which is not being . . . sufficiently developed or exploited'. It has, in fact, acted as a liaison rather than a development agency, not undertaking major expenditure itself, but seeing that inventors are put in touch with sources through which development can be ensured. By June 1951, it had itself taken out or applied for some sixty patents other than those arising from its functions as a government patent pool.

The lack of liaison between research and production agencies is a very general difficulty in the way of applying scientific discoveries. It has been a continuing problem of the cooperative research associations, and government departments have been forced to take considerable interest in it in their own fields of research, as notably in agriculture. The difficulty lies not only in the link between research institutions and firms but in that between research and production staffs within firms. To gear in any 'functional' department with production, without confusing responsibilities or creating ill-feeling, is one of the most difficult problems of management. It is liable to be particularly difficult with research, for research by definition deals in projects which are half-baked, will show their value (if any) only in the rather remote future, and meantime can be tried out only at the risk of considerable disturbance to production. ('You don't have to be crazy to work here,' an American research director recorded above his desk, 'but it certainly helps.') It could be said in 1946 by an experienced research director that this human element was the 'commonest cause of frustration' in converting research results into production.

A factor which has undoubtedly played a big part has been the lack of men with scientific, and still more with social scientific, training at the production end. The Cotton Working Party discovered in 1945 that four-fifths of the firms in the spinning, weaving, and finishing sections of the trade, with about two-thirds of the employees at that date, employed no graduate in science or technology in any capacity whatever, let alone research. This, clearly, is not a state of affairs in which the laboratory's contribution is likely to find an easy market. The employment of scientists, and to a smaller extent of arts and social science graduates, has increased steadily since the war, but not as yet sufficiently to fill this gap in the more old-fashioned industries. It would indeed be surprising if the gap had been filled; for in 1945-6 the total number of scientists working as such was barely equal to the number of industrial firms, with no allowance for the schools and universities, for research associations and government service, or for the very large numbers of scientists employed by big firms in industries such as chemicals or electrical engineering and equipment. It is especially, of course, the smaller firms in which the lack of men with scientific training is apparent, and it is for them in particular that local liaison agencies on the lines of the Manchester Joint Research Council can prove valuable.

.

THE CONTROL OF RESEARCH

The mechanisms available for deciding how much research is to be done, and on what, are the same as those considered in previous chapters; but the balance between them is naturally rather different.

Economic competition plays, and by common consent should continue to play, a big part. That it does play a big part is apparent from the fact that the largest single contribution to civil research comes from private firms, most of them in competitive industry. A further substantial contribution comes from the research associations, which have, in effect, to sell their services to subscribing firms.

The history of the research associations is as good a test case as any of whether the determination of research expenditure by the market is satisfactory. The associations *could* be financed otherwise. Their D.S.I.R. grant could be made to cover a hundred per cent of their costs, so putting them in the position of government research stations such as the Building Research Station or the Forest Products Research Laboratory. Alternatively, they could be financed from a compulsory levy on each industry under the Industrial Organisation and Development Act of 1947. The most thorough investigation of the associations in recent years concludes, however, that neither course would be desirable. The fact that firms have to be individually convinced, and kept convinced, of the value of an association's work ensures that its staff have an incentive to keep closely in touch with firms' and therefore consumers' requirements. The fact on the other hand that firms have individually put their hands in their pockets to find a subscription gives them a closer interest in the association's work than where finance is by one or other form of block grant. The gap between the laboratory worker and the producer is bridged from both sides.

On the other hand, some research is necessarily in fields too remote from the individual firm in its competitive market, or yields results over too long a time, to attract its interest and support. Other research is in fields where economic competition does not in any case work well. These heads cover much of the fundamental research in the universities, and of the military or health or educational research

167

(or even such work as that of the Geological Survey) carried on by the Government. Research, furthermore, is of all activities the one most concerned with change in the social framework, with proving the inadequacy of current practice and introducing, incidentally at the price of substantial threshold costs, new ideas and techniques. Once this systematic analysis and re-shaping of current techniques become standard practice among the leading firms of an industry—provided, of course, also that it is carried on in a way, and on a scale, which yields worth-while results—competition will make others follow suit; or, if the research is a cooperative venture, join in. But they will do so only when, and to the extent that, the leaders or 'representative' firms lead the way; and it will often need some force other than that of the market to give this first push.

The history of the cooperative research associations is again a good case in point. The First World War and the initial impact of the offer of D.S.I.R. grants gave the first push. But few industries joined the movement after the first rush; only six new names appear from 1923 to 1937. Further, many of the established associations failed to reach a level of activity which would have put their value beyond doubt even in their own industries. It is estimated that an association, at pre-war costs, needed an income of £30–50,000 a year to yield the best value for its subscribers' money. In the first half of the 'thirties the actual average income of associations was about £12,000. It is not surprising, in these circumstances, if associations often found great difficulty in convincing their subscribers that the relatively remote background research, which is, after all, their main objective, was worth while. The tendency mentioned above in the case of the pottery industry—to treat the associations as intelligence agencies or at most as doers of odd jobs for particular firms—was widespread. It took the Second World War to provide the further jolt which lifted the associations to a more economic level of activity, and at the same time doubled the number of industries participating.

This need for an initial push justifies the University Grants Committee in reviewing and stimulating universities' programmes of scientific development, or of the D.S.I.R. in making grants to research associations. The D.S.I.R. accepts a general responsibility for keeping in touch with non-governmental as well as government scientific research in all fields, and providing a centre of information and forum for discussion. Other departments have begun to do the same in their own fields. The Board of Trade, for instance, set out, about 1948, to stimulate research on the location of industry. But it is significant that in all these cases the accent is laid on stimulation, or cross-fertilisation—in any case on discussion and consultation—rather than on outright direction. Direction is appropriate when and to the extent that the questions to be answered and the methods of answering them have been defined. But it is precisely the fact that this has not been done which makes research necessary; which implies that in planning research it will normally be possible only to decide broadly that attention should be given to such and such a field, not to specify the action to be taken within it.

This is of course specially true of fundamental research at the university level. At this level it may be possible to say, for example, very broadly, that there is a case for more research on human relations or nuclear physics. But the precise amount of effort which it is worth devoting to a certain field, or the way in which the task should be tackled—the order of attack and the methods to be used —can often only be defined in the course of the research itself. At the university level, therefore, it is generally agreed that the most that can properly be done in the way of direction is, as the University Grants Committee has sometimes done—though it has usually been reluctant to go even so far—to earmark a grant for some broad field of research. It remains for the research workers themselves to determine its use, subject to the control of scientific public opinion, expressed through the learned societies and journals and personal contact between colleagues. The creation and maintenance of scientific standards depends much more on maintaining and developing this intricate system of consultation, on A.S.L.I.B.'s bibliographies or the N.I.E.S.R.'s *Register of Research in the Social Sciences*, than on any attempt to direct or pre-determine what is to be done; and it is, in fact, in this way that the D.S.I.R., for instance, has understood its relationship with university research.

But the same is also very largely true of even applied research; even, indeed, of operational research, concerned with the detailed problems and processes of production or military action. A striking example of this is the experience of Britain and Germany in radar research during the war. An official history offers its account of the British research machinery under the illuminating heading 'Sunday Soviets'. It was never assumed in British practice that the armed forces could correctly state even the questions to be answered.

'Admirals, generals, and air marshals came from the very first to see what was being done. They did not tell the scientists that they wanted this or that, but stated their problem and asked what science could do about it. The staff officers got into the habit of bringing rather diffuse problems to the scientists and general discussions went on between admirals, air marshals, lieutenants, pilots, scientists, laboratory assistants, development engineers, and anyone who could help.' (From *Science at War*, H.M.S.O., 1947.)

This happened notably in the Sunday free-for-alls from which the title of Sunday Soviets was taken. German practice, on the contrary, was for the consumer, the Army or Air Force, to specify exactly what he wanted, leaving it to the scientists merely to settle the technical details. The result was that German equipment was often superior to British in technical detail, but tended to be well behind in scientific inventiveness; and scientific problems and possibilities which were spotted early in Britain, where scientists were more closely associated with operational decisions, tended in Germany to be missed.

This is not, of course, to deny that direction can properly be more detailed in applied than in fundamental research. It is merely to insist that direction is useful only in so far as it is clear what direction to take; and in research, whether in the natural or the social sciences, the area in which consultation is necessary before this can be known is always wide.

Chapter 11

PROVISION FOR THE FUTURE (III)

III. PHYSICAL AND MENTAL HEALTH

EDUCATION and health are wanted for their own sake; they are themselves wealth, not merely means to its production. So indeed to many people is the state of being engaged in research and the pursuit of knowledge. But the last chapter was concerned with research not from this point of view but as a means of production alone. And so also it is as investments which may (or may not) lead to a high national income in future that education and health are considered here. For it is in this sense, as having money costs and advantages, that they become subject to the economic sanction and a matter for the economist.

It is not possible to pick out from health in general, or education in general, those aspects which specially contribute to the national income. Health is a matter not only of physical well-being but of psychology, and notably of social psychology:

'The individual is regarded not only in terms of a body that reacts to environment in its physical, chemical, and micro-organic aspects but also in terms of a life, or soul, that reacts to environment in its psychological (or social) aspects.' (Halliday, *Psycho-Social Medicine*, 1948, p. 9.)

Physical health largely determines psychological, and psychological health physical.

On the side of education, production obviously requires training in many highly specialised skills. Beginning in the last quarter of the nineteenth century, fears have again and again been expressed that too little is done in Britain, compared to other advanced Western countries, to give young men and women training of this kind. These fears are often justified; and this has been true, in particular, since the Second World War. But specialised skills alone are not enough. Even in recent years, and in the face of these fears, business men and specialists in education for industry have laid at least as much stress on general education, designed to develop character rather than technical skill: an open and adaptable mind, sensitivity to others' needs, energy, leadership and initiative, and

171

reliability and balance. Concluding a review of the wartime emergency schemes for training technicians, the Chairman of the Government's Technical Personnel Committee notes that technicians proved easy enough to train, but:

'What disturbed us was the number rejected by the Services . . . for want of what was termed "Officer qualities". . . . In my experience in peace and war the qualities of leadership and character are harder to find and even more important than technical capacity.' (Lord Hankey in Ministry of Labour, *The Worker in Industry*, 1952.)

What, asks another statement by a committee of business men and educationists, is industry to ask of the boy or girl leaving school at the statutory leaving age?

'*Not* . . . that they shall have received at school any specific vocational preparation for the occupations which they are about to enter; and there can be no greater misunderstanding of the real needs of industry than to suppose that it should. The demand which industry should make of these entrants is that they shall be as intelligent and as adaptable as is possible in both hand and mind . . . and . . . inspired with a zeal to give of their best and with a creative and forward-looking spirit.' (Nuffield College, *Statement on Industry and Education*, 1943.)

The school leaver of sixteen to eighteen should suffer neither from premature specialisation nor from an education designed primarily for those going on to a university. He should have, as the Nuffield statement says, 'a rounded education . . . the broadest and deepest possible development of general intelligence and initiative, and therewith a sound basis of general scientific and mathematical knowledge'. The value of university education, in its turn, lies certainly in producing competence in science and technology. But it lies still more in producing a certain quality of mind, able to study a situation objectively and to see the wood in spite of the trees, and matured, if possible, by the life of a college community.

Not merely is it necessary to pursue specialist knowledge and all-round development together; one is actually the foundation of the other. The man with an all-round education is not one who, by attempting to know something about everything, ends by knowing nothing about anything. He is one who, because he cannot learn everything at once, has focused his attention on a comparatively narrow field; but who, precisely because he has done this, has learnt to see it in all its aspects and relate it to its wider context. So also specialisation is all the more effective if the specialist learns to see the limits and possibilities of his craft, and the variables which determine these at any moment, by studying the wider social framework within which it functions.

172

THE COST AND ECONOMIC VALUE OF EDUCATION AND
HEALTH SERVICES

The fact that health and education are based on so very wide a
range of factors makes it difficult for the economist to keep track of
their costs and benefits. All-round health and development are the
product of nothing less than the whole of a civilisation. To decide
which educational or health measures add most to wealth, or how
great the net addition is, involves in principle following out the
action and reaction of possible changes throughout the whole field
of culture, institutions, personality, and political, economic, and
social action. This is nothing less than the total task of all social
science.

Leaving this breath-taking prospect aside, it is possible to make
a more modest and practicable beginning by concentrating on the
services which fill the gaps and cure the defects of education or
health. These fall into four broad groups:

(1) Education, in the sense of instruction.
(2) Medical services.
(3) Other physical environmental services, including nutritional
    services, housing, supply, sewage disposal, and the Factory
    and related Acts.
(4) Community-building services.

(a) *Overall cost and economic return*

No attempt has been made to estimate separately the present cost
of community-building services, including such headings as town
and country planning, personnel management, community associations, or marriage guidance. It is very small compared to that of
any of the other three groups. The main component of instruction,
public authorities' expenditure on education, amounted in 1950–1
to 2·1% of the gross national expenditure in Britain (Table 1).
Medical services amounted to 3·3%, and nutritional and certain
local authority environmental services to 1·5%. Some allowance
must in each case be made for amounts paid by private individuals.
In the case of most of the medical services these were in the year in
question too small to make any substantial difference to the total
shown in Table 1. The one exception is private spending on drugs
and pharmaceutical preparations, which is estimated for 1948 as
£35 millions at *wholesale* prices. The additions were more substantial in the case of education. 92½% of the children of compulsory
school age were in publicly maintained or grant-aided schools, and

173

TABLE 1. Current expenditure on certain educational and health
services and current cost of sickness, Great Britain, 1950–1

		£ millions	% of gross national expenditure
Public authorities' expenditure on education		280·7	2·1
National Health Service (including local authority services)	439·5		
Industrial rehabilitation	2·8		
Total medical services		442·3	3·3
Local authorities' current expenditure on:			
Water supply, sewage, refuse disposal (1947–8)	73·8		
Housing (1950–1)	74·2		
Nutritional services (school meals and milk, welfare foods, etc.)	56·9		
Total environmental services		204·9	1·5
Loss of production through sickness (approximately)[1]		167·0	1·2

[1] Average weekly number of insured workers absent from work through sickness, multiplied by the average weekly earnings of all operatives in October 1950, multiplied by 52. No allowance is made for higher paid earners or for inefficiency caused by illness which did not involve absence from work.

Source: *Monthly Digest* (especially May 1952), and *Annual Abstract of Statistics.*

accounted for approaching nine-tenths of all students receiving full-time education. But the balance, consisting mainly of students in secondary schools and in universities and other centres of higher education, were expensive to educate; and much of this expense was met by parents from other, private, means. In the case of food and accommodation the environmental services' expenditure constitutes only a small part of the total; but here the difficulty of deciding what is and what is not relevant for the purposes of this chapter comes up in full force.

In neither the medical, the environmental, nor the education services is it easy, at the present stage of these services' development in Britain, to say how the economic return on any further (or existing) expenditure may correspond to its cost. In countries where gross deficiencies of nutrition, sanitation, doctoring, or teaching exist this question is much more straightforward. A recent study by the World Health Organisation is able to quote cases where malaria control programmes permitted increases of 25–30% in production at a cost so small that the return exceeded the expense in some instances by twenty to one. Similar results are quoted for campaigns against hookworm and sleeping sickness. British labourers, in the middle nineteenth century, were better fed than their opposite numbers on the Continent. As a result they could demand far higher wages, and yet work at a rate which, as Clapham records in his *Economic History of Britain*, made it worth while for continental railway contractors to hire them in preference to local men. A little later in the century, Burn comments in his *Economic History of Steelmaking*, British steelworkers could earn more and yet produce at lower cost than German for the same reason.

Deficiencies as gross as these either are already, or are rapidly coming to be, a thing of the past in Britain, though some dramatic gaps remain.

(b) Education

To take first *education* (Tables 2–6); as lately as 1933–4 it was estimated in Britain that, of the most intelligent 25–30% of primary school-children, not more than 40–45% had the chance to continue their school education up to or beyond sixteen, and, whether they left school or stayed, their abilities were largely wasted for lack of vocational guidance. The proportion of boys and girls staying at school to age sixteen or later rose from 9–10% for those born in 1877–86 to 16% for those born in 1922–6; but even 16% was still a very low figure. Probably about a third of the boys and girls leaving school at or about the statutory leaving age in the 'thirties—at that time fourteen—went on to some kind of further education, usually in the form of evening classes or courses in technical colleges. The rest dropped out of formal education altogether. Even of the one-third, a substantial proportion failed to complete their courses, and

TABLE 2.   University education, numbers of staff and full-time students in Great Britain

	Students	*Staff*[1]
1938–9	38,557	3,994
1946–7	68,452	5,561
1950–1	85,314	8,490

[1] Excluding college staffs at Oxford and Cambridge.
Source: University Grants Committee, *University Development 1947–51*, 1952.

175

TABLE 3. Further education in England and Wales

	Full-time	Part-time, day	Evening	Total
Student hours (millions):				
1937–8	15·0[1]	11·0[1]	72·0[1]	98·0[1]
1949–50	44·0	41·8	95·5	181·3
Students attending, 1949–1950	54,046[2]	283,969[2]	2,023,796[2]	2,229,842[2]
Percentage of time given to group of subjects, 1949–50:				
Vocational	60	78	26[1]	—
General science and maths.	8	3	11[1]	—
Domestic and women's⎫			17[1]	—
Other (including art, ⎬ not in art schools ⎭	5	13	40[1]	—
Art schools	27	6	6	—
Age of students, 1949–50:				
15–17	—	—	—	704,421[3]
18–20	—	—	—	312,625[3]
21+	—	—	—	1,218,138[3]
Part-time day release of students by firms:				
1937–8 (no. of students)	—	—	—	40,000[1]
1949–50	—	—	—	240,000

[1] Approximate. [2] Eliminating overlap. [3] Not eliminating overlap.
Data from Ministry of Education, *Education 1900–1950*, Cmd. 8422.

TABLE 4. Adult education in England and Wales. Students attending classes of the W.E.A., university extra-mural departments, and certain colleges giving similar instruction

| 1937–8 | 56,700 |
| 1949–50 | 163,000 |

Cmd. 8422 and Ministry (previously Board) of Education reports.

the courses they did complete were commonly inferior in character-building quality if not as a means of acquiring technical competence. An engineering degree or its equivalent (Higher National Certificate) could, for instance, be acquired after about 750 hours of evening classes, as compared with about 2,700 hours normally required in

TABLE 5. Percentage of the child population in school, England
and Wales

(a) Aged 14 and under 18, in grant-aided schools   1910–1   4·0
                                                     1937–8   14·9
                                                     1950   32·8
(b) Aged 15 to 18, in grant-aided schools and   1946   9·3
    others recognised as efficient   1950   12·1

Cmd. 8422 and *Annual Abstract of Statistics.*

TABLE 6.   School leavers, local education authority schools and
direct-grant grammar schools. 1949–50. England and Wales

	Percentage of all leaving in year	
Age on leaving	For further full-time education [1]	For paid employment or other reasons [1]
14 or 15	2	78
16	1	11
17	1	3
18 and over	3	1
	7	93
Percentage of all children, 1950, aged 5–14 who attend grant-aided schools		92·5

[1] Not including pupils transferred to other primary or secondary schools.
Cmd. 8422.

a university; but the former course gave a purely technical competence, with none of the broadening characteristics of the latter. At
the end of the Second World War it was estimated that about 2%
of the young men and women of the relevant age groups were studying at universities; whereas not less than 5% had abilities as high as
those of the best 50% of the actual university students, and were on
the face of it equally well able to profit from a university course.
Not all of these should necessarily go to universities. There is a long
tradition in this country of training for the professions—the law,
for example, or engineering, or town and country planning—either
on the job or in technical colleges (full-time or part-time day courses)
or other vocational institutions. For many students of high ability
this may well be the best form of training. But the committee responsible for the estimate just quoted were of the opinion that, in

12   177

the case with which they were particularly concerned, that of scientists and technologists, the universities could with advantage double their pre-war output.

Apart from medicine, the universities have, in fact, approximately doubled their output; rather more in science and technology, rather less in arts. Probably at least three out of five of all boys with intelligence justifying a university education now reach the universities. This has been made possible by, among other things, a big increase in scholarships and grants. Of students entering universities in England and Wales in 1950, and normally resident in Great Britain, probably about three-quarters had major awards, entitling them in many cases—though by no means all, and subject to a means test—to a grant covering full fees and maintenance. Another 10% or so received minor awards. An official working party has recommended that as a long-term policy the proportion of major awards to entrants normally resident in Great Britain should be fixed at not less than 70%. In the opinion of the University Grants Committee, expressing a view widely shared by those who do the actual work of selecting university students, it would now be difficult to increase the universities' numbers much further without taking in candidates below sound university standards: for many of the boys and girls of high intelligence who do not come to the universities are already well provided for in professions like the banks, local government, or the law. This is not, of course, to deny that there may be a case for switching the emphasis of university teaching from one branch to another: for attempting, for example, to secure more students for advanced technology at the expense of some of the arts subjects.

The universities are lucky in that, though they have been short of space, they have been able in one way or another to house their increased number of students without lowering their standards of teaching and research. They have also been able, though again sometimes with difficulty, to hire the necessary staff. Schools and centres of further education have been much less happily placed. The Education Act of 1944 established the principle of full-time compulsory education for all children up to age sixteen, with compulsory part-time education beyond this up to eighteen. In 1945–8 national and regional councils were set up to coordinate further education and advise on its development.

But the actual realisation of the plans sketched in this way still lies well in the future. The 93% of all children up to age fifteen who attend publicly maintained or aided schools are taught at the primary stage—five to eleven years—in classes of, on the average, thirty pupils each; 30% of all classes having forty pupils or more.

178

Four-fifths of them leave school for reasons other than transfer to other full-time education—nearly always, that is, to go to work—at or about fifteen. Nine-tenths leave before they are seventeen. Further education fails to reach two-thirds, perhaps even as many as four-fifths, of those aged fourteen to twenty who have already left school. Twenty-one engineering, steel, and allied workers, twenty-one woodworkers, and nineteen clerks, per thousand men and boys in each occupation, were attending educational establishments part-time in 1951; but only five building workers, four mine-workers, and four-fifths of a farm worker. The county colleges in which compulsory part-time education up to eighteen is to be provided remain merely a hope for the future. Given the difficulty experienced since the war in recruiting teachers, and the slow rate at which, in the light of other commitments, public authorities have thought it right to issue permits for educational building, it may well be twenty years or more before the intentions of 1944-5 pass fully into fact.

It can, however, at least be said that the aims of 1944-5 have not been abandoned, and that their achievement will, in fact, eliminate the grossest defects of the British school system. Very substantial advances along this road are being made. The statutory school-leaving age has been raised from fourteen to fifteen. Uncertificated teachers accounted for 18% of all teachers in the primary schools in 1937-8, and no more than $3\frac{1}{2}\%$ in 1950. The increase in the numbers of children staying on into the higher forms is shown by the number of candidates passing the Higher School Certificate, which was multiplied by $2\frac{1}{4}$ between 1938 and 1950. Reorganisation of the school system to take account of differing abilities has made steady progress, and fees have been abolished for the great majority of children attending secondary as well as primary schools. The number of student-hours in technical colleges and other further education establishments has doubled since before the war, most of the increase being in full-time and part-time day students, with comparatively little in evening classes. Nearly 16,000 students in England and Wales obtained Ordinary and Higher National Certificates in different branches of technology in 1950, as compared with less than 4,500 in 1938; and there was also a big increase in technical college students working for university degrees. More is being done for advanced technology. Six colleges specialising in particular branches have been set up since the war, and more are in prospect. The Government announced in 1952 its intention of developing an existing technical college into a university specialising in technology, on lines already familiar in America and the rest of Europe. On the less

179

exclusively vocational side of further education, it is worth noting that the number of students in approved courses of the W.E.A., University Extra-Mural Departments, and other courses of the same standing increased between 1937–8 and 1950 from 57,000 to 163,000 for England and Wales alone.

These measures of education in educational establishments are supplemented, finally, with services of vocational guidance, apprentice training, and training for supervision and management, which have improved rapidly in recent years. Apprentice training was covered by a joint declaration of the British Employers' Confederation and the Trades Union Congress in 1945; and within the next four years the Ministry of Labour *Gazette* was able to record some thirty-odd industries, beginning with trades as large as engineering, building, printing, boot and shoe, and coal, which had, in fact, set up schemes for this purpose. The Employment and Training Act of 1948 consolidated the already established Youth Employment Service. At the other end of the scale, there has been a considerable improvement in the work of university appointments committees, and a technical and scientific register, and a higher appointments department, have been established by the Ministry of Labour. In addition to the measures for management training referred to above, considerable efforts have been made to improve the training of supervisors. A training-within-industry scheme was introduced by the Ministry of Labour for this purpose in 1941, and by the beginning of 1950 over 150,000 supervisors, from 2,400 firms, had taken at least one part of the course: some 1,500 of firms' own staffs had been trained actually to give courses.

(c) Medical and environmental services

The history of the medical and environmental services in Britain in the last century is broadly that gross deficiencies in physical health have been wiped out, but that psychological or social health has degenerated. Taking 'medical and environmental' services in the rather narrow sense in which they are marked off from such community-building services as town planning or the youth service, it would seem that these services have themselves been brilliantly successful, but that the community-building services, with the great contribution they have to make to psychological health, have failed to keep pace with them.

The success of efforts to improve physical health is illustrated in Table 7 by the fall in the infant mortality rate from 142 per thousand in 1900–2 to 36 in 1948. Success on this scale is the product of three or four main lines of development. The ideal of the *nutritional expert*

TABLE 7. Infant mortality rate, United Kingdom, 1870–1948 (deaths of infants under one year per thousand live births)

1870–2	150
1900–2	142
1930–2	67
1939	53
1948	36

Annual Abstract of Statistics.

is, to quote Lord Boyd Orr, a 'state of well-being such that no improvement can be effected by a change in the diet'. By this standard the diets of 10–30% of the population of Britain, including up to half of all children, were grossly deficient as recently as the early 'thirties. During and since the Second World War all but a small margin of this deficiency has been wiped out; though it has not yet been possible to provide a diet which both corresponds to consumers' tastes, at free market prices, and is nutritionally adequate. *Working hours* have been reduced from the fantastic levels of the early and mid nineteenth century—which added nothing to output —to about the level at which output (total, not merely hourly) is maximised. The *Factory Acts* enforce standards of health and safety high enough to eliminate gross dangers; though there is room for improvement in the identification and treatment of industrial disease, and much rebuilding remains to be done before all places of work are brought fully up to these standards. About £35 a family a year is now spent on *hospitals, doctors, and related services.* Nearly all of this is now spread over the population as a whole in proportion (since the beginning of the National Health Service in 1948) to medical need, and seems, once again, to be enough to eliminate at any rate gross deficiencies in the supply of services of this kind. The biggest remaining gaps are in the treatment of chronic sickness and the care of old age; and border, significantly, on the community-building services.

The biggest remaining gap in the *physical and environmental health services* is probably that in housing and town planning. The long fight waged by local and national authorities against insanitary conditions has had its great successes. But the older and larger towns still suffer, by comparison with those built since 1918, or with the countryside, from acute overcrowding of houses on the land (and to a smaller extent of people in houses) and from atmospheric pollution. These conditions substantially affect health.

The striking difference in health conditions which, in spite of these remaining gaps, separates the advanced Western countries from the

181

rest of the world is brought out in Table 8. Having discussed fields to which priority should be given in building up the health services of under-developed areas, including such matters as water supplies and sanitation, maternity and child welfare, the control of malaria,

TABLE 8. Health and health services in developed and under-developed areas

	Developed areas	Intermediate areas	Under-developed areas
Proportion of world population	$\frac{1}{3}$	less than $\frac{1}{6}$	$\frac{2}{3}$
Annual income per head, U.S. $	461	154	41
Food supply, calories, per head, per day	3,040	2,760	2,150
Physicians per 100,000 people	106	78	17
Expectation of life at birth, years	63	52	30

Quoted by Winslow, *The Cost of Sickness and the Price of Health*, World Health Organisation, 1951, p. 12.

tuberculosis, and venereal disease, and the development of nursing, health education, and industrial health services, the World Health Organisation report from which this table is taken concludes as follows:

'In North America and Western Europe, *where all the objectives listed above have been approached with reasonable effectiveness* (our italics), the problems of mental hygiene and mitigation of the degenerative diseases, geriatrics, and the care of the aged and infirm are today the next steps in the evolving public-health programme.'

(d) The community-building services

The lag of the *community-building services*, as compared with education, medical services, or public health, can be illustrated in several ways. It was shown very strikingly in the last chapter, in the low rate of expenditure on research in the social sciences as compared with that on medicine or technology. It can be seen from the rise in recent generations in such indices of 'social sickness' as infertility, suicide rates, or the diseases (gastritis and peptic ulcer, for instance) associated with worry. It appears also from studies of actual social situations, which bring out the very limited extent to which, in the home, the neighbourhood of working group, the problems of community-building have been solved.

It can be seen also from the history of the community-building services themselves. Some of these are now solidly established and operating on a mass scale; but only very recently. This is true of management, and especially of personnel management; the mass extension of professional personnel management dates from the last ten to fifteen years. The experimental period of town and country planning, which deals with the physical aspects of the design of neighbourhoods and regions, dates from 1909. But the charter of town planning, the measure which ensured its mass application, was the Town and Country Planning Act of 1947; and the preparation of the first development plans under this Act was completed only in 1952. The revival of the parish council dates only from the 1940's; it has affected different parts of the country in very different measure. There are other services which have not got even so far. The ancestry of the Youth Service runs well back into the nineteenth century. Yet a survey in 1949 showed that approximately half of all Birmingham boys aged fourteen to twenty, and not in full-time education, had no connection with it, and three-quarters of all girls. The community association movement has existed for most of a generation. But it is doubtful if as many as 5% of the country districts or town neighbourhoods big enough to support an association, and prima facie needing one, have, in fact, a satisfactorily constituted association, or, indeed, any at all. In the country as a whole the number of full-time salaried wardens of community centres seems to have increased from 27 in 1945 to 176 in 1950; proportionally a rapid rate of progress but a mere flea-bite by comparison with the work to be done. In general, community associations and other community-building services have had low priority since the war, in such important matters as the grant of building licences, compared to the older-established medical and environmental services, or to schools.

Here, if anywhere, is the field where gross deficiencies in the health and educational services are still to be found, and the return on comparatively inexpensive measures may prove to be very great.

(e) Conclusion. The economist's contribution

The picture as a whole is, however, of very substantial effort and expenditure, sufficient to remove at least the worst defects. This puts on accountants and economists a heavier responsibility than in the days when gross deficiencies remained; for it now becomes a matter,

183

not of mere common sense, but of careful and accurate analysis to discover where good value is or can be obtained by spending more or less. This is beginning to be appreciated by administrators; above all, perhaps, in the case of the National Health Service, on which expenditure has greatly outrun the original estimates. A report in 1951 speaks of 'medical economics, a science virtually unknown in Britain, which we neglect at our peril'. A vigorous effort has, in fact, been made, since the beginning of the Service in 1948, to develop standard costing, especially for hospital services. One of the by-products of the National Insurance Act of 1946 was a vast improvement in statistics of sickness and absence from work, thanks to which it should be considerably easier than in the past to estimate the gain or loss to production through changes in the sickness services. But it must be recognised that analysis of this sort is not simple. A recent study of nutrition attempted to answer the question: 'What difference will be made to sickness and health in Britain by small improvements or deteriorations in existing, post-war, standards of nutrition?' It proved impossible to obtain a precise answer. The effects of gross changes, starting from or ending at a level of seriously inadequate nutrition, can be expressed in statistics. Changes in the present position in Britain produce far vaguer and less distinguishable effects. A figure of the cost of sickness, of the type quoted in Table 1, is only a very short first step towards the analysis which is required.

The standard just quoted for nutrition, one 'such that no improvement in well-being can be effected by a change in the diet', or its parallels in other fields such as those of housing or medical services, has, of course, no absolute ethical validity. It may quite genuinely be the case that, when account has been taken of other commitments, the resources to achieve so high a standard may not be worth providing. Such a standard does, however, as was shown in discussing consumption, provide at least the starting point of an economic enquiry; for, so long as it is not attained, there is the certainty that additional expenditure on the service in question will bring some—though it may not be an adequate—return in welfare and in productive capacity.

THE MECHANISMS CONTROLLING EDUCATION AND HEALTH EXPENDITURE

(a) *Economic competition*

For some of the services considered here, and for certain classes of the people, economic competition seems capable, unaided, of raising expenditure to the level at which productive capacity is maximised. For a fair judgement on this it is necessary to go back to pre-war conditions, when the market for many of these services was much freer than it is now.

In the case of medical services, after allowing for changes in prices and the cost of living (including taxation), it seems that in 1937–8 families spending about £450 a year (£1,050–1,100 at the prices and tax levels of ten years later) were spending about as much on these services as is spent today for an average family in the whole population under the National Health Service. The incidence of sickness is of course uneven from year to year and between families. But this, apart usually from maternity and chronic sickness, could be provided against by insurance. Families with incomes as high as this, however, accounted for no more than 20% of the whole population. The rate of spending by poorer families (Table 9) fell far short of the 'saturation' level: even when allowance is made for the compulsory National Health insurance of wage-earners.

TABLE 9. Expenditure on instruction and sickness services (other than that financed through rates, taxes, and national insurance) by households in Great Britain, 1937–8

Household expenditure		*Expenditure per week*			
£ per annum	*Shillings per week*	*Shillings and pence*		*Percentage of total expenditure*	
		Instruction	*Sickness services*	*Instruction*	*Sickness services*
149	57/4	–/1¼	1/2½	0·2	2·1
221	85/–	–/3¾	1/8	0·4	2·0
354	135/11¾	–/10¾	4/11¼	0·7	3·6
451	173/4¾	3/3¾	7/4¼	1·9	4·2
592	227/9¾	7/11¼	8/10	3·5	3·9
836	321/8¾	14/5½	12/5½	4·5	3·9
Average weekly expenditure all British households, *including* expenditure from rates and taxes		5/8			

From Ministry of Labour, *Working Class Cost of Living Enquiry*, 1937–8, Massey, *Journal of the Royal Statistical Society*, 1942, and P.E.P., *Britain's Health Services* 1937.

In the case of housing, the average weekly expenditure by working-class households on rent and rates in 1937–8 was enough, without subsidy or other special aid, to cover the full cost and rates of a three-bedroomed council house of the least expensive pattern regarded at that time as satisfying 'human needs', in a sense parallel to that of the nutritionist. It fell somewhat short of what was needed to pay for a house of the minimum standard accepted today (Table 10). Craftsmen and many clerical workers, as well as all

TABLE 10. Expenditure on rent and rates and cost of housing, 1937–9

Average weekly expenditure on housing (including rates) by working-class families, 1937–8	10/10
Weekly unsubsidised rent excluding rates of a standard council house at costs of 1939:	
Pre-war standard (3 bedroom, 775 ft.²)	7/10
With interest at 3%	7/10
„ „ 3½%	8/5
Post-war standard (3-bedroom, 900 ft.², better amenities):	
Interest at 3%	9/8
„ 3½%	10/5

Based on Ministry of Labour, *Working Class Cost of Living Enquiry*, 1937–8, and *Report of the Committee on the Design of Dwellings*, 1944.

See also the data on owner-occupation in British Association, *Britain in Recovery*, 1938, Chapter 12.

higher paid workers, could and often did then buy housing of a standard such that no improvement would have added much to their health or productive capacity. But this was more rarely possible in the case of semi-skilled workers, and was impossible, in a free market, for the unskilled. Housing costs have since risen more sharply than wages.

The interesting and comprehensive studies of the effect of environment on health made for the Royal Commission on the Distribution of the Industrial Population showed that professional and business families, even in the big towns, can and do in a free market buy conditions of life which save them from the worst effects of overcrowded land and atmospheric pollution. The town solicitor, or manager, is not markedly less healthy than his opposite number in the country. This is, however, not yet true of the general mass of the population.

In the case of nutrition, the relevant pre-war figures have already been quoted. In the middle 'thirties about half the population could and did afford diets on the nutritionist's 'ideal' standard; another 20% were not far off; and 10–30% suffered from gross deficiencies.

It is a point of much importance for practical policy that these figures represent a snapshot of a changing situation, at one particular moment now fifteen to twenty years in the past. Table 9 illustrates how, as incomes rise, so also does the proportion of the people who can and do buy for themselves health (or educational) services such as to eliminate gross deficiencies. In the case of nutrition, for example, it was estimated in 1948 that if a free market were re-established at the unsubsidised food prices and with tax levels and income distribution of that date, a substantial number of the people (though fewer than in the 'thirties) would be unable to buy an 'ideal' diet. But if household incomes after tax rose over the next thirty years at the rate actually experienced in 1870–1937—including, it is worth noting, a world war and a period when capital exports to under-developed countries equalled or exceeded the proportion of the national income now called for from this country by the experts of the United Nations—practically the whole population would be willing and able to buy such a diet.

(b) Where competition fails

The mere fact that, in a competitive market, some people cannot and will not buy as much education or health as would maximise their working efficiency does not necessarily prove that competition is ineffective as a means of social control. If there are not enough resources to go round, it need not follow that the right thing to spend them on is more doctors or school teachers. But one will often have a shrewd suspicion that more doctors, teachers, or perhaps simply more proteins and vitamins, would be a good investment. And, in fact, it is generally agreed that even in a country with very high individual incomes, still more in one with incomes at or below the present British level, the pattern of expenditure on health and education which emerges from economic competition is unlikely to be, and is not, in fact, ideal. The factors of which competition fails to take sufficient account operate here as in other fields.

Firstly, of course, the background factors, too remote or diffused for individuals to bother with or effectively control. Since, for instance, the amount people spend on health or education depends on their income, it may well happen that a redistribution of incomes, such as is outside the power of individuals or small groups to achieve, can add more to welfare or productive capacity by ensuring fuller use of these services by poorer families than it takes away by reducing the expenditure of the well-to-do.

187

Again, the return on much health or educational expenditure is remote, and difficult for even the expert to define at all precisely; still more for the average consumer. The doctor's skill, the relative merits of a grammar and a secondary modern school, the value of a patent medicine, are cases in point. A child is in no position to assess the true value of different types of education; and even the average parent will find it less easy than, say, the Ministry of Labour to forecast the probable demand for school-leavers or graduates with training of particular types. This latter problem has not hitherto been serious in Britain, because of the comparatively small output (by the standards of the rest of the Western world) of men and women with higher education, and of the very wide range of openings available for them. In other countries it has been a major cause of social unrest and even revolution.

Instability is also an important factor here. Truancy does not help schooling: nor do frequent changes of school. When Halliday comments, in *Psycho-Social Medicine*, on the rising curve of suicides and gastric ulcers in the advanced Western countries, he is thinking of the impact of the disintegration and the ups and downs of modern life. It has long been recognised that unemployment, particularly prolonged unemployment, produces not merely poverty but what a sociologist has called the 'tired community'. The parks of the little Austrian town of Marienthal were beautifully kept while the town's textile industry was busy. When in due course it collapsed, people were left with unlimited time on their hands. But the grass in parks grew three feet high; and they were too tired to care. Psychological ill health such as this can easily turn over into physical ill health as well. So also many studies of migration—Londoners in Watling, Welshmen in Cowley, Irishmen in Birmingham—have shown that when people are rooted up from their established communities, often by factors outside their control, such as the lack of local jobs, it may take a generation or more to knit up again the broken ends; and in the meantime they suffer a greater or less degree of psychological and sometimes also of physical ill health.

Group loyalties, again, come into the picture, for better or for worse. If twenty-one per thousand woodworkers enjoyed part-time day release to attend courses in 1951, but only 0·8 per thousand farm workers, that does not tell one much about the initiative of individual woodworkers or farm workers, or about the need for skilled teaching of their trades. But it does say a good deal about the attitudes common in the two trades, and the power of public opinion to compel individuals to conform to these.

And, finally, the task of the educational and health services is

188

often to break through the existing social framework and create new physical and biological environments, new personality patterns, institutions, and standards of conduct. Education aims not merely at transmitting an existing culture but at encouraging useful new mutations of it; new personality patterns. The health services need their pioneers; like the specifically so-called 'Pioneer' Health Centre at Peckham. Both the doctor and the teacher are liable to be faced from time to time with situations in which a population is so weakened by disease or (more relevant to British conditions) by lack of experience of satisfactory human relations as to be unable without outside help to break through the crust of its existing customs and repair its own physical or psychological health.

And all these are cases of the kind where competition may be of some help in allowing new developments to emerge, but where it cannot force and often fails to induce them to do so.

(c) The role of direction and consultation

The choice between direction and consultation as means of supplementing competition in the educational and health services depends on much the same factors as were mentioned in discussing consumption. Direction is, in fact, already extensively used for this purpose. We have in Britain a National Health Service, an (in practice) almost equally national education service, and extensive control and supervision of the community-building services. The Ministries of Education and of Housing and Local Government, for example, and local housing and planning authorities, are largely responsible for providing community centres, and wholly responsible for the physical design of communities. Recent landmarks in the growth of direction in these fields are the Education Act of 1944, the National Health Service Act of 1946, and the Town and Country Planning Act of 1947.

There are, however, the same reasons for expecting that direction alone will be inadequate as a supplement to competition as there are in the case of consumption. The problem is not merely to enforce established standards but to promote novel mutations, and these can be encouraged to emerge by consultation, but not—since it is not known what they will be—ordered into existence by direction. Also, there is enough variety among individual personalities, and what constitutes psychologically and even physically healthy behaviour for each of them, to make fully detailed direction an impossibly complex task. From the point of view of any higher authority, many of the factors in individual cases must remain impossibly 'remote'. The individual may be *helped* to make his own adjustments, but cannot in practice be *directed* what to do.

189

And here comes in another factor special to the fields of education and health. One element in the concept of 'total health', or of the 'whole man', to which they are directed is the capacity of each individual himself to operate, in appropriate cases, each of the three main types of social control mechanism. He must know how to stand up for himself in competition, to behave when appropriate as a man in or under authority, and also to consult and benefit from consultation. And he can hardly learn these things without actual experience of all three mechanisms.

When competition has to be supplemented, there will often thus be grounds for preferring, other things being equal, consultation to direction.

'It is important to state that, in our opinion,' write the founders of the Pioneer Health Centre at Peckham, 'self-maintenance of a health centre is not only a possibility but is an *essential* for the maintenance of any institution *where health is the object*. The family's power to handle affairs, including the responsibility of adjusting a financial balance, is no less an expression of function—of the wholeness of apprehension of environmental circumstances—than any other capability . . . Nevertheless, the balancing of his budget is an experience from which . . . the working man's family is cut out from all·but his immediate domestic sphere. . . . Management and knowledge of the family's social and local affairs in a place like the Centre are the next steps in an education long overdue. . . . In the case of *sickness* we are faced with a quite different proposition. The very essence of sickness is withdrawal from the environment. . . . The doctor's work is thus to assume responsibility for the sufferer . . .' (From Pearse and Crocker, *The Peckham Experiment*.)

It is a commonplace that unless the members of a community centre or of a group in the Youth Service identify themselves with it and take responsibility for its running, it is not merely less efficient than it might be but is failing to do its most important work at all. The dependence of industrial working groups and their limited control of their own activities often, similarly, account for their relatively poor psychological health compared to that of farm working groups.

Although direction, and especially State direction, has grown steadily in the education and health services throughout the last century, the administrators and politicians themselves have not allowed the case for consultation to drop out of sight. The Minister of Education in introducing his *Report on Education*, 1900–50, writes:

'If this report comes into the hands of readers from overseas, as I hope it will, they may be expected to look first for a substantial chapter on educational method and the curriculum of the schools. They will not find it. This does not of course mean that the schools have made no response to the new knowledge about the nature and needs of children or to the changing conceptions of the function of education in a democratic community. The reason is that the Department has traditionally valued the life of institutions more highly than system and has been zealous for the freedom of schools and teachers. In all matters, therefore, affecting the curriculum and methods of teaching it has been content to offer guidance by means of suggestions, and in the main to rely on Your Majesty's Inspectorate.'

'Education in a democracy,' the Report adds, 'is determined not by the State but by the general will of the community.' Recognising this, the Ministry has laid special stress on consultation with experts and interested parties, and claims in this way to 'have made a special contribution to the art of government'. In the community-building services the accepted conception is likewise one of partnership through consultation between the State, local authorities, and independent associations; and this sector has, in the National Council of Social Service, one of the most remarkable instruments for fostering and shaping new services through consultation that is known to administrative history.

The National Health Service also set out to base the relation of the family doctor to his local executive council, and of the hospital to the Ministry, chiefly on autonomy (competition) plus consultation. This objective has been achieved in the case of the doctors by paying a doctor a flat rate per patient registered with him. He competes for patients; his actual work is not normally checked or controlled, at least in detail. Hospitals' incomes, on the other hand, are related to their actual budgets. In the first year or two, consultation between the Ministry of Health and hospital administrators, without the backing either of competition (the need to go out and earn an income by selling services to consumers or donors) or of effective direction (budgetary control), proved ineffective in keeping expenditure within bounds the Government would accept. Detailed direction—control of hospital budgets—was then imposed. But it is recognised that this state of affairs is unsatisfactory. There have been various suggestions for applying to hospitals, as to doctors, the system of a flat rate of payment per bed or in proportion to the population served, or of a block grant fixed over a period, like that paid to the universities.

In so far, of course, as the health and education services are run by local authorities, these authorities have a large degree of autonomy based on direct election, the possession of their own income, and the various services' statutes.

It may well be that the tightening up of direction in the last decade has gone too far in these services, and that more use should be made of competition for patients' or consumers' support and of consultation. This is certainly true of the National Health Service, not only for the reason just mentioned—the need to increase local autonomy, whether by block grants or by decentralising the source of hospitals' funds—but also for that pressed by the authors of the Peckham Experiment: that in a health service, as apart from a sickness service, personal responsibility on the part of the patient, and identification with an institution or group, should count for more than it does in the National Health Service now. This may well come to the front when the health centres envisaged by the Act—though as centres of medical treatment, rather than combined medical and social centres on the lines tried at Peckham—come to be built. It is probably also true that control has been tightened too far in education, and, generally, the local government services.

To say that direction has been tightened too far may mean either that direction brings benefits obtainable in no other way, but that the disadvantages associated with tight control outweigh these; or that direction has been tightened in the hope of obtaining some benefits which can, in fact, be obtained otherwise. There is some reason to believe that the latter is true in the case of the National Health Service and local government service. Pre-war experiments—the Gloucestershire Medical Services scheme, the Highlands and Islands scheme, the hospital coordination schemes promoted by the Nuffield Provincial Hospitals Trust, notably in the Oxford region—showed that it is possible to obtain very high coordination of the medical services of a region without bringing in direction; or rather without bringing in a greater measure of direction than is needed to promote consultation and the exchange of information. Mr. D. N. Chester has shown how simple-minded it is to believe that the coordination of local authorities, and of local and central government, is to be secured only or principally through law and orders. Subtler means can also work wonders: competition between political parties, and between local government officers anxious for professional distinction; the exchange of ideas through conferences, or through Her Majesty's Inspectors; the role of the Ministry as not the commander but the channel through which the wisdom of innumerable local experiments is combined and diffused; or, simply, a little unpleasant publicity for defective services.

Chapter 12

INTER-REGIONAL AND INTERNATIONAL RELATIONS

I. POPULATION

IT was noted above that the circle of solidarity relevant to economic policy is usually seen today as extending to the whole world. Everyone of every race is entitled to the benefits of equal pay for equal work, an income based on his and his family's needs, and the rest, as outlined in Chapter 8. This is, of course, easier said than done. In recent years four main bodies of experience relevant to it have been built up.

The first is that of the long series of efforts since the war to build up international policies on trade and development by agreement between independent nations. Some of these have been confined to particular groups of nations, as for instance the successive British Commonwealth conferences on the Colombo Plan for aid to under-developed areas in South-East Asia. Others have been in intention at least world-wide. Some of the earlier efforts of this kind were summed up in the Bretton Woods Agreement of 1944, under which were established an International Monetary Fund and an International Bank for Reconstruction and Development, and in the Havana Charter of an International Trade Organisation, agreed in 1948. Though the Charter was not in the end ratified by the leading economic powers, it is interesting as the most comprehensive statement on the principles of international trade ever to reach the stage of even preliminary agreement on a world-wide scale. And it is, in fact, an excellent summary of much of the thinking on these matters in the years just after the war. Particularly useful, among documents illustrating later trends, are the reports of committees of experts to the United Nations on *National and International Measures for Full Employment*, 1949, and *The Economic Development of Underdeveloped Areas*, 1951, and the regional and general reviews of trade and development published annually by the United Nations and the Organisation for European Economic Cooperation.

Secondly, there is the experience within various states, or state systems (including, for instance, a metropolis and colonies), of inter-regional development policies under the control of a single government. An outstanding example of this was the rehabilitation of the depressed areas in Wales, Scotland, and the North of England between 1934 and 1948. Another, and probably the most famous, has been the experience of the Tennessee Valley Authority in the U.S.A. The experience of colonial powers also provides a good deal of evidence.

Case (1) concerns inter-state action, and case (2) action within one state. Case (3), intermediate between the two, concerns areas in transition from one of these categories to the other. Europe has been making, via the European Coal and Steel Community or the customs unions (Benelux) between Belgium, Holland, and Luxembourg, the transition from a collection of sovereign states to a single economic area under one executive authority. Parts of the British Common-wealth, such as West Africa or the West Indies, are following the United States, Canada, Ireland, or India along the opposite road from economic unity with the United Kingdom to full independence, with common policies, where there are any, based purely on agreement.

Fourthly, there is a body of thought and experience which might be brought under the three previous cases, but has, in fact, usually been handled separately: namely, on the relation of population to natural resources, and especially to food supplies. For Great Britain this problem is particularly fully treated in the Report and papers of the Royal Commission on the Population in 1948: notably in the papers of the Commission's Economic Committee. On a world scale, an outstanding source is the series of reports of the United Nations *Scientific Conference on the Conservation and Utilisation of Resources*, 1950.

International and inter-regional economic policy, as these bodies of experience show it, centres round four issues:

(1) *Population policy*—the population which can be supported by a country or the world, and its distribution, by migration, between regions or countries.

(2) *Trade and employment policy*—freedom and restriction of trade, and the general level of demand and employment.

(3) *Investment policy*.

(4) *Relief and readaptation*. An 'ideal' degree of freedom of trade, or of capital development, cannot always (or even usually) be attained at one blow. Where a prolonged effort is needed, special measures may be required to maintain people in particular areas and industries during the transition.

It is convenient to take the first of these issues separately, and the other three together.

POPULATION POLICY

(a) *Population and world resources*

The population of the world rose from about 730 million in 1750 to around 1,600 million in 1900, and 2,450 million in 1951. It is increasing today at probably 1% a year. At this rate, will it not grow too large to be kept at a reasonable standard of living out of the world's resources, especially its food resources?

It is certainly the case (Chapter 11, Table 8) that there is today desperate hunger over a large part of the earth's surface. Indeed, the position actually got worse for some years after the war. Thus in 1951 food supplies in the countries of East and South-East Asia were about 100% of the average for 1934–8, whereas population was 113%; food supplies per head were down, therefore, by about 8%. But it would seem that this was due to failure to produce food rather than inability to produce it. One general estimate (Clark) suggests that world food supplies might well be made to increase by 1½% per annum, as compared with the annual population increase of 1%. Even allowing for the fact that as people grow richer they eat more, though not quite in proportion (a 50% increase in the national income in Britain or the U.S.A. would probably put 25% on to food consumption), supplies would thus keep ahead of demand.

A more exact estimate made in the late 'forties tried to show from what sources a full 'human needs' diet could be provided for the whole population of the world, allowing for different national tastes, by 1960. The standard taken was that quoted above from Orr; one, namely, so high that no improvement in the diet would lead to any further substantial improvement in health. It did not seem that a standard of feeding as high as this could be provided from existing crop-land, even allowing for possible increases in productivity. But existing crop-land includes only 7–10% of the available land in the world, or perhaps 20% of the really cultivable land. There are big reserves of fertile land in Indonesia, in Africa and Madagascar, in South America, and in Canada, the U.S.A., and the U.S.S.R. equivalent to 25–30% of the earth's surface. If from this area an amount equivalent to 4% or 5% of the world's surface could be brought into cultivation, the full 'human needs' diet could be found for the whole population of the world, including all prospective increases up to 1960, with a handsome surplus over.

There is no reason, hydrogen bombs apart, to suppose that the world's population will stop increasing in 1960. Looking further ahead, however, it seems not unlikely that supplies can still be kept adequate to demand even without any deliberate attempt to persuade parents to have fewer children than they would wish on their own. Still more of the reserve of cultivable land can be brought into operation. Other forms of food supply can be developed. Some of these may be useful supplements, but do not as yet look like yielding a massive increase in production; soilless cultivation, for example, or the micro-biological production of food yeast. But there are others from which mass-production might well be expected. The world has learnt in the past to take a harvest from the sea, but hardly as yet to cultivate it. The cultivation of fresh- and sea-water algae is already beginning to yield interesting results. 'The unicellular aquatic organism,' as one medical paper says, 'should certainly be capable . . . of providing the human race with such nutriments as are required from it.' Call it seaweed marmalade if you like; there can at any rate be a great deal of it, and it may not be as nauseating as the medical Press makes it sound. And we are still very far, in most parts of the West, from equalling the astonishing yields of fish which the Chinese have learnt to get from even small fresh-water ponds.

On the other side of the equation, there is every reason to expect the growth in world population to slow up after a time, as that of the Western countries has already done. Typically, the growth of a population shows three stages.

Primitive. Families of five to seven children typical. High infant mortality (anything up to 300 per 1,000 or more). Little or no net increase in the population.

Early industrial. Same typical size of family, much lower mortality (better health services), rapid net increase.

Mature industrial. Mortality drops further, but family size also drops. Increase slows down or stops.

Thanks to the lower infant mortality, families of typically three, four, or five children not only yield as big a net increase in population in the developed countries as much larger families do in backward areas, but also impose as big a physical and mental (not to mention for the moment financial) strain on parents. For the number of children actually alive and to be looked after in the family is the same, in spite of the lower initial number of births.

Western Europe has passed through all three of the above stages, and certain countries have reached the point where the population is no longer even replacing itself. In Britain, for instance, the average size of completed family is now between two and three children, which in British health conditions puts it just about at the margin of replacement. The birth-rate in Britain dropped below the replacement level in the depression of the 'thirties, rose well above it during and just after the war, and is now hovering around it.

In the less developed parts of the world a great many countries have moved in the last thirty years from the 'primitive' to the 'early industrial' stage, and it is to this that the comparatively rapid increase in world population in recent years has been due. They show signs, however, of moving on in due course to the 'mature industrial' stage, with the usual consequences. In Japan, for instance, the average size of completed family had already by 1940 dropped markedly below the 'primitive' level. As this trend develops—to complete it in the Western countries, it should be remembered, took a century or more—there is reason to expect the growth of world population to slow down from its present level.

The most important potential deficit in world supplies, after food, was until recently in fuel and power. Both coal and oil supplies were being rapidly exhausted, and water-power is unevenly spread over the world, and is in any case limited. Here, however, atomic energy has come to the rescue. A massive, world-scale review of resources in both the fuel and power and other fields is contained in the reports of the United Nations Special Conference on the Conservation of Resources.

By and large, then, it does not seem that natural resources will be inadequate to provide—by existing Western standards—an acceptable standard of living for all the people in the world, if population continues to follow what look like being its established trends. There remains, however, the question of getting the resources to the people, or bringing the people to the resources, and in either case of developing the resources and making them yield as much as they can.

(b) Migration as a means of adjusting population to resources

It is obvious in the first place that making the most of the world's resources must from time to time involve migration of people from one area to another. One can see this area by area. The white Dominions of the British Commonwealth need an inflow of a quarter of a million migrants a year to complete their development. Even bigger numbers might well be absorbed in Latin America. The post-war problems of refugees from Eastern Europe, and especially of the• refugee population of Germany, has had to be solved very largely by emigration. Ireland owes its present prosperity largely to the mass flight from the country in the years after the Great Famine of the 1840's, by which in the end its population was halved. Britain, if its population could be reduced in anything approaching the same proportion—say from 50,000,000 to 30,000,000—would be almost self-sufficient in foodstuffs; its balance of payments problem would disappear, its strategic vulnerability would be greatly reduced, and its town and country planning problems would become comparatively easy to solve.

The need for migration can also be seen problem by problem. One cannot, for instance, produce farm products without farmers. If providing adequately for world food supplies means bringing into cultivation the equivalent of an additional 4–5% of the world's surface, that is to say land equivalent to around 50% of all existing cropland, this alone must mean moving millions of families to the new land. And one reason why countries such as Canada and Australia have continued to encourage immigration is that they have learnt from experience that a small population in a large country means higher costs for such services as transport, gas and electricity, and generally for local government, and often in practice for industry as well. To the extent that countries are shut off from one another by trade barriers, a small population in each country means a small, possibly an uneconomically small, market for industry and inadequate competition. It is significant, for instance, that in the 'thirties, under growing protection, the productivity of Australian industries, other than those processing primary products, became practically stagnant; from being 16% above that of British industry in 1928–9 it dropped by 1937–8 to 19% below it.

To take a problem of quite a different sort, experience all over the world, and in Britain in particular, has shown that concentrations of population on the scale of Greater London, or Greater Manchester, or Glasgow, entail more economic costs—traffic jams, travelling to work, high building and health costs, and so on—than they are worth; not to speak of costs in terms of human relations. Where such concentrations exist, therefore, it may be necessary—as is, in fact, agreed to be the case in Britain—to break them up and shift their people to New Towns or old towns elsewhere.

On the other hand, there is evidence that *massive and rapid* movements of population entail economic costs which need not otherwise be incurred, and that *any* migration is liable to—in fact, usually will—involve costs in terms of human relations, which in addition to being undesirable in themselves may entail economic costs to offset them; special welfare measures, for instance, or the building of community centres, which might not have been required where people originally came from.

On a relatively small scale, these costs were much discussed in connection with the rehabilitation of the British depressed areas from 1934 onwards. It was at one time government policy to help as many individuals and families as possible to leave areas such as South

Wales and West Cumberland, and work in places like West London, Birmingham, or Cowley where industry was expanding, and could, it was thought, operate at lower cost than in the depressed areas.

Little by little, however, this policy was abandoned, under the influence of three considerations.

First, what might be called the 'sociological' costs of movements became clearer. If people are pulled up from their existing roots and resettled in communities new to them, it is likely to take years before the broken ends of their social life—their friendships, club memberships, and so on—are knitted up again. It will take even longer if, as often happened in those years, they move to places which are themselves newly populated, and where there is little social life with which to join up. They are socially amputated, and this reflects itself in every aspect of their human relations, including their work relations. Welshmen who came to Cowley in the 'thirties, for instance, tended to find Cowley and Oxford people unfriendly, to miss the chapel life and the Welsh language, to feel they had sold their souls for more material possessions. It is not surprising that the 'strike-proneness' of Oxford industries tended to vary with their recruitment of Welshmen. And this state of mind reflected itself also among men who had not moved, but feared they might be forced to. It is difficult to say just what effect this had in impairing labour relations and so increasing costs in the industries—especially mining —of the depressed areas. But it undoubtedly had some, probably a substantial, effect, and one which has lasted into the post-war years.

A survey by the present writer in Birmingham in 1938 showed how these costs might have been minimised, if not entirely avoided. At that time the whole outer ring of the city had become filled with new suburbs, to which people had moved in the ten or fifteen previous years out of the central wards. Social and political life (the percentage of local government electors who voted was one very useful index) in these new suburbs was at a low ebb. With one exception: that is in the group of wards in South-West Birmingham which radiate outwards from Bournville. Here alone a serious effort had been made, through adult education, community centres, effective political propaganda, to knit up the broken ends of migrants' social life. The effort was at least partly, though never wholly, successful. But the effort and expense involved were additional—an extra cost—to what would have been required if the migrants had not found it necessary to come there in the first place.

Secondly, attention began to be paid in the 'thirties to the direct economic costs of movement, and particularly to the cost of the new capital equipment—houses, roads, and so on—required by the migrants in their new homes. To anyone who has taken a bus ride up one of the Welsh mining valleys, this will seem a risky line of argument. Much of the capital equipment of these areas was obsolete even in the 'thirties, and more was becoming obsolete all the time; whether it was replaced in Romford or the Rhondda made little economic difference. But behind the less solid part of this argument lurked the substantial point that, whether or not the equipment of the depressed areas was ripe for replacement in the long run, its replacement quickly and at one blow would entail very high costs indeed. This side of the argument did not indeed apply in the 'thirties, when there were unemployed building workers and unused capital resources. But by 1944–8, the time when the rehabilitation of the depressed areas was proceeding fastest, any attempt to replace this equipment on a massive scale would have been very expensive indeed. Firstly, because building costs had risen relatively to prices in general. And secondly, because it would have involved diverting fully employed men and material resources from industrial building, war-damage replacement, and urgently required new housing, at a very high 'opportunity cost' to the community. Alternatively, it would have meant diverting more resources from consumption to capital development at a time when consumers were forcefully demanding some relief from the strains of the war. Its cost, whether in terms of the actual rate of interest paid to savers (if that were allowed to rise) or of the additional strain on consumers, would again have been very high.

A cost which might be classed as either social or directly economic —it has both aspects—arises from the fact that the people who migrate most easily are typically young, and either unmarried or only recently married. If they have been unemployed before migrating, they move more easily after only a short spell of unemployment —that is, while still members of the active labour force—than after a long spell. This may well lead to unbalance at both ends of the movement. At one end the community of origin loses its younger and often more enterprising or quick-witted members, and its social and economic life suffers accordingly. In South Wales, for example, there was deep feeling over this in the inter-war years; though the South Wales birth-rate was, in fact, so high that, even after heavy migration, the population contained much the same proportion of young people as that of the rest of the country. At the other end, the receiving community acquires a young and often enterprising labour force, but at the cost, often, of the social and economic problems of having a high percentage of its people concentrated in one age-group. At one point the schools are strained to bursting. At the next there is a strain on housing, as not enough older people are dropping out to release houses for the children of the first generation as they grow up. Then, a little later, there may be a surplus of old people. This evolution can be traced in miniature on many council housing estates. A classic example, written up by a University of Liverpool research team before the war, was that of the Liverpool Corporation's estate at Norris Green.

These difficulties may not be serious if the drain of population is small and spread over a long period. They become much more important if, as in certain depressed areas in the 'thirties, migration involves or threatens to involve a large part of the young people of a place within a matter of a few years. They can, of course, even in that case, be overcome by promoting the movement of complete families and of people of all ages. But there is an extra cost and effort involved in creating conditions in which the less mobile part of the people are willing to move. The 'mobile margin' of the people is (Chapter 3, p. 32) quite large. But it does not, at least in the short run, include the main bulk of them, and particularly of those who are elderly and set in their ways, or married with children. The elderly eventually die out, and both they and the parents with children can be persuaded to move one by one or family by family over a long time. But experience in Lancashire or South Wales before the war, or with the movement of miners from West to East Scotland after it, shows that to move these groups quickly calls for a massive effort of persuasion and very strong inducements. And receiving communities—this has been very marked in international migration in recent years—are, in general, very reluctant to accept responsibility for 'unproductive' groups such as the elderly, the sick, and the unskilled.

Thirdly, it began in the 'thirties to be seen that the depressed areas were in any case lower-cost sites for new industries than had been supposed, so that it was more economic to bring work to the workers than had been thought. As a general rule, British location of industry policy has insisted that factories should be taken to the depressed (now Development) areas only if there was a reasonable prospect of their producing at as low cost and competing as effectively from those areas as anywhere else; or at any rate of their doing so after the year or two required to overcome the initial difficulties of settling in a new area. On this basis, it has, in fact, proved possible to find a very wide range of industries suitable for location in what are now better called the ex-depressed areas. Plants to employ 45,000 workers were drawn into these areas in 1934–9, counting only those known to have been influenced by government action, and omitting a number

201

ECONOMIC CONTROL

brought in (notably in Lancashire) by such bodies as local authorities or local and regional development councils. In 1944-9 plants to employ a further 270,000 were brought in. And in each case these plants seem to have done as well, on the average, as could have been expected anywhere else.

All these arguments on the costs of any, or of massive and rapid, migration can, of course, be translated from the laboratory level of the British depressed areas to the larger-scale operations of international migration and development. There is now ample prima facie evidence, from the history of industrial development in such countries as Canada and the United States, Australia, Japan, or the U.S.S.R., that a wide variety of industries can operate at minimum cost in areas of the most diverse climate and culture. The high cost of massive and rapid movements of population applies as much to movements between Britain and Australia as to those between South Wales and Birmingham. Various estimates have been made of the rate at which countries can absorb immigrants without incurring higher economic or 'sociological' costs than they are likely to tolerate. A maximum sometimes suggested for 'new' countries like Australia is around 2% *total* increase in population, including natural increase, per annum. Indeed, the excess cost due to rapid and massive movements may be even greater with long-distance international than with relatively short-distance inter-regional movements. For the longer-distance movements involve not merely higher transport costs, but transport of kinds which do not in practice usually have as much space to spare for migrants as British railways and buses. Few, if any, extra train services were put on for Welshmen moving east, though some extra bus services were. But any great increase in, say, the British movement to Canada or Australia does mean extra ships and aircraft.

And, of course, great as may be the cultural differences between a Welsh miner and an Oxford motor worker, and the difficulty of one in finding himself and getting himself accepted in the world of the other, they are nothing to those experienced in many branches of international migration. There are Malays, Chinese, and Indians mixed up in Malaya, and Africans, Afrikaners, Indians, and British in South Africa. The relatively empty lands of America and Australasia are held today by people of a very different culture from those of the world's most land-hungry areas in South-East Asia, China, and Japan.

Migration, then, whether inter-regional or international, is costly and where possible to be avoided; though, for the reasons given, it is nevertheless sometimes worth while. But what then is the alternative—what is to happen to people who are poorly off where they are,

202

and yet would find it costly, both socially and economically, to move anywhere else? This problem does, in fact, arise in most of what are now the underdeveloped areas of the world, as it did in the 'thirties in the underdeveloped areas of Britain.

(c) *Alternatives to migration—(i) trade and investment*
The first possibility is to raise the standard of living of these areas by trade with other areas, and by investment for agricultural and industrial development. But rapid changes in the pattern of trade, or rapid and massive investment, as will be shown in the next chapter, often entail the same exceptional economic costs and social disorganisation as rapid and massive migration. Even when these costs are incurred, population growth in the 'early industrial' period may more than keep pace with the resulting rise in the national income. In Britain, for example, the national income rose by two-thirds from 1801 to 1841–7 in the full flush of Industrial Revolution, but the population doubled (1801–51).

The disproportionately high cost of rapid and massive migration, or rapid and massive changes in trade and industrial development, would apply even in ideal conditions of international and inter-regional relationships. But, in fact, there is no guarantee that international or inter-regional cooperation will be ideal. A speed and form of industrial development, for example, which might be quite appropriate with the help of capital investment from other countries, and in the hope of easy trading relations with them, may put a quite intolerable strain on an underdeveloped country which attempts it without these advantages. The sufferings and poverty of the Soviet Union—the fact, for instance, that real wages in 1950 were half, or less, those of 1913 or 1928—have been due very largely to thus attempting a massive development programme in isolation from the rest of the world.

(d) *Alternatives to migration—(ii) birth regulation*
The 'ethical imperative' as regards population growth is one of the most controversial questions of modern times. How far, where the choice exists, is it right to limit the growth of population so as to enjoy more material wealth? At one end of the scale it seems clearly wrong to multiply people to the point of causing starvation. At the other it seems equally clear that, once a tolerable standard of living is reached, the multiplication of personalities and human relationships is valuable in a far higher sense than the further multiplication of goods and services. If this order of values is accepted, there would seem to be no good reason, on the facts given above, to try to slow

up what would otherwise be the natural growth of world population. For supplies, though they are not now adequate to maintain everyone at a tolerable standard, can be made and kept so.

But, first, the "natural" growth of world population is that which results if the transition from the primitive through the Early Industrial to the Mature stage is completed. If that transition were to stop at the Early Industrial stage, when death-rates have fallen but birth-rates are still high, and if all countries eventually found themselves in that stage, world population might well go on doubling each generation until the end of time. There is no reason to think that world supplies of food and materials could be expanded at that rate. The "natural" growth curve, which *is* consistent with keeping the people fed, implies that the transition to the Mature stage will be made, and that parents will limit the number of children they conceive in line with the fall in death-rates and the increased chance of each child's survival. To that extent, it implies a regulation of births. And this regulation would seem to be desirable.

And secondly, the Early Industrial phase of population growth, coinciding as it by definition tends to do with a time of economic change and stress, may impose great strain on the populations concerned; especially if, for no fault of their own, they are shut out from the benefits of international cooperation. It may then be right to encourage them to pass quickly through this phase, lowering their birth-rates towards the "mature" level step by step with the fall in death-rates, instead of one or more generations later.

Policies of birth regulation, like those of migration or economic development, involve exceptionally high costs if pushed beyond certain limits. These costs are mainly 'sociological'. From the point of view, for instance, of the psychological health of children and of the family as a human group it would seem dangerous (Table 1) to reduce the typical size of completed families below three or four children. If the reduction of the birth-rate is carried so far as to lead to a marked increase in the proportion of older people in the population, it may also involve heavy economic costs. The increase in the number of old people may not in itself mean an extra net burden on the community, since it may be offset by a fall in the number of children—this has been substantially the case hitherto in Britain—and since many old people in any case can and do work. But a high proportion of old people in the population is liable also to increase the difficulty of adjustment to changing economic conditions, since older people are relatively hard to retrain for new work. And it may lead to less enterprise in management and investment.

TABLE 1. Women of 45 or over. Percentage who would have preferred
more, fewer, or the same number of children

Actual number of children	Would have preferred:			
	More	Fewer	Same	Not stated
0	81	—	4	15
1	81	1	15	3
2	51	1	46	2
3	36	3	60	1
4	30	7	62	—
5–7	18	19	61	2
8+	15	38	47	—

From 'Family Limitation,' Vol. 1 of the *Papers of the Royal Commission on the Population*, 1949, p. 161.

These arguments apply as much to the birth-rate and family size appropriate to a 'mature industrial' population as to the 'early industrial' stage. In the one case as in the other, they set a limit to the length to which the regulation of births can properly go. A typical family size of perhaps three to five children will, in fact, often be appropriate at the 'mature' stage. And the policy to which this points for the 'early industrial' stage would seem to be one of smoothing the rate of population growth, not by attempting to reduce the birth-rate to the greatest possible extent but by trying to bring it down as quickly as possible, in line with diminishing mortality and rising expectation of life, from the level appropriate at the 'primitive' to that appropriate to the 'mature' stage. The growth of population would be slowed up by getting rid of the awkward gap hitherto usual between the drop in mortality and the corresponding fall in birth-rates.

(e) Summary

Summing up all the foregoing argument, the mutual adjustment between population and natural resources may proceed along any of the three lines of migration, trade, and investment, or the regulation of births. Each of these lines of action involves much higher costs, economic and other, if pressed very far or fast than if used with more moderation. A practical policy will therefore usually involve some blend of the three.

It remains to consider the control mechanisms—more specifically, the *economic* mechanisms, since it is with these alone that we are concerned here—by which the right decisions under each of the three heads can best be promoted. Inter-regional and international trade and investment belong to the next chapter. We deal here, therefore, with the two fields, of migration and the regulation of births, which belong properly to a chapter on population.

ECONOMIC COMPETITION, DIRECTION, AND CONSULTATION AS APPLIED TO POPULATION PROBLEMS

(a) As applied to the regulation of births

The economic sanction, and in particular economic competition, influence the growth and decline of population in a way which could be guessed from what was said in previous chapters. The precise way in which it does so depends, as usual, on the social framework and the four main types of background determinant.

The most important background determinant ('keeping up with the Joneses') results in this case from the combined operation of group standards and the distribution of incomes.

(1) The expenditure standards of individuals and families are interdependent. In a society where economic competition plays an important part, they will tend to be fixed largely by reference to the number of times each person or family comes in contact, in his own 'social space', with superior goods or a superior supply of goods.

(2) There is no reason, other things being equal, to suppose that in a free economy the distribution of incomes will allow fully for family needs. In actual British experience it has done so only very roughly and insufficiently indeed.

These two findings were laid down in earlier chapters. In the light of them it seems probable—and does, in fact, turn out to be the case—that in a competitive economy standards of expenditure will be fixed by reference to the habits of small households (not, note, families). For these are by far the most numerous, and tend to have the highest incomes per head, and therefore the greatest amount and most 'superior' quality of goods.

The commonest size of household in Britain in 1951 contained two or three persons. Households of this size made up some 56% of all 'primary family units'. Altogether 87% of such units contained four people or less. Households of five persons or more, that is of what should probably be the minimum size of a typical family with children during the time when the children are all born but still at home, accounted for only 13%. Five-person households represented well over half of even this figure. Looking back at the age of fifty, the mother who has had only one or two children will no doubt wish she had had more. But the mother who has more than that number will suffer, all the time the children are actually at home and dependent, from a permanent 'invidious comparison' (Veblen's term) with the much greater number of neighbours who have either had fewer children or seen their children grow up and go away.

The distribution of incomes between classes (vertical distribution) may be important here, as well as that between families (horizontal). Where mobility between classes is easy, the higher standard of life of a superior class is likely to exert a strong pull on people near the upper edge of the class below it. How great a strain this pursuit of higher standards will impose on their budgets, and how much of a temptation to economise on children, will depend on the steepness of the income distribution; that is on the amount by which incomes and expenditure in the higher class typically exceed those in the lower. Instability of incomes and expectations may also play its part. War accelerates marriages. Slumps delay them. Social disintegration produces irresponsible parents, whose children may be either—among casual workers, for instance, or among rootless middle class groups —too many or too few.

And there is no need to emphasise the importance of the availability and cost of such key items in expenditure in general, and family expenditure in particular, as housing, education, and health services. In Britain in 1951, for example, 1,170,000 families were still without a separate dwelling of their own. The cost of education, particularly in England and Wales, has been a major reason for the fact that for half a century (if not more) the average size of completed family among non-manual workers has tended to run about 30% lower than that among manual workers. For the State in Britain has failed either to supply education of a standard which educated parents are themselves generally ready to accept for their children, or to make adequate tax or other concessions to enable these parents to provide suitable education on their own.

The social framework likewise plays its part. Summing up in 1948 the history of the birth-rate in Britain in the preceding century, the Royal Commission on the Population stressed notably such things as the change in what women expect of their lives (change in *personality patterns*), changing views on the application of science and planning to human affairs, or on the duty of parents to educate their children (change in *social norms*), and the decline of certain types of *institution* which once made children less of an economic burden. In family farming, for instance, children can give a hand from a very early age; but family farming, though more important than ever it was in the farming world, is much less important today than a century ago in the national economy as a whole. The Commission might indeed have commented with equal force on the absence in Britain of certain institutions which have grown up in other countries for the defence of the family in the face of changes of this kind; notably the family movements which have grown up in many parts of the Continent and act in effect as family trade unions. It is only in the years since the war that these have begun to appear in Britain, and then only, as in the Catholic Parents' and Electors' Associations or certain parent-teacher associations, in a small or tentative way.

The background controls over economic competition have been set in Britain in such a way that for a century and more this sanction and mechanism have exerted a steady downward pressure on the birth-rate, especially through 'keeping up with the Joneses'. Direction has been invoked mainly as a means of resetting the controls so as to counteract this. The Royal Commission's report contains a full and valuable account of the types of direction which are or might be used. They include:

(1) Alteration of the distribution of incomes in favour of families by:

bigger tax and family allowances;
bigger rent rebates;
encouragement of voluntary family allowance schemes set up by collective agreements in industry and the professions.

(2) Ensuring the availability of services important to the family, including housing, health services, nursery schools, home helps, laundry facilities, or parks and playgrounds.

(3) Maintaining full employment and income stability.

(4) Creating a physical environment—grouping the population—in such a way as to make it easy for group opinion favourable to the family to emerge. 'The family should be given a central place in town and country planning.'

(5) Research and education with a view to creating a sound public opinion—sound social norms—on the family.

This is excellent, but still leaves the usual question of how far direction is ultimately to go. Up to what point is it desirable to use direction to correct the deficiencies of competition, and how far should consultation be preferred? There is no need to repeat here what was said above, in the chapters on consumption and on education and health, on the advantages in many cases of education rather than compulsion. The argument there applies with equal force here. No form of direction can take full account of individual families' circumstances, or do all that might be done to call forth new and valuable departures in family life. The history of progress in family

208

matters in the last century has been largely one of individual revolt, sometimes merely destructive, usually disturbing, but often valuable and well directed, against the currently accepted conventions on which alone direction can be based. There is no reason to suppose that the present age has attained final wisdom in these matters. One has only to study family life and movements respectively in Britain and on the Continent to find a great many points on which each can even now learn from the other.

Above all, the special point made above about the mechanisms appropriate to the control of education applies with special force to the family. The family is, psychologically speaking, by far the most important agency in shaping personality, that is to say the most important educational agency. The object of the educational services, and of the family, is not merely, for instance, to drive certain knowledge into people's heads by the use of such mechanisms and sanctions as may come to hand. It is to teach them, by experience as well as precept, how to manipulate these mechanisms themselves. It is part of the family's business not only to accustom its members to the authority of direction but to teach them to use and respond to consultation—to discover and accept through discussion their responsibility to a wider community—and to take their responsibilities as free agents in a competitive system. And for this reason the role of direction must be limited. The experience of family movements, joining up with parallel experience in the fields of production (industrial relations) and consumption (see p. 137—the housewives' case) suggests that consultation itself, whether concerned with internal family matters or with each family's responsibility to the community at large, will be more effective the more it originates with and is conducted by the interested families themselves.

There is, in fact, a direct application of this to the regulation of births itself. Birth-control methods can be ranked in order according to the contribution they make to the development of personality. At one end are mechanical, chemical, and certain crude natural methods which can be used without serious self-restraint or sense of responsibility toward others. At the other is the self-devotion of the priest or nun who, stepping outside the family altogether, takes a vow of chastity to be free for a greater cause. In between come various methods—safe period, simple abstention, late marriage—which call in greater or less degree for responsible consideration and strength of character. The use of what might be called the higher forms of birth control calls for personal qualities which develop well under freedom and consultation, but can be produced to only a limited extent by direction.

14   209

Direction, in short, is necessary to set the framework within which the family evolves. But actual, detailed decisions about the number of children a family is to have are best left to each family itself, in the light of its position and problems relative to those of other families, and guided by consultation—preferably by and among families themselves—designed to educate families in their responsibilities both to their own members and to the community at large.

(b) The control of migration

The control of migration is on the whole a more—especially from the economist's point of view—straightforward and less controversial matter than the control of births. In the first place, there is now a mass of experience to show that the economic sanction in general, and economic competition in particular, are extremely powerful and effective means of persuading people to move from place to place. Some 53,000,000 people emigrated from Europe from 1846 to 1937, and of these over 18,000,000 came from the British Isles (including Ireland) alone; a number about equal to the total population of Great Britain, excluding Ireland, in 1841. Overwhelmingly the greatest incentive to this movement seems to have been economic; the difference in standards of living between Europe on the one hand and America or Australasia on the other. And the economic incentive took effect through competition, especially in the peak years of emigration at the end of the nineteenth century and beginning of the twentieth. For these were also above all others the years when emigration was free and uncontrolled.

That the 'mobile margin' of the population, especially the working population, is substantial, and moves quickly from job to job and place to place, was shown above in Chapter 3 from the internal experience of the British labour market. The *net* gain or loss by migration between different counties is small as a percentage, though large in absolute amount. In 1925–36 it averaged 173,000 a year for all Great Britain, or about 0·4% of the whole population. But post-war figures show that the *gross* movement of population from one local government district to another (in this case the smaller districts, not the counties) is nearer 10% of the total population per annum. And in particular cases the net gain or loss may also be large. The Merthyr, Pontypridd and Rhondda, and Rhymney and Tredegar areas of South Wales lost, net, the equivalent of 26% of their 1938 population by migration between 1929 and 1938. The counties of Glamorgan and Monmouth were losing population—again net loss, not gross—at 2–2½% per annum in 1927–31, and 1–1½% in 1931–6. The counties of Oxford and Buckinghamshire (including Slough) were gaining by migration at 1½-2% per annum net in 1927-31, and at around ¾-1¼% in 1931-6. Bedfordshire gained in 1931-6 at over 2% per annum. The population of the City of Oxford rose 40% in 1921-38, largely by migration; and in 1936 43% of all adult male insured workers there were from other districts. The County of London lost 1,600,000 people by migration (net) in 1901-37, and in 1931-7 had a net overall loss of population, even after adding back the natural surplus of births over deaths, of over 7%.

Oxford is an interesting case, as the variation of movement with the trade cycle, and the precise degree of attraction exerted by the city at different distances during the 'thirties, have been measured with some accuracy. Its attractive power, given an equal difference in economic conditions, seems to have been about ten times as great in the case of close and accessible counties such as Berkshire or Wiltshire as in that of, say, Hampshire or Dorset, and ten times as strong again in these latter cases as in that of Scotland.

Long experience has, however, shown that, effective as economic competition may be in inducing people to move, there are a number of points where it breaks down.

In the first place, competition may break down through natural or artificial monopoly. Serfdom may prevent or—as in Britain at the end of the eighteenth and early in the nineteenth century—Settlement Acts may impede migration. It is unlikely that as many refugees would have been as quickly resettled after the Second World War if an international refugee organisation had not been set up to press their case in the face of resistance from interested groups in the receiving countries. The framers of the draft statute for a European political community in 1953 found it necessary to lay down a legal right, to be enforced by the Community's courts and executive, to free movement over the territories of the Community's member states. In this they followed the provisions already in force for coal, steel, and certain other related groups of workers, under the Treaty of 1951 establishing a European coal-steel community. For without such specific directions as these they recognised that the barriers to free movement could not be broken down.

Secondly, the background determinants play their usual part. The distribution and availability of capital has its effect on the flow of migrants as well as—indeed largely because of—its influence on the growth of new industries. Reference has already been made, in Chapter 9, to the unevenness of the supply of capital to different places even within one tightly organised country such as Great Britain. The question of ways and means of getting capital to under-developed territories, on conditions acceptable to all concerned, has

211

been one of the main problems of international economic policy since the war.

Stability is a key factor in migration, in the sense not only that migration tends to fall off when there is depression in the receiving region or country but also that disappointment of established expectations on the part of an existing population is likely to provoke resistance to immigration, while disappointment on the part of immigrants is likely to be quickly reflected back to those who might otherwise follow them. The 'absorptive capacity' of a place or country depends on how far immigrants can be accommodated without frustrating existing inhabitants' expectations in the matter of—to name only economic aspects—wages, jobs, taxation, or the tenure of farms and other property, or of their chances of securing particular goods and services such as houses; or at least without frustrating them so far as to produce obstructions which cannot be overcome. Immigrants' experience, on their side, is quickly reflected in the flow of further migrants. The time of reaction in the case of movements within Great Britain seems, on Oxford experience, to be measured in days and weeks rather than months.

This argument must not be misunderstood. It is, of course, no criticism of competition to say that under it, if immigrants' experience is bad, immigration will fall off, or that if existing inhabitants find themselves under a severe strain they will resist further immigration. On the contrary; since policy is concerned with the welfare of the people, it is entirely right and proper that these results should follow. To this extent, instabilities or frustrations of expectation arising out of the movement of population are, under competition, self-correcting. But when one examines a case of movement in detail —say, for instance, the expansion of the town of Stevenage from 6,000 inhabitants to ten times that size after 1946—it becomes apparent that there are many such problems of stability which are too 'remote or diffused' for any individuals or individual groups to grasp or solve them fully. Problems (in that particular case) of property values, the tenure of farms and shops, or rents and the levels of local taxation could be solved with even approximate justice and satisfaction to all concerned only by collective action; in practice, by the decision of some public authority.

So also rail and road transport, houses, schools, and public utilities have often to be organised, in a developing area, well in advance of the immediate demand which may eventually enable them to be provided, or carried on, by competition. A bottleneck in housing, or public reaction to unemployment in some one trade, may hold up immigration even though conditions in all other respects remain favourable. And the attention paid to group relationships can well be decisive in the success or otherwise of immigrants' settlement. Many adjustments of this kind will come about under the influence of competition alone. Warner and Low, for example, show how in the free labour market of the New England town of Newburyport workers of different races and dates of immigration tend to group themselves into particular occupations, statuses, and departments on lines accepted and perhaps even approved by all concerned. But satisfactory group relations may also require action which immigrants cannot take as individuals, and are too disorganised, by the very fact of migration, to combine together on their own initiative to take collectively. It has been found, for example, that Irish and coloured immigrants to Birmingham need more than one generation to become fully assimilated into the city's life. For the first generation at least their culture must continue to be largely that of the countries from which they come. To retain and develop this culture they need to hold together as groups on their own. This requires for each such group a centre, and a degree of organisation, which they cannot in the first instance provide for themselves.

And, of course, in a new town, or region, or country, immigration involves the creation of a whole new social framework. Take simply one aspect of this: the geographical distribution of the people, whether between streets and neighbourhoods in a town or district or over a country as a whole. How chaotic this can become if left to competition alone is shown in a dramatic—perhaps over-dramatised—form in studies such as Lewis Mumford's *Culture of Cities*, or, more soberly, for Great Britain, in the Report of the Royal Commission on the Industrial Population (Barlow Commission, 1940). Both may be contrasted with more recent experience in establishing a planned environment in the New Towns, or earlier at Welwyn or Letchworth. On a larger scale, a case such as the contrast between the vast open spaces of Australia and the heavy concentration of its people in a few metropolitan cities also provides much food for thought.

The question is as usual one of ways and means. How far is direction appropriate for supplementing competition, and how far should consultation be used? It is useful to distinguish here between control over the investments needed to provide for incoming population and control over the movement of people themselves. The former is certainly often a matter for direction, but its discussion belongs to the next chapter. The latter, it would probably today be generally agreed, is a matter in the last resort for consultation.

213

Judging by recent international conventions and agreements, direction can acceptably be used:

(1) To break barriers to movement, as in the Treaty of the European coal-steel community.

(2) To stabilise movement, in the interests of immigrants themselves and of the losing and gaining communities. Regulations appropriate for this are defined in the *International Labour Code*, 1951, issued by the International Labour Office; particularly Articles 1207–1317, dealing with recruiting, migration, and forced labour in non-metropolitan territories, and 1493–1556, dealing in general with migration. The United Nations' *Convention Relating to the Status of Refugees*, 1951, does the same in its own special field, on very similar lines.

(3) To provide labour for basic services too 'remote or diffused' from the point of view of prospective employees to attract their services on reasonable terms. Examples, permitted by the *International Labour Code*, are military service, certain sorts of labour service 'which form part of the normal civic obligations of the citizens of a fully self-governing country' (compulsory labour service as an alternative to conscription would, for instance, presumably come under this), and service in case of floods, famines, and other emergencies.

(4) To require people to leave areas in which their presence is inconsistent with required changes in the social framework. Normally, this would only justify a (preferably temporary) ban on residence in some very small locality. An example would be the clearing of certain areas in connection with the replanning of a town. But it could also cover, as a quite exceptional case supported by very strong reasons, and subject to strict control of the methods of compulsion used, the compulsory removal of the Greek population from parts of Turkey after the First World War, or of the German population from parts of Central and Eastern Europe after the Second World War. In neither of these cases was the reservation about suitable methods of transfer in fact observed.

What would *not* seem to be acceptable is any permanent ban on the movement of people into labour markets which can or could be made to provide attractive employment for them (this is covered by the *International Labour Code*, Article 1506), or, subject to the limited reservation under (4), any ban on people leaving or returning to the place or country where they are at the moment established. A ban of this latter kind is forbidden by Article 13 of the United Nations Charter of Human Rights. Nor is it acceptable to maintain any discrimination against immigrant workers—for instance, by limiting the types of work they can do, paying them less than the standard rate, or refusing them access to publicly controlled housing or to social security—beyond the year or two after they enter a new country or region. Even in that period, discrimination can be justified only so far as really necessary to smooth migrants' way to settlement.

The reasoning behind all this was made clear by British war experience with conscription and the direction of labour, and has been indicated already in Chapter 5. Direction cannot be detailed enough to take account of the infinite variety of individual and family circumstances which may lead to or prevent migration, nor of the variety of personal adjustments which may be required. And yet migrants cannot simply be left to work out their destinies under competition, within only a broad legal framework. They need advice and guidance—consultation—on many matters where they are indeed well able to judge, but lack the necessary information; job prospects in different areas, for instance. They need it still more on others, such as the problem of how best to adjust generally to the new society they are moving into, which may call for more far-reaching adjustments in their personality. Advice of either of these types may be needed by the settled inhabitants of a receiving area as well as by migrants themselves. Much difficulty arose in 1952, for instance, over the immigration of Italians to certain British mining areas, not because of any complication on the side of the immigrants themselves, nor because of anything that could have been dealt with by a direction from the top level of management or the trade union, but through failure to consult in sufficient detail with local groups affected, to work through their problems and obtain their consent.

The question of information to settled inhabitants has been widely discussed in this country in recent years in connection with town-planning changes. For migrants, the *International Labour Code* calls on governments to make all the necessary information available. It will naturally be made available in the first place to individuals and individual families. But here, as elsewhere, experience has shown the value of also enabling groups of migrants—or, for that matter, of settled inhabitants—to work out their problems among themselves, give one another mutual support, and back their personal conclusions on the new problems facing them with the agreement on new group norms. Group settlement schemes, or the grouping of migrants round clubs or centres on the lines mentioned above, can be very effective for promoting mutual education of this kind.

Chapter 13

INTER-REGIONAL AND
INTERNATIONAL RELATIONS

II. TRADE AND INVESTMENT—THE ROLE OF COMPETITION

IN modern conditions of cheap transport, highly specialised production, and the hope and expectation of a high standard of life, inter-regional and international trade and investment have come to play a far more important part than they did even a century ago. They have indeed become a necessity of life, or at any rate of life in the style and on the scale to which we are all rapidly becoming accustomed.

Take, for example, the case of Western Europe, which has found itself faced since the Second World War with economic problems of two types. The first is poverty: about one-third of its inhabitants, or a hundred million in all, live in underdeveloped countries on the Mediterranean and Adriatic, with incomes per head ranging down to a quarter of those found in relatively well-off countries such as Sweden, Switzerland, or the United Kingdom, and to a sixth or less of that of the United States. The second is the balance of payments. A survey by the United Nations Economic Commission for Europe estimated in 1951 that, with fluctuations from year to year, Western Europe looked like having a permanent deficit of around £1,000 million a year in trade with the dollar countries. This deficit might be covered by special grants and loans; it would not be covered by normal transactions. A succession of other surveys has shown that these difficulties are unlikely to be overcome—or can be overcome only at greatly increased cost—unless by a great increase in the already substantial flow of goods, services, and capital from one Western European country to another.

One key problem, for example, from the angle both of poverty and of the balance of payments, is that of the low efficiency of agriculture in Southern Europe. The Southern European countries have, in round numbers, two-fifths of the cultivable land of Western Europe as a whole, but only one-quarter of the output of farm products. If the productivity of these countries (and of French) farmers could be raised to the levels customary in Northern Europe, the largest part of the gap in Europe's balance of payments would be filled, and a handsome increase in the standard of nutrition, and in general of living, could be achieved into the bargain; primarily in Southern Europe, but also in the north. But to do so would involve political and social as well as economic problems of a most formidable kind; changing the habits and customs of peasant farmers, displacing many of them and reorganising their farms, ensuring markets for the new and increased production, and financing and carrying out a massive programme of capital investment. It has become clear that rather little of this is likely to be done—and that slowly, expensively, and with much strain on relatively poor countries—unless the problems of capital supply and marketing are tackled internationally, on an all-European scale. The north has the capital, the markets, and often the technical knowledge; the south has the men and the land. The problem is to bring the two together.

A second key problem of Western Europe has been that of industrial specialisation. For a number of industries such as steel, motors, aircraft, atomic energy, or certain branches of machine and machine-tool manufacture, even the larger European countries do not today offer a big enough market to allow minimum costs to be attained. Even when their markets are not actually too narrow to allow a plant to operate on a scale which minimises costs, they are often too narrow to allow more than one or two such plants; technical efficiency can be attained, but at the cost of setting up a monopoly. The most prosperous countries of Western Europe, Sweden and Switzerland, which have built up their economies round industries of this type, have been able to do so only because they succeeded in enlarging their industries' markets beyond their own frontiers. A major question of European and, indeed, of world economic policy in recent years has been how to enlarge the market for other industries and other countries as well.

If the increase of inter-regional trade and investment is so important for the welfare of regions as large as France, Germany, Italy, or the United Kingdom, it must clearly be still more important for those smaller territories which face in an even more acute form the choice between high-cost production for a local market or specialisation for a wider low-cost market; or between pulling themselves up, in the matter of investment, by their own often rather stringy bootstraps, and calling upon guidance and finance from elsewhere. There is a great deal to be learnt about this from the history of small countries, such as Australia and Ireland, which have, in fact, attempted to cut themselves off from important sectors of international exchange. Colin Clark's findings on the productivity of Australian manufacturing industry, other than that engaged in processing the country's characteristic primary products, were quoted in the last chapter. It sank under a policy of protection from 116% of the British figure for 1928–9 to 84% in 1937–8.

At the other end of the scale it is clear that regions on the scale of Western Europe, the British Commonwealth, the U.S.A., or the U.S.S.R.—those which are so large that exchange between them might best be called intercontinental—can to a great extent be self-sufficient. At a pinch, the U.S.A. or the U.S.S.R. would both be able to maintain a high standard of life without outside help. This is reflected in the small share which international trade has in their economies. In the late 'thirties, for example, to take a time when trade was rather freer than it is today, these countries' exports represented 2–5% of their national incomes, whereas the corresponding figure for most of the individual countries of Western Europe, including Britain, was around 10–20%, rising to 30% or even 40% in the case of some of the smaller countries. Even these countries, however, have something to gain by international exchange. The United States has turned over within the last generation from being a net exporter to being a net importer of primary products. Its demand for a number of industrial raw materials—lead, zinc, copper, iron ore, cobalt, manganese, nickel, crude oil, rubber, sisal, wool—multiplied anything up to ten times over between 1937–8 and 1948–50. An American commission of enquiry (Paley Commission) anticipates a further increase averaging around 25% by 1975. In general, American willingness to enter into international trade has been increasing, and American tariffs dropping, since 1930.

The U.S.S.R. has pursued a policy of extreme nationalism, or more strictly of reliance on the resources of countries under Soviet political control. Nevertheless, in the early years of industrialisation, up to and including the time of the first Five Year Plan (1928–32), the Soviet Government found it impossible to do without large imports of machinery, electrical equipment, iron and steelwork, motor vehicles, and precision instruments, as well as of industrial raw materials and some foodstuffs. Aid to or investment in underdeveloped countries, Communist or not, seems, in fact, likely to be a—if not 'the'—major item in 'intercontinental' exchange in the next couple of generations. In 1951 a study by a group of experts for the United Nations indicated that to secure a 2% per annum increase in incomes per head in Asia, Africa, and Latin America, it might be necessary to transfer about £3,500 million a year from North America, Western Europe, and Australasia; after allowing, that is, for what the underdeveloped countries could reasonably be expected to do for themselves.

THE ROLE OF ECONOMIC COMPETITION

The prospect of economic gain, plus the competitive market, has in the past proved a tremendously powerful incentive to international and inter-regional trade and investment. This can be seen particularly clearly in the case of British experience, since Britain was the leading economic power in the days, up to 1914, when economic competition had the field most nearly to itself. From the 1840's to 1913 the volume of British trade—which already had risen very sharply through the first generations of the Industrial Revolution—was multiplied by eight. About £4,000 million of British overseas investments were outstanding by 1913, say £12,000 million at the prices prevailing after the Second World War. This money went mainly into government loans (national and local), railways, public utilities, and raw material development, in North America, Latin America, Australasia, and India, with sizeable contingents in Europe, South Africa, and East Asia. The next three chief lending powers (France, Germany, and the U.S.A.) contributed nearly as much again, though with a different distribution. Between these four countries, and adding in a few contributions from elsewhere and some post-war loans, Australia, New Zealand, and Canada had by 1928 about $1,700–1,800 a head of foreign capital (say double that figure at post-Second World War prices), and Malaya, Cuba, Chile, and the Argentine $800–1,100. Such countries as India, China, Indonesia, and Africa, exclusive of South Africa and Egypt, had at that date $20–70 of foreign capital a head. Looking at these latter figures; remembering the vast populations concerned; and remembering also how much countries like Australia have owed to the high overseas investment in them per head: it is not surprising that the United Nations experts should have talked in the apparently astronomical terms they did about the international investment needed today. This becomes even less surprising when it is seen that in the last years before 1914 British investors were adding to their overseas holdings at the rate of about £200 million a year, or between 8 and 9% of the national income per annum. This would be equivalent to investing £1,000 million a year (in round numbers) overseas today.

But competition as a means of controlling international trade and investment, highly effective as it is up to a point, turns out to have the same limits and defects as competition for any other purpose.

In the first place, it does not always exist. It is true that modern

219

means of transporting goods, distributing capital, and ascertaining prospects and possibilities increase the chances that competition will be continuous in time, place, and product (to use the terms from Chapter 2), that goodwill will be reversible, and that long views will be taken. But distance—the cost and convenience of transport, and the difficulties of understanding accurately the needs and possibilities of different cultures and far-off places—has not yet been wholly annihilated. Not every British business man has yet learnt to understand even the American market. The soil of East Africa still has traps for the unwary ground-nut grower who drafts his plans in Europe. These problems of time and distance are, of course, simply a magnification of what happens every day in the life of each town and district. The housewife has to push her pram to the neighbourhood shopping centre and take the bus to the main centre. The operation takes time and effort, and this limits the number of shops which can effectively compete for her custom.

Obstacles to competition arising out of market structure will in general be reduced the wider the geographical area over which competition extends, and the greater therefore the number of firms of any given size which can take part in it. But they may also be increased. It can, for instance, quite well happen that there is in one country an economy including many big firms, which compete vigorously with one another, and in another country a similar number of small firms, also vigorously competing, though at a lower level of technical efficiency and a higher level of costs. If now the two economies are brought into relations, it may very well happen that one—but only one—of the big firms in the former country will find it worth while to undertake the very substantial effort of building up a market in the latter. In that case it may well, through its superior efficiency, acquire a dominating, effectively monopolistic position in its new market, and also in the flow of trade and investment between the two countries. This is what has actually happened in a number of cases where big metropolitan businesses have staked out claims for themselves in underdeveloped colonial territories.

And, of course, legal or trade association obstacles exist in interregional and international trade as well as elsewhere. Other things being equal, international cartels are harder to build and maintain than those which cover only a single region or country, just because of the greater number of competitors or potential competitors. It is no doubt true that it is easier to organise aluminium or steel or heavy chemical producers on an international basis than to bring together farmers or shopkeepers on a national basis. But it will usually also be easier to bring together (rather few) aluminium or steel firms on a national basis than (rather many) internationally. And it is even more likely in trade over a large region than over a small that, if an association is formed and survives, it will be effective in stabilising output, prices, and market shares around the trend which competition would in any case cause them to follow, but not in diverting that trend itself.

However, for better or for worse, international cartels do in fact exist, and have some effect on competition. A study published in 1944, based on pre-war material, listed 110 case-histories from a much wider material, ranging from diamonds to bone glue, by way of submarines, steel, and false teeth. And legal restrictions on trade and investment are very widespread indeed in international trade, and also very effective—much more so than any but a few cartels. Britain was for long not only the leading economic power of the world, but also the leading free-trade country; but even Britain abandoned free trade (after various pieces had already been nibbled out of it) in 1931 and 1932. The free movement of capital was in effect stopped from the same date, though not by legal powers. Since the Second World War it has been stopped also by the law on exchange control. In Europe in the post-war years the Organisation for European Economic Cooperation has made it its objective to free 75% of the flow of trade between West European countries from quantitative controls. But it has not always been possible to achieve even this degree of freedom; and there has been little question, except between the six countries of the European Coal and Steel Community, of removing control by tariffs even from the 75% of 'liberalised' trade. Also, 'liberalisation' applies only to private trade. A number of countries—Britain in the war years, the U.S.S.R. as a matter of permanent policy—have secured results equivalent to those of tariffs and quantitative restrictions by putting part or all of their foreign trade in the hands of a state monopoly.

Not only does competition in international trade and investment not always exist; it also fails, as usual, to take due account of factors which appear remote or diffused from the point of view of those immediately concerned in competitive decisions.

In the first place, there is no more reason to expect competition to lead to a fully satisfactory distribution of income and wealth in a wide region than in a narrow one. The ratio between the average incomes per head of the 10% of the world's population who live in the richest countries and the 50% who live in the poorest is actually about the same as that between the richest 10% of the population of Britain and the poorest 50%; in each case taking incomes before tax. If the sharp contrast between rich and poor which emerges in

221

Britain under competition is regarded as wrong, and needing to be corrected by taxation or other non-competitive means, it is difficult to see why the same argument should not apply to the contrast between, say, Britain and India. The figures given above for the distribution of foreign investment down to 1928 are also illuminating from this point of view. It is not difficult to see why, in the light of immediately obvious considerations, British investors preferred to put their money in Australia rather than in China. It is much more difficult to see how their choice could be justified on a comparison of relative needs (the 'ethical imperative') or of the—from individual investors' points of view— 'remote or diffused' reasons for paying more attention to those of the Chinese.

Secondly, competition will not necessarily provide the basic services needed for the development of an area, where these do not promise an immediate profit to competitors, nor will it ensure the conservation of the area's natural resources. This has been apparent even on the comparatively small scale of the British economy. One of the decisive factors in the recovery of the British depressed areas between 1937 and 1948 was the provision of industrial estates, offering, in advance of the demand, prepared sites, public utility and other services, and even factory buildings to let. Such estates *may* be developed as a profit-making proposition as a result purely and simply of competition; examples are the estates at Slough or at Trafford Park, Manchester. But in the actual case of the depressed areas it was necessary to secure their development through public utility companies, brought into existence by government or other non-competitive action, and financed by the State.

The conservation of natural resources has not been as big an issue in Britain as in many other countries, thanks largely to Britain's climate and geography and to the sound tradition of British farming. Even in Britain, however, it has had to be discussed in the case of coal, and has actually arisen in the case of timber. The Forestry Commission had to be established to develop State forests, as the prospects of gain were too remote to attract competitive investment. It has arisen also over farm-land. When electric and motor local transport came in at the beginning of the twentieth century, towns all over Britain—as in other countries—'exploded', and began to eat up farm-land at an alarming rate. It is reckoned for England and Wales that an area equal to Gloucestershire was taken for non-farm uses in 1927–39 alone. British town and country planning procedure now has special arrangements to save cultivable land from being unnecessarily diverted to building or other non-farming uses. Town and country planning, in its broad sense of the control of land use in country and town alike, is, in fact, the chief example of deliberate, non-competitive planning for the conservation and development of resources in Britain today.

Other countries have faced problems of conservation and basic services, arising out of inter-regional or international relations, on a much bigger scale. The United Nations committee of experts which reported in 1951 on the development of underdeveloped areas urged 'most strongly' that the more advanced countries should make grants (not investments) to the underdeveloped parts of the world at the rate eventually of rather over £1,000 million a year, to cover such purposes as research and education, public health programmes, and subsidies to farm credit and to a variety of public works, including soil conservation, afforestation, roads, and water supplies; all having in common that they are services necessary to the development of a country, but too 'remote or diffused' in their impact to attract enough investment under competition.

Then, thirdly, and extremely important, international trade and investment is very liable, under competition, to instability. This has been a fundamental factor in international and inter-regional economic policies throughout the world.

First of all, international trade and investment fluctuate even more widely in a competitive economy in the course of the trade cycle than trade and investment within individual countries, and so consequently do the incomes and employment depending on them. This was true in the classic age of competition, as British experience at that time showed, and has remained true under the less competitive conditions prevailing since the First World War. In the slump of 1929–32 the national income of the United States dropped some 43% from its peak, but the dollars made available by America to the world, through current purchases and investment, fell 68%. In 1948–9 a quite minor recession in the U.S.A. reduced the volume of American imports from Europe by one-third within a few months.

What these wider fluctuations in international trade mean to a particular country depends on the type as well as the size of its trade. There is in any case a tendency for fluctuations to be greatest in the case of the *output* of durable goods, which can be done without in a slump, and the *price* of primary products, demand for which depends little on price and a great deal on the level of incomes.

The difference between the effects in the two cases is due to the fact that durable goods are typically produced by industries, which can cut their output short and sack their workers when demand drops, whereas primary products are also largely farm products. Farm output at any moment is for technical reasons fixed for

223

anything from a year to several years ahead. And the farm labour force, consisting as it often does of the farmer and his family, cannot be much reduced; it is more profitable to go on growing *something*, even at a miserably low price. In a slump the price of farm products thus tends to drop rather than the output; and, since demand depends little on price, the price cut may have to be very severe and prolonged to get all production taken off the market. It is this which accounts, for example, for the fact that Britain (an importer of primary products and exporter of industrial goods) was able in 1936-7, after the slump of the early 'thirties, to import, in real terms, 5% more goods than in 1929 while exporting 20% less, and yet to have only the same deficit as in 1929 on the resulting balance of payments. The same process operated in reverse, that is to Britain's disadvantage, after the war, when primary products became scarce relatively to industrial goods.

A country whose national income depends firstly on a big export trade, and secondly on the export of durable goods and primary products, is thus likely to be hit doubly hard by the fluctuations of a competitive market. In the slump of the 'thirties this was notably the case with certain countries whose general economies were under-developed, but which had important export trades in one or two lines, usually mining or farm products. There were in all in 1938 some dozen primary producing countries—Malaya, for instance, or Bolivia—which obtained a fifth or more of their national income from exports.

The United Nations committee in *National and International Measures for Full Employment*, 1949, after a general review of the international effects of the trade cycle, centred its recommendations round three ideas.

(1) Overdraft facilities, whereby countries which maintained full employment could be enabled to spend as much on imports as if other countries had done so as well. Countries which allowed their imports to fall as a result of unemployment would be bound to deposit with the International Monetary Fund an amount of their currency equal to that of which the fall deprived their foreign suppliers. Each supplying country would then be entitled to acquire and use an amount of this currency equal to the loss caused to it.

(2) Each country to establish stable programmes of imports, exports, and capital investment overseas: so ensuring stable markets to, notably, primary producing countries.

(3) Regular and continuing consultation between countries on these and related matters.

Another form of instability with which competition fails to deal fully, especially in international and inter-regional trade, arises out of the process of adjustment from one set of economic standards and institutions—one social framework, that is—to another. Dislocation may, of course, happen in any case of change. A firm retooling for a new line of production, for example, has to consider what to do to prevent dislocation in the change-over. But this factor is specially significant for international and inter-regional trade, because the time and effort needed for any change tends to increase in proportion to the number of people involved and to the area and the number of distinct societies and groups over which they are spread. To solve the problem of the British depressed areas, making also many incidental changes in prosperous districts, took about a quarter of a century from the time when the problem first appeared; that is, from about 1923 or 1924 to 1948-9. There was, it is true, a break in this progress during the Second World War; but this cut both ways, accelerating change as well as slowing it down. Today, the world economy is adjusting to the new importance of the United States and the U.S.S.R., the rise towards maturity of the present underdeveloped countries, and the dislocation of Europe through the war and its sequels: this change looks like being spread over two or more generations.

To the administrator or diplomat, anxious to ensure that all factors are duly balanced together before a final solution is decided on, progress at this rate will not seem unduly slow. But people live from day to day and year to year, not from generation to generation. The business man left at sea in a period of major structural change in the economy of his country, or the worker caught by the collapse of his region's main industries, cannot be expected to see things in the administrator's or diplomat's way. And, indeed, dislocation in the course of change does not help the change itself. Early in the 'thirties, for instance, when the gold standard collapsed, there began a period of major change and readjustment in international monetary relationships. For a time, this proceeded on a basis purely of competition between countries, in effect without any rules at all. A nation which made a useful and appropriate adjustment in its exchange rates might find the effect of this cancelled through—perhaps quite unjustified—retaliation by irritated neighbours. And no country could be sure what its neighbour would do next. This was a nuisance to business men, whose international contracts must run through time. But it was also a nuisance to governments and central banks, for it prevented the *orderly* readjustment of relationships. No one wished to *abolish* competition in the international money market. It was apparent that no one agency, national or international, had the knowledge needed to direct the establishment of 'correct' exchange rates. The free, competitive initiative of individual countries, each in the light of its own circumstances, seemed essential as a means of feeling the way to a more permanent new structure of rates. But it seemed essential to *stabilise* competition round its trend. A first step towards this was to set up national exchange equalisation funds. This was followed in 1936 by a Tripartite Monetary Agreement between Britain, France, and the U.S.A. in 1936. These steps led on after the war to the establishment of a permanent international monetary authority—if at first a somewhat ineffective one—in the shape of the International Monetary Fund.

The importance of this problem of preventing dislocation in the course of structural change has, in fact, been recognised in many post-war agreements on international and inter-regional trade. Thus, for example, the U.S.A. supplied $14,727 million of grant aid to Western Europe between 1948 and 1953 (Marshall Aid), to tide over the period of recovery from the war, as well as other special contributions such as a loan of $3,750 million to Britain. Britain in its turn made grants totalling some hundreds of millions of pounds to other countries of Western Europe (notably Germany) and the Commonwealth. Later discussions have tried to put provision of this kind on a more permanent basis. So, for instance, the Treaty establishing the European Coal and Steel Community, and the draft statute for a European political community, both of which aim at major changes in the structure of European trade and investment, provide for:

(1) Delays in the application of measures of structural readjustment, to allow consequent adjustments to be worked out. These delays may run into several years.

(2) Permission to apply or maintain special measures, such as subsidies or tariffs, to keep in operation obsolete parts of the European economy during the period of adjustment.

(3) Grants and loans to assist the re-employment of displaced workers, and where necessary the creation of new industries.

It being also assumed:

(4) that displaced workers will receive relief and maintenance from their own national authorities.

There has been a great deal of argument, in this country and elsewhere, over the type of economy most likely to minimise dislocation in times of stress and change. Much of this discussion has concentrated round the idea of a diversified economy. Internationally, the problem of underdeveloped areas is typically that the working population is concentrated in a small range of overcrowded occupations, chiefly agricultural, and often producing largely for the less stable sections of the export market. If in a case like this workers are moved from primary trades (farming and mining) into secondary (industrial) and tertiary (professional and service) trades hitherto under-represented, it is possible at one and the same time to raise incomes per head, cut down dependence on unstable markets, and create a broader and surer base for further development in future. This is, in fact, the typical line of advance for underdeveloped countries.

So also in Britain, the depressed areas of the 'thirties were specially hard hit because they were:

(i) dependent on a narrow range of industries, which at that time were—in Britain as a whole—overcrowded, and so suffering from low wages and stagnant or falling employment;
(ii) dependent largely on the production of durable goods, and on export markets;
(iii) poorly placed, because of the narrow range of their existing industries, to develop new types of industry. The growth of expanding trades in those years was typically in proportion to the employment in these trades which each region already possessed.

The slump of the 'thirties would in any case have made itself felt in these areas as elsewhere, and changes in their economic structure to meet new long-term needs would in any case have been required. But it was widely argued at that time that these changes would have come about more easily and with less deliberate effort, and that they and the slump would have caused less immediate dislocation of economic and social life, if the depressed areas had had more diversified economies and the burdens of the 'thirties had been spread more evenly over the country as a whole.

Arguments of this kind contain a great deal of truth, but are scrutinised today with more care than they were twenty years ago. More often than not it pays to concentrate an area's industries round one or two main complexes: farming, engineering, steel, or whatever it may be. Costs are cut and the social consistency of the area increased. It may still be dangerous to concentrate heavily on this or that group of trades. But these dangers can often be dealt with in other ways. It may be useful to spread the burden of fluctuations in exports or in durable-goods production more evenly over the country, or the world. But it is better still to cut off these fluctuations at their source by measures to ensure a permanent high level of demand. Or, if productivity and incomes in farming are low, the answer may be to improve productivity in farming and not to transfer farmers to other jobs. A common mistake in colonial development has been to concentrate on large-scale 'modern' types of production, including mining and plantation agriculture, and neglect what are often the even greater possibilities of raising productivity and income by helping small-scale 'traditional' farmers without trying to turn them into anything else. If the problem is to secure the transition of a region's economy from one pattern to another without dislocation on the way, one way to do it is certainly the 'natural' process of a diversified economy, in which the contraction of one trade tends to be offset by the expansion of another. But it can also be done by a deliberate location of industry policy, such as was in the end actually applied to the British depressed areas.

The last of the 'remote or diffused' factors of which competition may fail to take account—and once again one important for international and inter-regional trade—is the existence and solidarity of social groups. An excellent illustration of this at the international level is provided by an article in the British Iron and Steel Federation's *Statistical Bulletin*, March, 1954, discussing the British attitude to the European Coal and Steel Community. If the United Kingdom were to join the Community, the article points out, it would no longer be possible to grant to Commonwealth steel firms the margin of tariff preference thanks to which 'the developing steel industries of Canada and Australia have latterly been exporters to this country'. If the factor of Commonwealth solidarity were ruled out, it would indeed seem a lunatic policy to bring steel from Australia when it can be had from the Ruhr. There is no doubt that, if the open, competitive all-European market proposed by the Community existed, the Australian producers would sell very little in Britain. Whether Commonwealth solidarity, which has economic as well as political and social advantages, does actually justify bringing steel from Australia is too complex a matter to argue here. But it is beyond question that this is an important factor, and one which the Federation was right to bring into the argument.

National, regional, and even, as in this case, international solidarities are, in fact, among the most important factors with which economic policy has to deal. If there was political dynamite in the depressed-area problem in Britain twenty years ago, it was largely because people in those areas felt themselves to have been let down by a national community to which they belonged and which owed them help. It was also because the whole of each of the depressed-area communities—South Wales, Tyneside, or whatever it might be

—was in the depression together. When, for instance, hunger marchers from Jarrow tramped to London to demand aid for their town, it is significant that they carried credentials from each of the main political parties, not from one side alone. It was as a whole that Jarrow suffered, and as a whole that it fought back.

It is impossible to judge, within the limits of a purely economic discussion, how far a pattern of industry which takes account of these solidarities will differ from that which would emerge under competition. But it is certainly possible to serve simultaneously the two masters, minimum cost and respect for the solidarity of local and national communities, more often than might be thought. In 1934-9—to refer again to figures quoted in the last chapter—factories whose eventual employment reached at least 45,000, and probably more, were settled in what are today the British development areas. In 1944-9 others to employ a further 270,000 were added. These jobs were largely in trades unfamiliar in these areas, and often for women who in most of them, traditionally, had not worked much in industry, The development areas themselves are scattered round the periphery of Britain, outside the central belt in which, under the influence of competition, most new industrial development has tended to take place.

Nevertheless, the new industries in the development areas on the whole did well. It would seem that a great many of the lighter in- dustries in Chart I of Chapter 3 (those handling less than forty tons of fuel and materials per operative per year) can operate so as to sell their goods at a competitive price from almost any region in Britain, *provided* that their initial settlement is carefully planned. Firms which have paid careful attention to such initial factors as techniques for training raw labour, the design of an appropriate management struc- ture, and relations with the local community, have sometimes found that it paid to be directed into a new area instead of expanding, as tends to happen under competition, in the old-established centres of their trade. For, though entering a new area has its risks and costs, it also offers the chance of breaking away from bad old traditions and setting up new levels of expectation and output.

Britain is admittedly a favourable case. It is a small country, with well-developed transport and relatively well-educated and adaptable people. There ought therefore, compared to other countries, to be little difficulty in finding and training workers and managers in any fairly populous part of the country. And the differences between regions from the point of view of access to materials and markets are relatively small. There are also relatively few regional an- tagonisms. The regions of Britain, even those which, like Scotland or Wales, are themselves nations, have been more interested in demanding jobs and wages than in trying to tie managements' hands with more far-reaching nationalist demands. There has, for instance, been some resentment of English managers, key workers, and capital coming into Scotland and Wales. Firms which have allowed for this, for example by insisting on training local men for key jobs instead of bringing in managers and key workers from outside, have found this policy to pay. But resentment of this sort has not usually been strong enough to break out on the surface, and has never had the support of the accredited leaders of these countries. The Scot who wrote to one of his national papers just before the war to suggest that at least 65% of the capital in businesses north of the Border should be of Scottish ownership and origin, and that Scottish property owners should unite to prevent 'English or other alien concerns' from obtaining premises, could safely be written off as belonging to the lunatic fringe. Internationally, by contrast, the question of the ownership and control of capital and of the staffing of foreign firms has been a major source of disputes. But with all these reservations, important as they are, British experience of the possibility of serving the two aims, low cost and community solidarity, without sacrificing one to the other, still contains a substantial lesson for other parts of the world.

After this catalogue of the 'remote or diffused' factors of which competition may fail to take full account, it is hardly necessary to add that changes in the pattern of international trade and investment may involve or be intended to produce changes in the social framework of the countries concerned. As usual, competition may permit or even encourage the emergence of these changes, but cannot be relied on to compel it.

'There is a sense,' write the United Nations experts in discussing the development of underdeveloped areas, 'in which rapid economic progress is impossible without painful readjustments. Ancient philosophies have to be scrapped; old social institutions have to disintegrate; bonds of caste, creed, and race have to be burst; and large numbers of persons who cannot keep up with progress have to have their expectations of a comfortable life frustrated.' (*Measures for the Economic Development of Under-Developed Countries*, 1951, par. 36.)

New social norms are needed: belief in the value and possibility of progress through industrialisation, or belief in the rightness of social mobility. New institutions must emerge: forms of government, new administration, new firms and industries, a capital market, new patterns of land tenure or of family or tribal or community relationship; and new status systems, offering prestige in return for industrial service. New personality patterns are needed, adapted to the new and changed conditions.

Once the attractiveness of these new solutions to new problems has been brought home to people by launching them into practice on a substantial scale, competition (economic, political, or social) will often do the rest. But the initial push must very often come from outside the competitive system. The political, educational, and economic development programmes of the governments of under-developed countries are designed, not merely to attain 'remote or diffused' objectives within an established social framework, but to break through the old social framework and set in place the elements of a new one; of one which otherwise would only straggle into existence sporadically as the chances of competition might provide.

Here also one can learn a good deal from recent British studies of the location of industry. The outstanding development in these studies in recent years has been the emphasis now laid on initial or 'threshold' costs. A firm will often need a (non-competitive) helping hand to settle it in a new location, but can compete successfully without further aid once this threshold is past. The case for similar help to 'infant industries' has long been recognised in the theory of international trade and development. This 'infant industries' case is from one point of view simply a matter of 'remote or diffused' factors involving no change in the social framework. Business men do not think it worth while to locate in a development area rather than in an established centre of their industry because the extra initial cost falls on them, whereas the special advantages of locating there are spread over the community as a whole or realisable only after an uncertain running-in period. But very often the problem is not one of thus balancing competitive advantages within an existing social framework. It is that local and foreign business men have a blind spot for the possibilities of development in a certain place. South Wales is on the map for light industry today; it was not so in the 'thirties. What has happened in between is not simply a change in the actual cash advantages of operating in South Wales: it is, and probably much more, a change in expectations (social norms) about South Wales. And to bring about this change it has been necessary to bring about a whole series of parallel changes in social structure and personality: to establish new firms and new branches of public administration, to train new managers and try to develop new personality patterns and a new class structure in the ex-depressed areas, and so on.

Chapter 14

INTER-REGIONAL AND
INTERNATIONAL RELATIONS

III. TRADE AND INVESTMENT—THE ROLE OF
DIRECTION AND CONSULTATION

(A) IN THE RELATIONS BETWEEN FIRMS AND NATIONAL, REGIONAL, OR INTERNATIONAL AUTHORITIES

THE discussion of State or other governmental controls over inter-regional and international trade and investment was confused, during and just after the Second World War, by doubts as to whether such controls were needed at all, apart at any rate from the two or three years of immediate post-war readjustment. Events and Dr. Balogh have swept these doubts away, leaving only the question of the sort of controls needed to supplement competition in each particular case. Discussion of this has tended to settle down along the lines already marked out in Part II. Direction is appropriate when some superior authority has, or can without disproportionately high cost get, information about factors which are 'remote or diffused' from the point of view of the firms or other agencies which actually carry on trade or development. It is also appropriate where the superior authority can (as in the relations between developed and underdeveloped countries) draw a firm's attention to some practice or opening novel in the firm's own country—and so requiring a change in that country's social framework to adopt it—but not novel elsewhere. Consultation, on the other hand, is appropriate for helping the discovery and development of genuine novelties, and for dealing with cases where the factors in question are 'remote or diffused' from the point of view of those immediately taking a decision, but cannot without disproportionate cost be known to any higher authority which could issue a direction.

(i) *Relations between public authorities and traders* (*international or inter-regional*)

Direction, it was said above in Chapter 5, breaks down at the point where it causes a sharp rise in 'managerial costs'—though not, usually, in 'direct' managerial costs, which cover such things as

232

administrative staffs' salaries and accommodation. More commonly the impact is felt in 'indirect' managerial costs, which are measured by the difference between what the cost of any operation would be if men and machines were used with the greatest economy technically possible, and what the cost in fact is.

In line with this, discussion of the flow of trade between the more and less prosperous regions of Great Britain has led to broad agreement to *rule out* directions intended to provide:

(1) Any permanent subsidy or other aid to depressed-area industries, not equally available to industries elsewhere.

(2) Any similar aid, even temporary, granted otherwise than on the authority of the national government and within limits defined by it; or so as to discriminate for or against one of two or more similar firms in the area protected, or against sales in that area, or in markets served by its firms, by suppliers from any other region of Britain; especially if discrimination takes the form not merely of a preference but of a rigid bar on entry into this or that market. Some depressed-area towns, for instance, at one time ran 'buy local' campaigns, tried to ban the placing of local authority contracts outside their area, or made trade treaties with other towns in or out of Britain granting (even if only on a small scale) preference in each other's markets against goods from other towns or regions.

Approval, on the other hand, has been given to:

(3) Permanent measures of general advantage to all regions in the country, even if incidentally of special advantage to the less prosperous regions. These would include national full-employment policy (policy for maintaining a high and stable level of demand), or unemployment insurance or assistance, or the decision in 1932 to introduce—mainly in the interests of full employment—a general tariff on goods entering Britain as a whole.

(4) Temporary protection to the trade of depressed areas, to tide over periods of adjustment, if given on nationally approved lines and, preferably, without discrimination against any firm within a place or region outside the depressed areas. Thus the Government itself in the 'thirties administered a scheme for giving preference in armament contracts to firms in the depressed areas. This scheme discriminated in favour of depressed-area suppliers, but not in favour of suppliers in one or another region outside these areas. All who were equally well placed from the point of view of cost and military strategy (especially the danger of air attack) had the same chance.

The danger of direction of types (1) and (2) is that it is specially liable to raise indirect managerial costs, and indeed direct costs as well.

If, for instance, a firm is granted a permanent subsidy, it may rest on its oars and fail to increase its efficiency to the extent that it could and should. *Either* this danger is allowed to materialise (increase in indirect managerial costs), *or* extra staffs have to be engaged to check the efficiency of firms on behalf of the authority giving the subsidy (increase in direct managerial costs). Uncoordinated local measures of protection are unlikely to be taken with proper regard to the interests of other regions, since these, from the point of view of the authorities of any one place or region, are 'remote or diffused'. The resulting confusion and cross-currents represent an increase in indirect managerial costs. So also discrimination against this or that firm or area can be misused to advance sectional interests. And a rigid ban on entry to a market may stifle valuable new departures in trade. Once again, *either* indirect managerial costs go up *or* direct managerial costs go up in an (often, experience suggests, unsuccessful) attempt to stop this happening.

Exactly the same arguments have come to be applied in international trade. Post-war discussions and agreements have approved without hesitation national or international administrative measures (directions) designed to raise the level of activity and flow of trade in and between all countries; national and international measures for full employment, for example, or the provisions of the International Monetary Fund or European Payments Union for smoothing out the flow of international payments. They have also recognised that countries may need to take temporary non-competitive measures to check or increase the flow of trade. But they have insisted that:

(1) Such policies should be applied on internationally approved lines, and be subject to international review. The General (Geneva) Agreement on Tariffs and Trade (1947), for example, and the Code of Liberalisation of the Organisation for European Economic Co-operation (1950–3) both provide for reviews of this kind.

(2) They should preferably stick strictly to their purpose of protecting or increasing the trade of the country applying them. They should not discriminate in favour of or against any one or group among the states with which that country trades, nor between trading firms. It is recognised that this may not always be possible. The chief exception in post-war trade has been the relationship between the dollar countries and the rest of the world. It has been possible for the non-dollar countries to increase their trade among themselves, to their own benefit and no one else's loss, by keeping up protective measures against dollar imports and abolishing or reducing those

against imports from each other. It can be shown that if they had dropped the barriers against dollar imports as well, little or no increase in dollar trade would have followed, and the chance of increased trade among the non-dollar countries would have been lost.

(3) They should take the form of tariffs, subsidies, or similar measures which leave traders with some freedom of action, rather than of any rigid administrative ban on entering a certain market, or compulsion to enter it.

The tendency has been to concentrate on a few well-defined types of control, including tariffs, exchange control, export and import quotas, and inter-governmental commodity agreements. Efforts have been made to cut out other types of control which add little to what these can achieve, and which do on the contrary, by their number or character, complicate international trade and add to indirect managerial costs. These include restrictive practices in connection with customs formalities, marks of origin, the publication and administration of trade regulations, and the transit of goods through foreign territories; also purchases and sales on non-commercial grounds by State enterprises: and, in general, private cartels.

If direction is limited on these lines, traders (international or inter-regional) will be left much freedom to make their competitive contracts as they wish. They will find their choice weighted in a certain way. But they will not find any roads absolutely barred, nor (the rule of non-discrimination against firms) will *individual* firms receive directions other than those applicable to them under the general law. Will direction, limited in this way, be sufficient to fill all the gaps of competition, and achieve the objects of stability, respect for the solidarity of nations, and so on, outlined in Chapter 13?

Experience shows that the answer is 'no'. Though there are limits to the amount of direction which can profitably be imposed on traders, it is possible and useful to go a good deal further by consultation. For often traders (interested mainly in their competitive position) and directing authorities (which have a different and in some respects a wider view, but cannot afford to direct individual traders in much detail) have a mutual interest which only consultation can bring out.

A government, for instance, has often wider sources of information than are available to individual businesses, and can use these to help businesses to find new openings (a change in the social framework) or become aware of existing openings (within the established framework of transactions) of national as well as individual importance. It can, within limits, particularly in dealing with relatively large and secure firms, draw on the forces of group solidarity. Thus it is unlikely that the special attention paid by many big firms in Britain to export markets since the war has been due solely to their individual self-interest. It has been due at least in part to their consciousness—without any actual direction—of common responsibility, as important members of the national community, for the nation-wide problem of the balance of payments.

In a modest way, consultation between authorities and traders goes on even in inter-regional trade. The Local Government Acts authorise local authorities to provide or subsidise information services about their areas' industries and possible openings for business between them and the outside world. Authorities in places with a tourist trade make a good deal of use of this. Some of those with industrial interests, in Scotland and Wales, for example, have used these powers to support regional development councils which conduct general information and propaganda work and run trade fairs.

At the international level, consultation between firms and planning authorities is well developed. The British Government, for example, maintains a network of information services throughout the world for the benefit of British traders. It encourages industries to provide similar services by collective action; under the Industrial Organisation and Development Act, 1947, an industry can be empowered to raise a compulsory levy for this purpose. Government departments also confer regularly with trade associations and big firms, to encourage interest in what seem, from the national point of view, important export fields, or to promote the replacement of imports by home produce. These consultations may on occasion, as, for instance, in the motor trade since the war, end in a more or less formal agreement about the percentage of an industry's output which is to be exported and the direction in which exports are to go.

(ii) *Public authorities and investment and development (international or inter-regional)*

Very similar ideas have come out of recent experience of international or inter-regional investment and development. In British location of industry policy, for instance, a basic though not always an explicit principle has been that neither a firm nor a planning authority can have, by itself, all the information needed for a satisfactory decision about a site. Neither, therefore, is in a position to take the final decision on its own. The firm draws from its experience of the competitive market detailed knowledge of how best to serve consumers' interests, and, in particular, of the conditions in which it can produce what consumers want at minimum cost, or develop a new product. The Government or local authorities can get this knowledge only with a disproportionate effort, if, that is, they can get it at all. They are not, therefore, in a position to direct location. On the other hand, they know far more than any firm about the relative needs and possibilities of different local communities. The firm is therefore unlikely to pick a site suitable from all points of view if it chooses its own location in the light of its knowledge of the competitive market alone, and ignores the information in the hands of public authorities.

In these conditions it seems reasonable enough for planning authorities to use direction to bring needs and possibilities as seen by the authorities to firms' notice, but not to force them into any given location. Competition is left its share of influence. Facilities are offered in favoured areas—prepared sites, factories ready to buy or rent, loans, open or concealed subsidies, building priorities, housing allocations—and permission is refused to build new plants in areas regarded as overcrowded. But these measures are applied so as to avoid:

(1) Any permanent subsidy or other special assistance to a firm. There has been no objection to offering firms special help with their threshold costs. But after four or five years, if not sooner, they have been expected to stand wholly on their own competitive feet.

(2) Grants and other forms of aid and protection, unless awarded under a nationally approved policy. This does not necessarily mean that grants and aid should be given only by some national authority. It does, however, mean that, if local or regional authorities are, for instance, to develop their own trading estates, they must do so on lines laid down by a national authority in the light of the relative needs of all localities and regions.

(3) Any rigid determination of firms' location. Except in the war years, it has never been the practice to direct firms to this area or that. At certain times the power to ban new building in 'over-crowded' areas such as Greater London has been vigorously used. But there has never been any ban on acquiring *existing* buildings, even in these areas, and a choice has always been left open between sites in other parts of the country.

(4) Discrimination between firms, except so far as is necessary to induce them to come to a particular area. Also discrimination which creates gross inequalities or goes beyond the limits imposed by con-dition (1)—no permanent subsidies. Since location at a given site is a once-for-all operation, usually planned well in advance, and since

far fewer plants are looking for locations at any time than are making decisions about international or inter-regional trading transactions, it is practicable for planning authorities to consider location cases one by one and discriminate among them in a way which would not be practicable in the case of trading transactions. Even so, discrimination has proved acceptable only in rather narrow limits.

Applied on these lines, direction leaves firms a great deal of scope to follow their own competitive inclinations. But there remains the further possibility of limiting this discretion by consultation, and this has played an important part in British location of industry policy. Firms have an inducement to consult not only because they want sites from which they can compete effectively, but because they want to get in a position to take advantage of the inducements and avoid the penalties for which planning authorities' directions provide. The planning authorities on their side recognise that they cannot push direction far enough to reach all the results they want, or at any rate cannot do so without stifling useful initiatives and contradicting firms' correct knowledge of what the market requires. Both parties have an interest in coming together and trying to work out a mutually agreeable solution. The Board of Trade's files, especially between 1944 and 1949, when the pressure to get firms into what are now the development areas was at its height, contain voluminous records of exchanges of views of this sort. Most of these did, in fact, end in an agreement satisfactory to both sides.

(B) THE RELATION BETWEEN INTERNATIONAL, NATIONAL, AND REGIONAL AUTHORITIES

(i) *National and regional authorities*

The above argument leaves in the background the question of *which* authority is to apply direction, or to consult with a firm, when one or other of these measures is needed. What is to be the relationship between the local, national, or international authorities responsible for trade and development policy? Consulting once again British location of industry experience, the answer would seem to be something as follows.

First, competition exists, and is useful, between local communities as well as between firms. This is very obvious in the tourist trade, where the unit of attraction to the holiday-maker is at least as much the town or district as, say, the individual hotel or boarding-house. No one seriously suggests that the flow of tourists to this place or that should be determined, in the main, by anything but the competition between resorts; whether this competition takes the form of individual enterprise, or of collective action by each town or district council. On the industrial side, interlocal competition of one or other of these kinds pioneered all the methods later used with success to revive the depressed areas. Trading estates were developed at Letchworth, Welwyn, Slough, Liverpool, Manchester. Loans to firms were available at Liverpool and Manchester (the Birmingham Municipal Bank had some possibilities here which were never followed up), or through the Scottish Development Council. Liverpool subsidised new plants through the sale of land below market value, and other towns did the same by judicious adjustments of rate assessments and public utility charges. Systematic research was carried out into local industrial needs and possibilities, information services were created, and intensive propaganda campaigns were undertaken by regional or local development councils in Lancashire, Cumberland, the North-East Coast, Scotland, Wales, and a number of more prosperous areas such as Bristol. Competition between regions and localities—Birmingham's stout efforts, for example, to avoid being put at a disadvantage by the activities of the then depressed areas—did much to clarify the problem of the depressed areas and the issues of policy arising out of it. It cleared the way for measures of direction in due course.

Secondly, competition between local communities and direction by some higher authority are to some extent interchangeable, at the risk of incurring the dangers, outlined in Chapter 5, which any unnecessary extension of direction involves. These dangers, as was pointed out there, are subtler than appears on the surface. They may be summed up as the risk of *general* overloading of the branch of administration in question. The effects of this *general* overloading will not necessarily make themselves felt in that *particular* area of direction whose extension has proved the last straw. That area may not get its full share of administrators' attention. But it very well may; and in that case the impact of overloading will be felt elsewhere.

In a country where direction and in particular State direction are as highly developed as they have been in Britain in recent years, this risk is a very real one. From 1944 onwards—after a transitional period in 1937-9—most of the work previously done in the then depressed areas by local or regional agencies, on a competitive basis, was taken over by central government departments, principally the Board of Trade. The Board at that time was a large and somewhat unwieldy department, and the camel's back creaked noticeably under this (and other) straws. The depressed-area problem was at

239

that moment important enough to secure a great deal of attention, and the effects of overstrain showed more elsewhere. An example might be the Board's relative failure, in negotiating for the creation of development councils under the Industrial Organisation and Development Act of 1947. Later, when problems of the location of industry had a lower priority, the boot came to be on the other foot, and location suffered. By the early 1950's overstrain was showing in, for instance, the Board's slow response to the need for industry in the new towns round London. And a little later, in 1952–3, the Board was failing to make an adequately detailed scheme for transferring and resettling workers displaced through the supersession of the older tin-plate mills of West Wales by modern continuous mills.

In view of this risk of administrative overloading, competition—in this as in other fields of administration—is in a modern State preferable to direction where the two are interchangeable. If local or regional bodies can provide trading estates or industrial finance, or conduct research and information services, it is better that they should do it rather than have some central administration do it for them. But there remain, thirdly, several purposes for which directions from the central government to local communities have proved necessary as a supplement to competition, at points where competition *in any case* breaks down. These include:

(1) Requiring local communities to act according to (from their point of view) 'remote or diffused' considerations which, even if known to them, would not otherwise come home to them with enough force to make them do what is required. It was, for instance, necessary for the revival of the former depressed areas that planning authorities in Greater London and the Midlands should severely restrict the building of new plants in their areas in the years just after the war. It is very unlikely that they would have done so to the extent called for if the Government had not taken power, first under Defence Regulations and later under the Town and Country Planning Act of 1947, to compel them to do so.

(2) Requiring them to apply in their areas what from their point of view may be novel standards (representing therefore changes in the social framework in which they operate) worked out elsewhere. Thus, under the Town and Country Planning Act of 1947, every county and county borough must prepare a development plan, covering among other things industrial development; and the Ministry of Housing and Local Government has the right to review these plans and impose on them standards derived from general experience.

The Act also directed the creation of a new planning structure, under which planning powers were transferred from county districts to counties.

Fourthly, since no national directing authority can expect on its own to obtain all the information it would need to formulate a complete location policy and impose it on local or regional authorities, consultation between the national and local authorities becomes necessary to arrive at an agreed policy, as well as to foster and spread a knowledge of new techniques and developments. Local and regional authorities have the knowledge of local needs and possibilities which they derive from their own competitive initiative. They see in the national government, armed with its powers of direction, a body which can greatly help or hinder their development. The national government, for its part, has its own wider view of the comparative needs of different regions, and needs local guidance because of the limits to what it can achieve by its own direction. In these conditions, consultation becomes valuable to both sides.

In the formative period of depressed area policy, down to 1939, there was, in fact, very close and continuous consultation between the central government, local authorities, and the various joint or voluntary bodies concerned with local and regional development. This died down in 1944-9, when policy was broadly agreed and its execution was (though probably excessively) concentrated in the central government's hands. It has tended to re-emerge since 1949-50, when, after the virtual solution of the old depressed-area problem, the direction of policy became less clear and new priorities had to be debated. The counties and county boroughs which are the primary town-planning authorities under the Act of 1947 are much more formidable bodies than the county districts which had primary planning powers in the past. They have begun to make their weight felt. In Scotland, the North-East Coast, Wales and Lancashire regional development councils, and some related bodies—the Manchester Joint Research Council, for instance—have shown what a few years ago would have seemed an unexpected power of survival, or have been recreated. And various new agencies, such as new town corporations, have joined in the battle.

Consultation between local and national authorities is, of course, not confined to formal meetings between local and regional authorities and government departments, or between their officers. It overflows into the meetings of professional institutes—the Town Planning Institute, for example—of propaganda bodies such as the Town and Country Planning Association, and of political parties, or of

16   241

departmental committees and royal commissions. Once the debate
starts it may proceed at any of these levels. And its purpose, as
Mr. D. N. Chester in particular has recently very well brought out,
is not merely to keep all concerned informed of problems and possibilities within the existing social framework but to encourage and
spread a knowledge of new initiatives in development, such as have
so often emerged from competition between local communities and
regions in the past.

The direction to which local communities in Britain have been
subject is that of the State. But State direction is not the only kind.
Probably the most famous regional development authority in recent
history is the Tennessee Valley Authority. This has powers to impose
certain forms of development and promote others in some seven
States of the U.S.A.; but it is not itself a government nor a branch
of government. It is a public corporation, chartered by the Federal
Government to perform certain limited functions in a specified area
for a certain time. So also the High Authority of the European Coal
and Steel Community, which has powers over the mining and steel
industries of Belgium, Holland, Luxembourg, France, Italy, and
Germany in many ways analogous to those of the T.V.A.; only,
instead of being chartered by a superior government, it has its
authority from a treaty between these six countries. Legally, its
status is very like that of, say, a joint water board established by a
group of local authorities, which agree, within limits and for purposes laid down at the start, to accept its authority.

(ii) *National and international authorities*

This distinction is important when the question comes up of
relations, not between regional and national authorities but between
national and international authorities. These latter relations have
developed since the war at three levels, becoming more and more
similar to those between national and regional authorities.

First, there has been greatly intensified consultation through a
whole host of agencies, new and old. There is the United Nations
Organisation, with its various commissions—the Economic Commissions for Europe, Latin America, and Asia and the Far East, for
example—and associated bodies such as the I.L.O. or the Food and
Agriculture Organisation. There are the institutions of the British
Commonwealth—the Commonwealth Economic Conferences, for
example—of the French Union, or of the emerging community of
Western Europe. There is a variety of intergovernmental committees
dealing with the affairs of Europe (the Organisation for European
Economic Cooperation, in particular), with Africa south of the

Sahara, with the Caribbean, with South-East Asia (the Colombo Plan). And so, one might almost say, *ad infinitum*.

Secondly, from this consultation has emerged agreement on the need for direction in certain fields, to require countries to take account of the 'remote and diffused' consequences of their actions, or to apply within their borders experience gained elsewhere but novel to them. The characteristic type of direction of the latter kind is that which metropolitan countries exert in their colonies, or which the U.S.S.R. exerts in its satellite States. Outside the Soviet world the number of cases in which relations of this sort exist—still more, the number of whose existence opinion in the free world approves—has rapidly diminished since the war, as one country after another escapes from colonial status into independence. India, Ceylon, Burma, and Indonesia have taken that road already, and a number of other British, French, and Dutch territories are well advanced along it.

The other type of direction, designed to make free countries allow for the remoter consequences of their actions, has on the other hand been increasing, taking the form not of the emergence of a World State but of the creation of international 'public corporations'. The Geneva Agreement on Tariffs and Trade, the articles of the International Monetary Fund, or the Treaty of the European Coal and Steel Community each establish an authority of the 'public corporation' or better of the 'joint water board' type, with limited but effective powers to require countries to do or refrain from doing certain things.

The European Coal and Steel Community is a particularly good illustration of the type of thinking which has led up to the creation of authorities of this kind. Debates on the economic future of Europe have for some time made it clear that the countries of Europe need to come much closer than they at present do to free trade among themselves and to common investment, employment, and location of industry policies. The Organisation for European Economic Cooperation has for several years tried to secure these objectives by consultation, but with only limited success. Though it has had the bulk of trade within Western Europe freed from quantitative restrictions, it has not broken down tariff barriers, nor secured any notable coordination of investments. From the point of view of individual countries, the advantages to be obtained have been too 'remote or diffused' to lead them to take the necessary action. But the High Authority of the European Coal and Steel Community, armed with executive authority, was able within a year of its establishment to abolish not only quotas but tariffs and the majority of other restrictions, subsidies, and miscellaneous protective measures within its particular market, and to take important steps towards a common investment and employment policy.

Finally, these developments in international consultation and direction form the superstructure of a system of international economic relations whose foundation is still competition between independent nations, each with an economic policy which it decides for itself alone. Few, in the Western world, would quarrel with this in principle. No world government is likely to have the information it would need to direct, efficiently and at reasonable cost, the main course of international trade and investment. Only competition can effectively and cheaply guide the variegated decisions involved and reduce them to order. And it is in and through the competition of national states that the trade and investment practices which international authorities are now trying to generalise or control have been and are being pioneered. But the growth of international direction and even of consultation in their present form and scope is new, and it is probably true that international economic relations even in recent years have been overweighted on the side of competition, as they certainly were in the past. This is in interesting contrast to policy on inter-regional relations within Great Britain, which since 1944 has almost certainly been overweighted on the side of direction. A profitable line of enquiry, for anyone who wished to pursue the matter of this chapter further, might be to examine in detail these differences between recent inter-regional and international experience and see what lessons each might have for the future development of the other.

Part IV

ECONOMICS IN ITS
WIDER SETTING

Chapter 15

WHAT AN ECONOMIST IS

ECONOMICS, to go back to the definition in Chapter 1, is the study of social relationships in so far as they 'can be brought into relation with the measuring rod of money'. That is, economics is the science of which accountancy is the art. But it is only in very recent years that the two have joined forces. Till within the last generation the field of monetary analysis could be pictured as a large sheet of blotting-paper, with an ink-spot in each corner. One represented the economist, formulating hypotheses about monetary relationships in the market, or between nations, or between employers and workers; but having very little in the way of actual accounts against which to test them. The other represented the accountant, grappling with the actual financial records of business and the public service, but in the light of day-to-day needs, and without much concern for wider or longer-term hypotheses; for scientific analysis or reflection on the material on which he worked. The two spots spread gradually, putting out feelers towards one another. But only in the last ten years have they begun to coalesce really rapidly, and this has been due very largely to the appearance on the paper of a third spot, falling precisely between the first two. This represents social accounting, the analysis of the accounts of the whole economy of a region, nation, or international group. Social accounting has come to the fore because, like business accounting, it serves urgent practical needs. It necessarily makes use, as will be shown, of the techniques and concepts of business and public authorities' accounting as already established. But it has been created for the most part by economists to answer the questions posed in economic hypotheses. In this field the accountant and the economist have had perforce to lie down together, and have ended by each discovering that the other is not bad company after all.

BUSINESS ACCOUNTANCY

The origins of business accountancy (including the accounts of public authorities) as we now know it date back at least to the fourteenth century. An organised profession of accountancy emerged in

Britain in the nineteenth century. The chief associations of accountants in general practice—there are other more specialised societies such as the Institute of Municipal Treasurers and Accountants—date from between 1850 and 1890. In 1886 the two leading associations in England and Wales had 1,802 members; in 1913 some 7,370; by 1937 the figures reached 19,784. But the art which this numerous body of professional men administered remained for many years narrowly empirical. It grew piecemeal, by common-sense judgement, and without allowing ideas to wander beyond what could be justified by immediately available facts and figures. The spirit in which its practitioners were trained is well summed up in a comment by *The Accountant*, in 1893, on a proposal for university courses. 'There is no immediate danger,' observed the editor with emphasis, 'of universities taking up this idea. . . . Service under articles is the only real way of training.' As late as 1933 it was possible to write off the scientific study of accountancy in the words:

'Nothing has yet been done by the profession in the way of organised study or research.' (Carr-Saunders and Wilson, *The Professions*, 1933, p. 266.)

The accountant remained in principle, and only too often in practice, a mere book-keeper.

A number of forces have conspired, in the last fifty years, to raise accountancy above this empirical and unreflective level. Something may perhaps be attributed to the occasional idealists who have proclaimed the possibility of something better. The first Lord Stamp reminded the Society of Incorporated Accountants and Auditors in 1921 that they and their colleagues held 'practically a monopoly grip' of the data for concrete economic analysis, at least in the world of business, but in the last half-century had not yet made 'a single substantial contribution to economic science over its own field of the analysis of the results of industry'. Others, more often in America than in this country, have warned accountants of the dangers which some of their conventions, too narrowly focused on the affairs of individual firms, may hold for the economy as a whole. Price-fixing conventions may ignore the possibilities of bringing down costs by lower prices and expanding demand. Particular methods of forecasting yields may make investment seem unnecessarily unattractive.

More important, however, have been changes in the scope and practice of accountancy itself. The techniques which the accountant is expected to have at his finger-tips, and the range of purposes for which they can be used, have multiplied. The first concern of accountancy was with financial accounting; balancing costs against receipts in an enterprise as a whole. Inflation in the last few years has forced accountants to take more seriously economists' debates on what their accountancy conventions mean. What, for instance, is meant by 'income' or 'true profit' when prices are rising? This is a change within the traditional field of accounting; but new fields have also been opened. In the first two decades of the twentieth century, interest grew in cost ascertainment and budgeting, and was greatly accelerated by the First World War. More recently has come in the technique of standard costing:

> 'The utilisation of the whole accounting technique to locate errors and inefficiencies at the source, by setting up standards as a basis for judging actual operating performance.' (Institute of Chartered Accountants in England and Wales, *Developments in Cost Accounting*, 1947.)

There is a shift here not only in the technique of accountancy but in the purposes which it serves. The older accountancy was concerned with the profitability of each firm, which is a matter of limited and particular interest. For a firm may earn a profit in spite of avoidable inefficiency, if it holds some degree of monopoly, or the general level of technique in its industry is low, or the inefficiency of one competitor in one sphere offsets that of another in another. The newer accountancy concerns itself directly with efficiency in the actual use of resources, which is a matter of general public interest to producers and to consumers alike.

The wider the area on which the standards used in standard costing are based the more useful they are likely to be. A generation ago proposals to organise the exchange of firms' data for this purpose were rejected by many accountants as little better than Bolshevism. This older tradition of business secrecy and particularism is not yet dead. But, in view of the obvious value of wide comparisons in the newer branches of accountancy, it is dying. The steady tightening of the Companies Acts requirements on information to be given to shareholders and the public is hastening its demise. So, to a less extent, is the increase in the information which firms have to supply to public authorities.

The accountant has also become more of a manager; though this applies more to those employed in trade and industry than to accountants in professional practice. The commercial and industrial, or for that matter the Government or local government, accountant is often a major department head in his own right. About 70% of all accountants are reckoned to attain to some administrative responsibility, and the chief accountant or controller of a large firm may have under him a staff of hundreds or even thousands. This does not, of course, imply anything directly about the technique of accountancy, but does necessarily affect the way the accountant himself looks at it. It is difficult for the head of a major administrative branch to retain the outlook of a mere book-keeper.

This is all the truer since, with the widening range of accountancy techniques, accountants are becoming more and more deeply involved in decisions on general management policy. Wherever a choice between alternatives arises, or a complicated sequence of transactions is to be sorted out, the accountant's analysis of costs, prices, and money flows comes into play. His relation to business policy is very much that of the economist to ethics. He might be regarded simply as one who answers questions which others have defined, and clarifies issues on which others will take executive decisions. But in practice it is often very difficult to disentangle the answer to a question from the definition of the question itself. The way the accountant selects and presents the material of which he and he alone is the master will often determine the way his colleagues view a situation and the decision they take. That the accountant should bear a share of responsibility for management is thus not merely convenient but, often, inevitable. This has, increasingly, been formally recognised by the inclusion of accountants in boards of directors and executive committees.

With the growing range of accountants' techniques, and their rising responsibility for management, their work has moved over a great extent from recording past transactions, whose framework is given, to prediction and to the design of accounting systems to answer new questions; to what an economist would call model-building. The profession insists on keeping its feet on the ground; it will not depart from that which can be justified by reference to actual, historical, facts and figures. But it has always been recognised that what questions the accountant asks, and how he answers them, is to a great extent a matter of convention and even (as regards, for instance, transactions not completed at the end of a financial year) of hypothesis. The newer tendencies to model-building and prediction are thus a natural development of the older accountancy, not a new graft upon it. But they represent a substantial shift in accountancy's centre of gravity.

These shifts have been apparent for at least a generation. The point they have reached now, in some though by no means all parts of the profession, is well summed up in a recent study by the Harvard Business School. It centres round an engaging character known as the 'broad-gauge controllership executive': keen eyes, a little past middle age, a whiff of cigar smoke and the board room. The young accountant will necessarily begin, in his first job, as a technician of book-keeping, working under direction. If, however, he rises to the top he is as likely as not to find his work nine parts management to one of technical accountancy. In a few swift strokes the author of the Harvard study contrasts the book-keeper and the accounting executive. One administers payroll procedures; the other takes an active hand in wage negotiations. One records past sales; the other forecasts sales in future. One provides standard cost figures; the other correlates these with other financial data as a basis for pricing. One checks the legality of expenditure, the other its soundness. One collects accounts due; the other studies collection costs in relation to receipts. One makes standard analyses of department costs; the other uses these to spot problem areas and define new questions. One fills up the tax forms; the other makes taxation an element in general management policy. One takes stock; the other shapes buying policy. One ascertains profit; the other interprets it to shareholders and the public. One helps operating management to set standards on the basis of current practice; the other sets up a long-term forecast of expense, and uses it to clarify organisation problems.

The 'broad-gauge controllership executive' turns out, in fact, to be none other than the economist—the analyst of social action in monetary terms—skilled in 'figure know-how' and dressed up with executive power. 'Accountancy', to quote a recent definition, 'may be thought of as a systematic record of the working of the economic structure of society in terms of monetary symbols. As it takes on and develops notions of economic order it gradually points to what should be by accuracy of statement in regard to what is.'[1] No economist could say fairer than that.

This change from book-keeper to economist has been progressively recognised in the profession's schemes for study and research. Economics and statistics found their way into accountancy syllabuses (beginning in Scotland) by the beginning of the 'twenties. University graduates were permitted to qualify as accountants after three years' articled pupilage, instead of the normal five. In Scotland, though not in England, students were required to attend university courses. Chairs of accountancy were established.

Eventually, in the Second World War, arrangements were made, and are now in force, for university degree courses in economics, accountancy, and law, designed specifically for prospective members of the accountancy profession. In 1937 the Society of Incorporated

[1] F. S. Bray, *Precision and Design in Accountancy*, 1947.

251

Accountants set up a Research Committee, and in 1942 the Institute
of Chartered Accountants in England and Wales set up a Taxation
and Financial Relations Committee, which has likewise carried on
research into accounting principles. The tradition that accountancy
is practice without theory, though not as yet entirely overcome, is
at long last passing into history.

ECONOMETRICS

If accountancy in the nineteenth century was practice without
theory, economics was theory without practice. What is known today
as econometrics springs from two sources. On the one hand economists, engaged in formulating abstract hypotheses about economic
relations, have felt more and more the need for clear-cut mathematical formulations leading to statistical tests. The great precursor
in this field is generally reckoned to have been the French economist
Cournot, whose major work was published in 1838. By the beginning
of the twentieth century the need for a mathematical-statistical
approach was being vigorously pressed by writers such as Alfred
Marshall or Sidney and Beatrice Webb. The necessary statistics were,
however, still lacking, and in two senses. First, statistical series suitable for economists' use were still comparatively rare. Statistical
techniques, secondly, were being vigorously elaborated, especially in
the field of the biological sciences. But their possibilities in the
economic field were barely beginning to be grasped.

From then onwards, however, and especially after the First World
War, the alliance between economic analysis and statistics developed
fast. By 1931 it was far enough advanced to justify the formation
of the international Econometric Society, whose journal, *Econometrics*, remains the chief (though by no means the only) focus for
work in this field. The number of specialists in econometrics is still
comparatively small. There were fewer than a thousand members of
the Econometric Society in all countries together in 1949, more than
half being in the United States and a mere forty-odd in Great
Britain; this may be compared with the 5,557 members of the Royal
Economic Society at the same date. But econometric methods have
become part of the standard equipment of every economist.

Econometrics has been defined as the 'statistical observation of
theoretically founded concepts'. Both parts of the definition are
essential, and the two together imply that econometrics is the application to the economic field of the standard methods of natural
science. The variables apparently relevant to a particular problem
are picked out, in the first place, on a basis of observation and

common sense. A hypothesis about the reaction of an individual, or group, to changes in the variables is set up. It may be timeless (static) or concerned with changes through time (dynamic). It may deal with the reactions of an individual, or a group which can be treated as a unit (micro-economic analysis), or with a multitude of important agents (macro-economics). In any case, it defines a set of questions for the statistician to answer.

It is then checked against the facts. The facts to be collected are defined by the hypothesis. But statistical technique will usually have to be called in for two purposes even before analysis begins. Sampling technique may be needed to minimise the labour of collection; and, where the facts required are numerous, miscellaneous, and difficult to use without prior treatment, it may be necessary to set up an accounting framework in which they can be presented in an orderly and convenient way. This is obviously true, for example, where one of the facts, or rather sets of facts, required is the national income.

The facts have then to be analysed. Once again, the economist has defined the questions to be asked. But statistical technique is again called in (correlation analysis and curve-fitting) to disentangle the influence of each variable, and to eliminate irrelevant factors; by, for example, eliminating trends, or smoothing over seasonal, cyclical, or random variations. The result may be to prove the initial hypothesis defective; in that case it is necessary to redefine the hypothesis, or look for new variables, or even to restate the whole problem, as a preliminary to new statistical tests. It will never be to prove the initial hypothesis absolutely correct, for no statistical test can guarantee that a more comprehensive and satisfactory hypothesis will not be found in due course. Provided, however, that the hypothesis is open to no objection for the moment, it can be temporarily approved and used, alone, or as a component in a larger system, for prediction.

Though materials have multiplied in the last generation, and especially since 1939, the chief difficulty in the way of the econometrician is still today the lack of data. Discussing in the *Economic Journal* (September 1950) the life of a government statistician, a member of the staff of the Oxford Institute of Statistics has observed that, in the present state of the science, advanced mathematical methods in the economic field serve chiefly in the hands of the honest to reveal that the evidence on which policy is based is not worth the paper it is written on: and in those of the less honest to earn repute and promotion by clothing departmental cases in language which other departments cannot see through. The number of variables which can be simultaneously handled with any precision is small even when the basic data are fairly exact. In quite a number of the problems facing economists today, as for instance those of under-developed territories, or the labour market, or the location of industry, variables which have a significant effect on calculations appear from every corner of the map of social action. A backward people's culture, institutions, and even personality pattern, for instance, are likely to be completely transformed well within the length of time which the economist has to envisage in a development programme. Even where the effective variables are fewer, the data available are usually somewhat rough and ready. The econometrician finds himself over and over again able to analyse accurately action and reaction in a narrow area, but forced to fall back on the rough, qualitative estimates of the 'practical' economist for variables outside that area: variables possibly more important, even for action within it, than any of those which the econometrician can as yet measure.

It is an accident of history that econometrics is new, whereas the technique of accountancy is long established. When the logic of the two is argued out, it is clear that the econometrician and the accountant are doing the same thing. They each start from a problem ('How is the business to earn a profit?'—'How will purchase tax affect the demand for cotton piece-goods?'). They formulate, explicitly or implicitly, a hypothesis ('that consumers react to a change in price in a certain way': 'that the business, by proceeding on the lines followed in the last financial year, earns a profit'). They define the relevant variables, and design a system of money accounts to bring out not only the extent to which the hypothesis as a whole is, in fact, fulfilled (financial accounting) but (costing, standard costing) the influence of each variable on it. They then use the results for prediction, as a pointer to further variables which might be examined, or to throw up alternative hypotheses on which the problem might be more effectively solved. Econometrics is in principle simply the formal mathematical expression of the economic logic which runs through business accounts as well. It is the experimental, pioneering fringe of the art whose established procedures the accountant applies. In the newer development of accountancy the two meet.

SOCIAL ACCOUNTING

In practice, however, over and above the fact that economics has traditionally had a theoretical slant and accountancy a practical, the two have been kept apart because they have been concerned with different parts of the economic system: the economist with nation-wide or international relationships, or with firms' or workers' relationships in so far as they are common and repeated from case to case; the accountant, on the other hand, with the concrete, individual case. This also is a main reason for the different degree of attention to theory in the two professions; for whereas the economist in his special field has been starved for exact, and indeed often for any, data, the accountant works in a world where he is buried in data of a very precise kind up to his neck. It is here that the third type of economic measurement, social accounting, has bridged the gap by facing the economist with data like those of the accountant, and bringing the accountant right into the traditional field of the economist.

Social accounting is concerned with money flows within and between territorial communities as such: what may be roughly called national income and outlay, provided it is remembered that the 'nation' in question may be anything from a village to the world as a whole. Scattered attempts at it go back a long way. Colin Clark's massive collection of national income estimates (*Conditions of Economic Progress*) includes a number of specimens from the nineteenth century; to say nothing of Gregory King's famous, and probably fairly accurate, contemporary calculation of the British national income in 1688. But the moment at which social accounting began to set the world on fire can be dated fairly precisely in 1936, the year of the publication of Keynes' *General Theory of Employment, Interest, and Money*. Keynes showed that there was no automatic force ensuring that the amount of money spent in an area would be just enough to maintain full employment without inflation. Three streams—investment, consumption (in each case both public and private), and international transactions—contribute to the total volume of demand. Their contributions must be studied separately and in detail; for they and their component series do not always move in step, or change in the same order. The data required for this will be not merely a global estimate of the national income, but a detailed analysis of the whole of the nation's accounts.

The Second World War gave a further stimulus to social accounting. It became urgent to discover, not merely the total of the country's resources, but where in detail they were to be found and how they might be mobilised. A great step forward was taken in 1941, when the first White Paper on national income and expenditure was published. A third stimulus has come from the continued high level of demand since the war, the great shortage of resources in relation to it and need for careful allocation, and the greatly increased interest in problems of the distribution of incomes.

Social accounting data have been rapidly built up, but are still far from complete. The specialists in this field overlap with those in econometrics, and are still comparatively few. The art they practise is new. Many important problems have accordingly not, as yet, been fully solved, and others have not been attempted in even a rough and ready way. We have, for instance, no estimates, with any pretence to accuracy, of the cost of overcrowded and badly designed towns, the effect on incomes in a region when new factories are settled there, or the contribution made to production by the unpaid services of housewives and members of their families. But social accounting has already grown far enough to prove not only that the logic of accountancy and econometrics is the same, but also that it is possible to combine their actual procedures in a system which uses the methods and experience of traditional accounting (including its newer developments) to answer the more fully thought-out questions which the econometrician poses.

This fusion of procedures applies first of all to the accounting framework itself: the definition of categories and design of accounts. There are still, admittedly, detailed points in dispute. The most important concerns the valuation of capital. Economists, who have been chiefly responsible for designing social accounts, treat a machine or a stock of goods as an asset for earning future income. Before it can be admitted that a profit or true surplus has been earned, enough must have been set aside to maintain the (real) income-earning capacity intact, by repair or replacement. Traditional accountancy prefers to treat invested capital instead as a delayed cost, whose original price—or rather the proportion of it represented by wear, tear, and obsolescence in a given period—must be recovered from income. The two methods give very different results at times of rising prices, when depreciation allowances based merely on the original cost of goods will leave a firm with far less than it needs to replace them with others of similar (real) income-earning capacity.

This is essentially a difference of terminology and the design of accounts, not of underlying logic. A committee of accountants may still describe profits computed on traditional principles as 'true profits',[1] which to an economist is nonsense. But on further analysis it turns out that the most serious objection of the committee to any alternative method of computation is that it 'involves departing from known measures of value and dealing in abstractions'. With much justice, accountants insist that to base what purports to be an

[1] Report of the Committee of the *Taxation of Trading Profits*, 1951 (Cmd. 8191), pars. 118 and 98.

historical record of a company's (or the nation's) activities on anything but actual, historical, receipts and payments will open the door wide to all manner of uncertainties and manipulation. There is no corresponding objection, however, to appropriating a certain sum out of the (historically recorded) surplus, on the ground that depreciation allowances arrived at on the basis of historic cost are too small for replacement; and an increasing number of accountants agree with economists that, in times when the value of money is changing rapidly, this may rightly be done.

This apart, the framework of social accounts differs from that of business accounting only in that it is concerned with the total effects of which business accounts analyse the component parts. Social accounts are built up, as regards at least those sectors of the economy where business accounting is in use, on ordinary business data. Business accounts are not standardised, nor does social accounting require that they should be, except in their broadest outlines. But it is already possible to design a single 'invariant' framework within which most of the available business data can be fairly easily assembled. In this country, the Department of Applied Economics at Cambridge has done particularly valuable work on this.

Certain remaining difficulties arise not from the nature of business accounting data but over their availability. The information actually published in business accounts, especially that compulsorily published under the Companies Acts, as apart from the more detailed data in firms' books, is often insufficient for economic analysis. It has therefore to be supplemented by enquiries such as those of the Censuses of Population, Production, and Distribution, and by more frequent specialised returns of employment, production, or the consumption of particular materials or finished goods. These will sometimes cut across the structure of firms' own accounts, or at least call for more information than they contain; for the information needed to decide a question of national policy is not necessarily important, or even relevant, to the affairs of each firm within it.

Social accounts, econometric inspiration and all, are not only produced but used in essentially the same way as business accounts. Income, as in traditional *financial accounting*, is balanced against expenditure, and reveals a surplus available for investment or distribution, or a deficit to be made good by additional income or by cutting expenditure. This is essentially the way in which the Treasury prepares for the Chancellor of the Exchequer's Budget statement, which is today recognised as the occasion for reviewing not only the Government's accounts but those of the nation as a whole. There is one important practical difference. The income of any *one* firm

17   257

(the number is important) will with only slight exceptions be earned whether or not the firm decides in advance how it is to be appropriated. The nation's will not. What the firm, by way of wages or dividends or purchases of equipment and materials, puts into the hands of the public has little to do with what the public in its turn spends on the firm's products. For the public as a whole, however, even in a country with a big volume of foreign trade, income is mainly determined by expenditure. What the public pays out determines what the public produces and takes in. If therefore the social accounts show a prospective surplus of receipts (production) over expenditure, it has to be remembered that this surplus will take the concrete form of unemployment and idle machines, not of disposable income and production, unless a corresponding amount of expenditure is arranged for in advance. A firm's surplus can be allocated after the event: the nation's must be allocated before it.

But this is a practical difference, not one of accounting principle: and even the practical difference is smaller than it at first sight seems. Even the individual firm's expenditure does in principle, and in some slight degree, influence its income; and the aggregate expenditure of all firms does very substantially influence their income. The tendency of accountants, with their eyes fixed on the single firm, to ignore this, has, in fact, in recent years been one of the most substantial and practical grounds for criticising their practice.

In other respects the parallel between the use of social and business accounts runs very close. In social as in business accounting the margin of error in *forecasting and budgeting* becomes far less when all relevant data are assembled into one accounting framework, and the inevitable gaps can be filled and errors cross-checked by reference to the rest of the figures. Some beginning has been made with *costing* on the national scale; with estimating, for instance, the real cost of different ways of regulating international trade. Social, like business, accounts show up *weak points in the economy*, by comparison with a general standard; low productivity in one sector, failure to cover depreciation in another, the dangers of a runaway rise in prices if rationing is withdrawn in a third. Once comprehensive national data have been collected on a standard basis, *international comparisons*, and analysis of the international effects of national policies, become much easier; precisely as the collection of business data from a wide selection of firms makes possible more informative firm to firm comparisons and more reliable standards. This has, in fact, been one of the most useful services of social accounting in recent years.

In general the social accountant, by presenting complete and consistent data in a framework designed specifically for answering economic questions of practical importance, clarifies the choices of public policy, narrows their margin of error, and, by his selection and presentation of material, substantially influences and takes responsibility for them. And this is precisely the role in which the business accountant, in his own more limited field, has in the last two generations emerged.

SYNTHESIS—THE ECONOMIST AND ACCOUNTANT. THE PROBLEM OF CLARITY

A working economist needs—to sum up—to understand the logic and practical use of accounting material of three kinds:

(1) Business (and public authorities') accounting practice and documents. This means not only financial accounting (operating accounts, profit and loss accounts, appropriation accounts, balance sheets), but also budgeting, costing (including standard costing), and its converse, productivity measurement.

(2) Social accounting practice, meaning, in particular, practice and standards in making up national income accounts.

(3) What might be called the scientific basis: the econometric techniques which express the underlying logic of both (1) and (2), and supply the chief tools of pioneering and experiment. This will cover the design of mathematical models in the light of economic hypotheses, and the statistical techniques for collecting and analysing the data by which these hypotheses can be related to facts.

Care must be taken here over the different language in which these three forms of accounts are expressed. Though social accounting and business accounting are increasingly well correlated, and use similar concepts, the relation between them is not always apparent. The Government's accounts are not yet fully adjusted to the economic concepts of econometrics, nor to the conventions of business and social accounting. On the other flank, economics and the econometrician use a terminology, that of marginal analysis, different from that of traditional accountancy. Marginal analysis is, of the two, the more precise way of expressing economic relations, and can be applied successfully to large aggregates of data. But it is not easy to apply to the data available for an individual firm or other small accounting unit. The confusion which this causes can be removed by abolishing one form of analysis in favour of the other; but this, whether or not it will ever be possible, is certainly not practicable in the immediate future. The alternative is to keep clearly in mind and, when necessary, to explain carefully how the two sets of categories are related, so that analysis in one set of terms can be easily translated into the other.

Clarity does not always depend on the economist–accountant alone. The extent to which he can clarify the choices facing administrators depends a good deal on the layout of the transactions with which he has to deal. This can raise, especially in the field of public finance, some very thorny issues. One or two examples might be:

(1) It is wished, for what may be assumed to be good reasons, to fix rents too low to allow the full replacement cost of houses to be recovered out of them. This can be done *either* by limiting rents to less than the replacement level, *or* by fixing them at the replacement level, but paying occupiers a subsidy equal to the difference between this and the desired level. The second procedure makes clear to all concerned what is being done, whereas the first may create in occupiers' minds a very inaccurate idea of the cost of the supplying houses.

(2) The social accounts reveal a prospective surplus of expenditure over income (the value of production at current prices). It is wished to eliminate this by a tax, and thought that the best point at which to impose the tax is on firms. One way might be to impose a profit tax falling only on those firms which earn profits, and in proportion to the profits they earn. Another might be to tax firms in proportion to their turnover: the main form of taxation in, for instance, the U.S.S.R. The first method permits rather inefficient firms to obtain a relatively high proportion of the nation's spendable income (after tax), and encourages them to remain in business. The second allows net profits and losses to correspond to relative earning power, and so brings home to inefficient firms, in the sharpest possible way, the point of the accountant's calculation of profit and loss.

(3) Government expenditure is increasing, and it is wished to raise taxes. The choice lies between income tax, a purchase tax on finished articles, normally marked by shopkeepers on price tickets, and a customs duty falling mainly on raw materials and industrial equipment. Either of the first two taxes will bring home to taxpayers the extra cost of the new public services. The third will do so much less directly, if at all.

These are cases from current practice at the time of writing. Matters such as these are important political issues, and in the heat of debates on whether such-and-such a policy should be adopted at all the question of how, if it is adopted, it can be applied so as to maintain accounting clarity is often overlooked.

Issues of this kind are by no means confined to public finance. One of the thorniest points of company law, for example, and one notably discussed by the Committee on Company Law Amendment in 1945, has been the arrangement of company transactions, and especially of those between holding and subsidiary companies, so as to give shareholders and the public a clear picture of each firm's or group's affairs.

Accounting clarity is not an overriding requirement. If complicated transactions have to be carried out, the accountant, with those who use his information, must adapt himself as best he can. But, other things being equal, that arrangement of transactions which gives most clarity is obviously to be preferred; and, while this was always so, it has become more manifestly true today. Transactions have become more complicated, notably because State intervention in economic affairs has increased. As the debate over competition, direction, and consultation, and over the economic and other sanctions, has gone on, it has also come to be seen more clearly than in the past that wages, or profits, or money costs, are only an approximate index of real cost or welfare. The accountant and the economist alike continually find it necessary to look behind the money accounts and interpret them in the light of the technical factors or social relationships underlying them. It is obviously much more difficult to do this than simply to record and map a series of money flows, taking them at their face value. It is all the more important that the transactions which underlie any important money aggregate should have a logical and, if possible, a simple structure.

Chapter 16

THE ECONOMIST AND HIS
NEIGHBOURS

FOR some purposes it is convenient to think of the social relationships in any society as a sort of sea of simultaneous equations, in which everything determines everything else. Each person
is in relationship with a circle of others, each of these in turn with
a further circle, and so on until the interlocking system of relationships includes the whole population of the earth. A change at any
point in this system will cause further changes throughout all the
rest of it. No doubt the remoter effects will often be negligible. But
in principle, at least, the ripples will spread out from the first
point of disturbance till they reach the limits of the system as a
whole.

Economic theorists, in particular, have long used this approach.
For teaching purposes it has a great deal to recommend it. It makes
it easier to break away from the common-sense idea of a straight
sequence of cause and effect, in which A determines B and B determines C, and think instead, more correctly, of a system, more or
less in equilibrium, in which A, B, and C determine one another. It
also underlines the fact which emerges in one field after another of
social study that 'True laws . . . can only be established when we
study the reactions of the organism as a whole'. In the social as in
the natural sciences, departmental barriers tend to wither away as
knowledge increases. A common body of basic concepts emerges,
and the unity of the whole field becomes apparent. An interesting
example is the way in which Mr. P. W. S. Andrews' restatement of
the theory of competition has built a bridge between this branch of
economics and the theory of the small group, as developed by
sociologists and psychologists. It is instructive to use an approach
which emphasises this unity from the start.

However, for practical purposes it is necessary to be more modest.

> '. . . and still the wonder grew
> that one small head could carry all he knew.'

Maybe: but even the stoutest of small heads splits after a time. The
economist or accountant who sets out to master the field outlined

in the last chapter has a fair life's work in front of him. The need for specialisation is indeed greater in the social than in the natural sciences, because the data are so much less exact, and the ground which can usefully be covered in any one series of calculations is correspondingly more limited. One becomes used in social science to working with basic data carrying a margin of error of 5%, 10%, or 20%; and this seems likely to remain the case for as far ahead as can be foreseen.

Some social scientists choose to specialise in an *analytic* science, that is in the study of some one aspect (economic, political, psychological, sociological) of social situations of all kinds. Others specialise in a *synthetic* field, that is in some relatively narrow range of problems (public administration, industrial relations, local communities) which are studied from the angle of each and all of the social sciences. This is, of course, parallel to what happens in the natural sciences, where one man will specialise in physics or chemistry and another in engineering or metallurgy. Each type of approach is useful, and the two are complementary. Neither can claim to lead, by itself, to the whole truth. The industrial relations expert no doubt knows something of the economics or psychology of the labour market; but he is fooling himself if he thinks he knows as much economics as the economist or as much psychology as the psychologist. But these also in their turn are fooling themselves if they imagine that they can apply or even develop their special knowledge to the best advantage except in the wider perspective of those who 'study the reactions of the organism as a whole'.

This raises a problem of great importance for the practice of social science and the outlook of the social scientist. Do the various specialists in social science simply operate alongside one another, asking one another's advice as the occasion may demand, or do they more positively and actively contribute to building up one another's knowledge? Do they work in parallel, or constitute a team—and if the latter, then in what sense? This question has been particularly long and actively discussed in the case of the relation between economics and ethics.

ECONOMICS AND ETHICS

The classic British study of the relation between economics and ethics is Robbins' *Nature and Significance of Economic Science*. Here on the one hand, says Robbins in effect, are the natural resources of the earth, and the technicians with their knowledge of how to turn them to account. These are part of the economist's data. He should know what the engineer or the chemist can do with the materials at hand. But he has no responsibility for how they do it, nor for teaching them to do it better. He and they work independently, though taking account of each other's existence and actions. There on the other hand stand people, with their preferences or values. They have their indifference-maps, showing not merely whether they prefer one article or service to another but whether they prefer this bundle or combination of goods to that, or remain indifferent between them. These valuations also are part of the economist's data. By all means let him study people's values, both their more superficial, temporary, and localised cultural norms and the more fundamental and universal ethical values behind them. By doing so he will see more clearly how to do his own job: which is to show how these *given* preferences can best be satisfied out of the *given* resources and technical possibilities. But the accent is always on *given*. It is not for the economist to say what values and preferences are to be, nor to pass judgement on them: any more than he is to pass judgement on the activities of the engineer or the chemist. Or, to put it a little differently, the economist is concerned with what, as a matter of *fact*, is the utilisation of resources which best corresponds to the set of values given to him; and facts and valuations are things of quite distinct sorts, on different planes of discourse.

It is sometimes said that by this formulation Robbins, in some atheistical or agnostical way, drives a wedge between economics and ethics. He leaves economics 'value-free', in the sense that it need take no account of duties and rights. This is, of course, nonsense. Robbins is as well aware as anyone that economics is the handmaid of ethics. He is discussing which field of study is appropriate to the economist and to the moral philosopher; he is certainly not denying the connection between the two. But his reasons for making the division of labour as sharp as he does need more careful scrutiny. For to say that facts and ethical values are on different planes of discourse is at best a half-truth.

Ethics may be defined as 'the ultimate principles of integration of human society and action'. They rest on a small number of judgements which are accepted either *a priori*, that is because they seem self-evident, or on the authority of Revelation, that is from a supernatural source beyond human experience. For practical purposes these may be reduced to two:

(1) That it is right to put any person in what from his point of view—in the long run and all things considered—is a more preferred position rather than in one which is less preferred.

(2) That the preferences (arrived at in the long run and all things considered) of all human beings carry equal weight.

Both these propositions would be accepted by many people in many societies as self-evident; the first, probably, more easily than the second. In the Western world they have come to be very generally accepted on the direct or indirect authority of the Christian revelation; direct for those who are Christians, indirect for those who have absorbed from society cultural norms established under direct Christian influence at earlier times. The two propositions are, in fact, merely a 'natural law' statement of the two great Christian commandments, to love God and one's neighbour.

From these *a priori* or revealed propositions others can be directly deduced. Suppose, for instance, a case involving a conflict of interests: one in which, however the decision goes, someone must gain and someone else must lose. If all people's preferences carry equal weight, and it is right to put everyone in the most preferred position open, it may be deduced that the decision should be settled by comparing the intensity with which the gainer prefers his new position to his old with that with which the loser prefers his old position to his new. If the gainer is more in favour than the loser is against, the decision should be affirmative; and vice versa. Here also Revelation, for those who accept it, steps in to point out how, ultimately, all such contradictions can be reconciled, and all can reach what for them is the position of 'maximum' preference.

But cases which can thus be decided by referring directly or indirectly to *a priori* or revealed principles account for only a very small fraction of the whole range of ethical judgements. The judgement 'This policy is right' certainly implies acceptance of the basic *a priori* or revealed arguments. But it also implies some such strictly factual, scientific statement as:

'Consideration has been given to all the persons *in fact* concerned in this case, directly or indirectly: to what *in fact* constitutes a preferred position (in the long run and all things considered) for each of them: and to the intensity with which each *in fact* prefers any one position to any other. Consideration has also been given to the possibilities of action which are *in fact* open. In the light of these considerations, and offsetting gains against losses, the course of action which will put this whole group of people in—on balance—the most preferred position attainable is as follows. This therefore (given the initial *a priori* or revealed judgements) should be done.'

It is possible and indeed necessary to distinguish among the rules which emerge in this way from a combination of factual analysis and *a priori* judgements. Some are general, fixed, and permanent, while some, at the level of 'middle principles' (Chapter 1) change from one time and place to another. But at both levels alike, ethics represent the 'law of the situation' which satisfies human reason, and compels assent, because it completely corresponds, not only to one or two *a priori* judgements, but to reality as actually understood and experienced by individuals and social groups. If one thinks of society, as at the start of this chapter, as a sea of simultaneous equations expressing relationships all of which determine one another, one can also think of ethical rules as being those whose application would produce a state of total equilibrium in these relationships. That is, a state such that there was no longer any tendency arising from the 'law of the situation' for relationships and patterns of behaviour to change, apart from changes provided for in those patterns themselves. St. Augustine put the same thought more elegantly when he described the 'peace' which he defined as the natural goal of society as 'rest in good order'.

There is not much sign here of ethics being on a different plane of discourse from facts. For the most strictly factual investigations leading up to the formulation of scientific laws start, like ethical enquiries, from an *a priori*, unverifiable assumption; namely, that there is and will continue to be enough regularity and order in the world to make prediction on the basis of past experience possible. They go on, as do ethical enquiries, to consider all the facts relevant to the investigation. Finally, on this double basis of factual enquiry and *a priori* assumption, they conclude in the form 'this has the following relation to that', or 'if this is done, that will follow'. This is just the process of thought from which ethical propositions also arise.

There is, however, a half-truth in Robbins' formulation. Factual and ethical propositions are no doubt constructed in the same way, out of elements of the same sort. But ethical propositions, derived as they are from a summary of *all* human experience, are based on a particularly complicated analysis and particularly wide range of facts. Since there is never unlimited time for puzzling out solutions, they must often therefore be vaguer and less well founded than propositions of other kinds. People make propositions of various sorts. There are those which can be set out in full with scientific precision, and have been thoroughly verified by controlled observation and experiment. There are others belonging to the sphere of 'non-logical' thought, such as those which the craftsman makes after a lifetime's experience. These cannot perhaps be set out in full, but are nevertheless thoroughly verified. There are others again, whether logical or non-logical, for which verification is hoped in future, but has not yet occurred. And lastly there are metaphysical propositions of a kind which cannot within the range of ordinary human experience be verified at all. For some propositions evidence is easily and quickly available, while others depend on long chains of previous reasoning. Ethical propositions, because they are ultimate and depend on a very wide comparison in space and time, are of the latter kind. They tend therefore also to fall into the categories unverified or non-logical, if not metaphysical. Life must go on; action cannot be held up for ever while philosophers debate and computers count: there must be rules to guide it, interpretations to give it meaning. It becomes necessary to conclude on such evidence as there is that such and such *must* be the case, even though it has not been possible to work it out fully, or verify it completely. At any given moment current thinking about ethics necessarily includes a rather large dose of probability and of *a priori* argument.

Robbins points out how in the economic field this recourse to the unverified, non-logical or metaphysical may begin very low down. We can as a matter of verified fact compare the economic welfare— the purchasing power—of an individual this year and last. Suppose that the man in question, with his tastes as they are now, can buy more goods to suit these tastes this year than he could last year. Suppose also that, had his tastes this year been the same as last, he could still have bought more goods to suit those tastes this year than last. Then it can be said, in a perfectly factual sense, that his income or economic welfare has increased. This comparison can be repeated for any number of individuals. But suppose we want to compare the real income of a whole community this year and last? Normally, there will have been some change, even if only a slight one, in the distribution of incomes. Some will have gained, others lost. We can make the comparison only if we know whether the losers' loss outweighs the gainers' advantage, or vice versa. But this we can tell only by getting inside these people's minds and seeing how they feel. And this, Robbins argues, we cannot do. We have to get round it by some agreement on what 'must' be the case; as, for instance, that other things being equal a closer approach to equality 'must' increase welfare.

Robbins, it is true, overstates his case. If we admit that other minds exist at all, we can hardly deny—for the evidence is of the same kind —that we also know or can know something about the state of those minds. But it is also true that such knowledge can be precise only in the case of individuals and small groups. When it comes to judging, for instance, the effect on welfare of redistributing income between the United Kingdom and its Colonies, it becomes very rough and ready indeed. It can indeed be argued that it is practicable to judge how the welfare even of individuals and families changes from time to time only by bringing in some more or less verified conception of what their needs *must* be: for their tastes change in an irregular way, are often inconsistent, and are hard to know accurately. The *average* worker, or the *average* bank clerk, as he figures in the statistics, behaves consistently enough. The actual individual and his family do not. The margin between what is and is not clearly known is not permanent; social science has shifted it a long way in recent years. But it is still true that even for description, let alone for ethical statements, it is necessary to have recourse to a great deal of unverified estimation.

Here, clearly, is justification for the idea that 'facts' and 'values' are on separate planes. Economics is concerned with events and relations which can by definition ('the measuring rod of money' is after all the criterion of what does and does not belong to economics) be measured with some accuracy and checked. To move in this world is, or should be, a very different matter from moving in the world of ethical thinking. Here is good reason—even apart from the danger of loading one or the other group with more work than they can digest—for assigning the investigation of ethics to one set of men and of economic events to another.

What cannot be admitted is that this 'division of labour' necessarily implies 'different planes'. When Robbins says that 'there is no logical connection between the two types of generalisation', he seems to be making a double confusion. The first is between ethics and cultural norms. These latter—actual beliefs and motive patterns, as apart from the equilibrium, represented by ethics, towards which these tend—are facts: for practical purposes, very important facts. But they are not factual in the same sense as ethics: not, that is to say, the true 'law of the situation' deduced from a general review of the state of affairs in each time or place. People's ideas and norms are one of the facts of reality which ethics have to reconcile, but are in themselves at best approximations to ethics; not ethics but the current ideas about ethics. Secondly, Robbins seems to confuse the empirical facts of ethics and their symbolic underpinning. One of the chief functions of ritual, magic, and to some extent religion is to symbolise the fundamental beliefs of a society, notably those which reach beyond the level of scientifically analysed and verified fact, and to provide them with an emotional support. But the emotional scaffolding is not the structure itself. Ethics belongs, as much as economics, to the field of empirical statements, not to that of symbolism.

THE MANAGEMENT ANALOGY

All this, however, merely shows that ethics and economics (or other social sciences) make propositions of the same kind. It does not yet show that there is any special link between these propositions: that one group of them depends on another, as apart from merely existing alongside it. But in actual fact the propositions of the various social sciences do depend on one another. The right analogy for the relations between them would seem to be provided by management theory. Chester Barnard, in his study of *The Functions of the Executive*, points out how in any firm or department there exist various moral systems (as he calls them), or more correctly cultural norms. The chief and hardest business of the executive is to weld these partial, limited syntheses into a wider whole; to reconcile the claims of family, friends, departmental loyalties, professional codes, in the light of the needs of the common enterprise. The moral philosopher (anyone, that is, who makes ethical propositions) has also to make a general synthesis in order to arrive at his 'ultimate principles of integration of human society and action'. A synthesis of what? Clearly, like the executive, he will build up his general synthesis out of partial, local syntheses. He takes the conclusions arrived at by the economist, the politician, the sociologist, or the student or practitioner of industrial relations or family casework: their analyses of the possibilities open in their particular fields, and of how the factors with which they are each concerned can best contribute to the generally accepted purpose of raising people from less to more preferred positions. He observes how in a well-functioning society these separate analyses, by a process of successive approximation and independent adjustment—each taking account of the findings of the rest—become more and more consistent with one another. He projects this process into the future, and considers how the approximation could be improved. And so he arrives at his estimate of the rules of life most consistent with the 'total equilibrium' of relationships, or the 'peace' which is 'rest in good order', described above.

Since it is thus the case not merely that the moral philosopher's conclusions provide guidance for the economist but that the economist's syntheses are among the foundations on which the philosopher builds, the relation between philosopher and economist—to follow the management analogy further—is one not simply of a division of labour but of team-work.

David Lilienthal, in his study of the T.V.A., underlines the contrast between an enterprise where various specialists work side by side, coordinated only by some manager to whom they report, and one where all concentrate, certainly, on their specialities, but are conscious of their share in a common enterprise in which every part influences every other. It is not possible, in complex and technical matters, for some central manager to absorb from his subordinates enough of their knowledge of the facts and opportunities in their special fields to do the coordination entirely on his own. This is true especially because even in the most factual and technical field 'hunch', or non-logical thinking, often difficult to make convincing to outsiders, necessarily plays a great part. Each subordinate must take responsibility, not merely for applying general principles delivered from above but for considering in the light of his special knowledge how the common purpose can best be shaped and developed. To devise and express the common purpose of an enterprise is a matter of team-work, not dictatorship; though this is not, of course, to deny that Chester Barnard's general executive, or his counterpart the moral philosopher, has also his place as leader of the team.

And so also it is with the relation of ethics and economics. The economist, or practitioner in economics, must be aware that in devising his own analyses and syntheses, within his limited field as defined at the end of the last chapter, he is also contributing to define the common, general purpose expressed in ethics. No doubt his contribution covers only a fraction of the field, and it is not for him alone to take the final decision on where, if at all, it is fitted into the general framework. But his contribution is as important as that of anyone else, and it is one which only he can make. He must normally take all that is covered by ethics and the other social sciences for granted, and simply apply their findings in his own field. But he can see, with his technical knowledge, not merely where these findings are relevant to economics but where they in their turn need amendment in the light of economic experience; and often he can see this where no one else could. He has therefore a responsibility for shaping ethical as well as merely economic rules.

This analogy with management can be extended (Chart III) to cover the whole field of the theory and practice of the social sciences. It is usual to distinguish between 'line' management, concerned with all that happens in a plant, or department, or geographical area, and 'functional' management, the specialist concerned with some one aspect or technique covering only a fraction of a field of action. The specialist, functional manager may issue an order in his own right to his own specialist subordinates; among his own collaborators he has the status of a line manager. But he may not do so to anyone else

CHART III

The Managerial Structure of the Social Sciences

General Studies

(overall synthesis—general management)

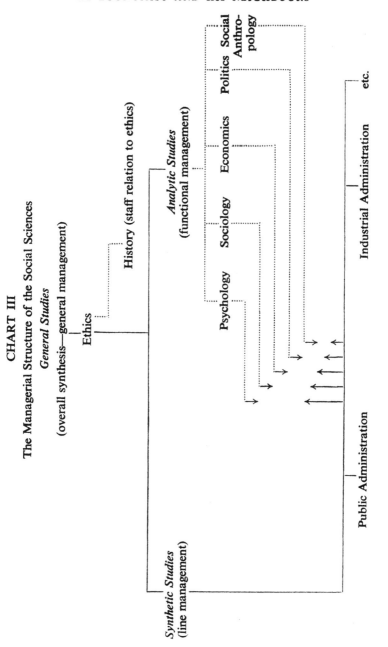

in the unit with which he works. His business is to advise and to draw attention to approved technical procedures, leaving the decision to the line manager; though his advice carries authority of two sorts. There is in the first place that of his own technical knowledge (the 'law of the situation' in his own field). Secondly, the line manager who ignores advice or approved procedures without good reason will find himself called to account by his own (line) superior. By this division of the roles of line and functional managers the unity of management is preserved, and the main decisions about what is to be done in any unit are taken by managers who have the whole of its activities in view.

A further distinction is that between line or functional and 'staff' management. Staff managers have no independent authority of their own. They are assistants to managers of one of the other sorts, supplying them with data, seeing to the transmission of their orders, but in all things acting as an extension of their superior's personality, with no independent authority of their own.

Following out this analogy (Chart III), it would seem that:

(1) *Ethics* corresponds to the highest level of 'line' management; that at which, as Chester Barnard says, all the various claims upon those engaged in any branch of social action have finally to be reconciled in the light of the experience and proposals transmitted from lower levels.

(2) *History* would seem to fall into a 'staff' relationship to ethics. For history attempts an overall, synthetic view of a certain range of events, and of the factors involved in them, but does not itself draw conclusions for action. This is precisely the function of the staff assistant to a general manager who is deputed to establish the facts on which the general manager can make a decision. He is establishing them at the level (so to speak) of the general manager, and not as they would appear to some more junior official. But he does this for and on behalf of the general manager, not in order to take decisions of his own.

(3) *Synthetic social studies*, and their practitioners, are concerned with the whole of some range of activities, such as 'industrial administration' or 'public administration' or 'social work'. They correspond to the lower levels of 'line' management. Like the general manager or moral philosopher, practitioners at this level take a comprehensive view of all the factors entering into their field. They are therefore particularly well qualified to prescribe what is to be done in it, though they may, of course, be overridden by 'general management' itself. Their views on what ought and ought not to be done in their

own fields will carry particular weight with 'higher management' when it comes to determining ethical rules, the equivalent of a firm's general policy. And they are entitled in their own field to take decisions even against the advice of 'functional' specialists such as economists, though they will be expected to listen and, normally, defer to these specialists' advice in their own special lines.

(4) *Analytic social studies*, and their practitioners, correspond to 'functional' management. The economist or the psychologist is sovereign over the accounts department or the vocational guidance office. As regards the broader purposes of society he advises rather than prescribes. But it is 'advice' with a sting in it. The distinction made in the last chapter between the book-keeper and the 'broad-gauge controllership executive' applies here. The economist or psychologist advise, not in a 'staff' relationship, as the mere extension of someone else's personality, but as independent managers in their own right, possessed of knowledge which may and should influence general policy in ways which only they can perceive, and entitled and indeed bound to press their view of what is to be done right up to the highest level of decision.

The relations between the 'functional' or 'analytic' social sciences themselves would seem to be similar to those between the functional departments of a business. An accounts department and a personnel department are both functional departments. But the accounts department employs personnel, and the personnel department keeps accounts, and in each case the relation between the two departments is the same as that between a functional and a line department. The personnel assistant who happens to be stationed in the accounts department has the same relation to the manager of that department as he would to, for example, the works manager if he happened to be stationed in the works. He is under his orders; but he is also bound to advise him in matters within his competence, and he has a right to expect that his advice will be taken unless there are strong reasons to the contrary. So also, at the academic level, the economist uses many concepts and much material supplied by the sociologist, and vice versa. It is for the economist to decide how much of this material is relevant to economics, and how it is to be used. But the sociologist has a right and duty to advise him of this, and the economist is bound to hear and respect this advice. And, of course, he is bound to do as much for the sociologist—or for any of his other colleagues in the social sciences—in return.

Chapter 17

THE CHANGING BACKGROUND

THE theme of this book has been the complex interplay of competitive, directive, and consultative mechanisms, and of the economic, political, and social sanctions behind these. The economist of a hundred or even of forty or fifty years ago lived in a relatively simple world, where the economic sanction and competitive mechanisms loomed much larger than they do today. That people today understand that a more balanced and complex analysis is necessary is due in part to the development of the social sciences themselves. But it is also and above all due to changes in the social framework in which the economist operates; the social norms, the personality patterns, and the institutions by which he is surrounded. Even where these have not actually changed, there is today often a new appreciation of what they mean. Though it is not the economist's business to analyse these changes, it is his business to understand them or even—as just described, in the last chapter—to promote and assist their analysis. Often enough, no doubt, he can take the existing state of culture and institutions for granted. But there are many economic problems—those of industrial relations or underdeveloped territories, for example—where changes in these variables may be far more important even in the short run, let alone the long, than any variable with which the economist as such is directly concerned.

CULTURAL CHANGE

The cultural changes most immediately relevant to economics over the last two hundred years were briefly summed up in Chapter 1 under the headings of the eotechnic, palaeotechnic, and neotechnic ages. The rise of modern machine industry opened the palaeotechnic age, the Dark Age when the struggle to bring industrial power under effective social control was barely begun. As this struggle has proceeded, in the course of the transition through the palaeotechnic to the neotechnic age, Britain has passed through at least three main phases. One was wholly within the first of these ages, one lies within the second, and one has been transitional between the two. These phases can be characterised in various ways.

First, in terms of wealth and its uses. In the first generations after the Industrial Revolution the accent was on production and the size of incomes. On the consumption side there was a tendency to vulgarity and ostentation, to accent the mere quantity of expenditure, which gave rise to Veblen's famous analysis of 'conspicuous waste'. In a second period, roughly since 1880, transitional between the palaeotechnic and the neotechnic ages, the accent shifted to the stability and fair distribution of incomes; production problems dropped rather into the background. In the last decade the accent has begun to shift again. The earlier emphases on production, stability and distribution are not forgotten. Production problems, indeed, have come back to their old importance. But there seems also to be a new and growing interest in the quality of consumption. It is less visible perhaps as yet in Britain than in America. But it is marked even in Britain in such matters as the design of houses and furniture, in clothing standards, or in changing food, drink, and leisure habits. And it is, of course, precisely what might be expected at the end of two generations in which for the first time the mass of the people have become able to earn a substantial margin over bare necessities, and the grosser problems of instability and inequality have been solved. The skilled design of expenditure by the mass of the people—not merely by a limited upper class—may well prove to be the hall-mark of neotechnic economics.

Secondly, and particularly relevant here, there has been a change in the relative importance of the different sanctions and mechanisms of social control. There was a liberal age. There has been, recently ended, a socialist age. And an age seems now to be opening which might best be called federalist. The accent in the generations immediately after the Napoleonic wars, the liberal age, was on individual aims and on competition—political, social, but above all economic —to attain them. From the 1880's to the 1940's it changed, and fell more and more on collective aims and non-competitive action, and especially on State direction and 'scientific management'. The characteristic interest of this age was in politics, in the wide sense of types or forms of social control sanctioned by formal, non-economic authority. Since the end of the 'forties the accent seems to be shifting again to 'social' objectives, that is to problems of less formal human relations in the family—as a human group, not as an economic problem—or in the neighbourhood, the working group, or the plant or firm. There is no question of going back on the findings of previous generations about the value of economic and political mechanisms, or of competition or direction. Direction and scientific management have come to stay, and so have political democracy

275

and economic competition. But consultation and the 'social' sanction —control by the informal pressures of group opinion—are coming into their own. And, significantly, the social sciences specially concerned with these things—sociology, social psychology, and cultural anthropology—have been coming rapidly to the fore alongside the hitherto dominant subjects of economics and politics. There is as yet no single word which sums up the new age, as 'liberal' and 'socialist' sum up those which went before. But, if one thinks of how in the liberal age the accent was on the individual, in the socialist age on the State, and how it is now coming to be spread more evenly over the whole range of intermediate social units, the right word would certainly seem to be 'federalist'.

Thirdly, as the three phases of recent social history have moved on, the area of the world of which the social scientist or the practical politician normally takes account has also changed. The liberal age was cosmopolitan, though in the sense not of world government but of competition between sovereign states. In the socialist age this cosmopolitanism in one sense broke down; the accent of social policy was no longer on free trade or overseas investment, but on the problems of direction, and particularly economic direction, within the largest units of executive authority then available, namely States. On the other hand, the socialist age was also the time when an important new range of machinery for international consultation and, ultimately, direction came into being. The British Commonwealth took its modern form. The League of Nations and the International Labour Organisation came out of the First World War; the United Nations and a wide range of other new international machinery, touched on above in Chapter 14, emerged after the second. In the present, federalist generation the conceptions of the two previous ages look like being combined. It is recognised on the one hand that the liberal age was right to insist on spreading trade and development over the widest possible area, and on respecting the existence, the solidarity, and therefore the independent sphere of action of national States. But it also seems likely, in view of the proved needs outlined in previous chapters, that the tendency to set up more and more international mechanisms of consultation and direction will go on.

Looking back over the trends in these three periods, it is not too fanciful to think of them as running together into one; the fulfilment of the prophecy of Marx and Lenin of the 'withering away of the State'. Modern industrial society, as the classic writers of Marxism saw it, may be expected to pass through three stages. One is the phase of liberal capitalism, with its accent on economics and competition.

A second is that of socialism, concerned with correcting the grosser defects of a competitive order and with guaranteeing a tolerable standard of life to all. Then comes a third stage, which both Marx and Lenin deliberately left vague, but which would seem to have two characteristics. The first is that supplies of at any rate the more important consumer goods reach saturation point; food supplies, for example, become such as to permit an 'optimum' diet as defined by Orr, 'a state of well-being such that no improvement can be effected by a change in the diet'. So, secondly, the 'managerial society' characteristic of the socialist age fades away. Management need no longer be coercive. It relies now on consultation, not direction. And in particular the power and influence of the State withers away.

The liberal and socialist ages, so far as Britain is concerned, are now past. The grosser defects of competition have been corrected, and a tolerable, if hardly luxurious, minimum standard of life has been guaranteed to all. A comparatively small further increase in supplies, and progress with existing programmes such as might well be expected within the next one or two generations, should make it possible to reach 'optimum', or at any rate highly satisfying, standards in such services as housing, health, education, or food. And meantime the accent of social policy is shifting, as predicted, from direction to consultation, and from the political sanction—formal authority—to informal social relationships. And the power and influence of the national State is being undermined from two sides. International mechanisms grow in importance, and—whether or not any State formally gives up part of its legal sovereignty—bind its decisions in fact in an increasing number of ways. And within each State the heavy concentration on State authority and politics characteristic of the socialist age seems to be giving way to a more even spread of power and influence among the social groups—family, working group, trade union, local community—intermediate between the State and the individual.

It might well be asked how it is that the progress which has led Britain from the comparatively simple economic, political, and social concepts of the nineteenth century to the more complex views of today has proceeded as smoothly as it has done. The credit for this goes to a further cultural factor, which may in the end prove more important than all the rest together. This is the framework provided by Anglo-Saxon Protestant theology and ethics, which proved most admirably adapted to maintaining continuity and direction at a time of rapid social change.

Major social and technical innovations were coming into the world in the nineteenth century, after the Industrial Revolution, at probably twenty times the rate of the fifteenth century, and two hundred times the rate of the Middle Ages. Yet the experience of social movements at that time showed—as it shows to this day—that each major stage of adaptation in a society's ideas may take anything from one or two generations up to five or six. The process described in this book, for example, whereby the new industrial forces have been gradually brought under social control, has already been spread over four or five generations, and is still incomplete. A typical process for solving a major group of social problems would be thirty or so years' discussion and experiment, leading in the last five or ten years of that period to the definition of the problems and the invention of working models for a solution; followed by thirty years' effort to secure the general adoption of these models, leading to a 'break-through' to success in the last ten or so of these years. This pattern has already been run through twice in British social history since the Napoleonic wars.

There is no necessary contradiction between this slow, stepwise pattern of learning and the flood of innovations in the last couple of centuries. For one of the things which can be learnt is, precisely, how to digest innovations quickly. Nevertheless, in the face of this torrent of new experience it has been hard to maintain continuity and direction. The art of rapid digestion is certainly being learnt. The progressive firm, the 'open' community, the 'open' family—open to the outside world and all its influences, not turned in on itself or confining its friendships and interests to a narrow circle—have become the ideal. But this ideal is even now not accepted everywhere. And meantime problems present themselves, and even in the most 'open' of societies may take a lifetime and more to solve. There is inevitably a danger of impatience, a tendency to be tempted away from the path of steady advance by superficial solutions and half-truths. And, once a wrong turning has been taken, it may take as long to regain the right road as it would have done to reach a correct solution along that road in the first place. These possibilities are strikingly illustrated in, for instance, the history of the anarchist-Marxist-Stalinist family of Continental labour movements.

In its classical form, as it existed, for instance, towards the end of the nineteenth century, the Anglo-Saxon Protestant ethic provided an extraordinarily successful formula for keeping control of a situation of this kind. It left the scientist, the politician, and the business man full freedom in their day-to-day activities. Detailed ethical rules were seen as emerging from current practice rather than from *a priori* logic. In a changing world, where only the practitioner can be fully up to date on the details of practice, only he, and not any outsider

—not even the moral philosopher or theologian—seemed likely to be able to formulate these detailed rules correctly. But, secondly, this freedom was limited and standards of judgement were provided by a body of firmly held views on the nature and significance of human nature, rights, and duties. The practitioner was to be free, but only within a firm and clear definition of the purposes to be served.

This approach—a few basic value judgements, worked out empirically into rules applicable to current facts—corresponds exactly to what was said in Chapter 16 about the right relation between economics and ethics. For guiding and yet encouraging change and development, it proved far more successful than any other approach tried in the same period. The relation between capitalism, the labour movement—British and American, above all —and the Protestant ethic has for this reason become one of the most striking and vigorously discussed chapters of economic and social history. It also, however, provides one of the chief queries for the future. For the religious belief on which the Protestant ethic and its twin standards of freedom and obligation were erected has now in Britain faded. What new foundation for the social framework will be laid in its place remains to be seen. Christian belief itself may revive, or a new, naturalistic ethic may replace it. This choice is of key importance for the future guidance of the complex British system of social control.

PERSONALITY

Personality studies and their practical application have advanced fast over the last generation, and have arrived among other things at distinctly unflattering conclusions about the attention paid to personality in economic life.

The methods traditionally used to fit the right man to the right job have come in for particularly powerful criticism. War Office psychologists estimate that in 1940, under traditional methods of selection, half the men recruited for the Pioneer Corps were capable of better work than they would ever be asked for, whereas half of those taken for tank regiments were incapable of doing the ordinary duties expected of them. An Industrial Health Research Board survey in 1942–4 showed $28\frac{1}{2}\%$ of the men and 36% of the women in a sample of light and medium engineering workers to be suffering from some degree of neurosis due to their home or industrial circumstances. A study in 1947 of the recruitment and training of nurses showed that about 30% of student nurses were below the standard of intelligence needed to profit by their training, whereas about a third of all unqualified assistant nurses could have profited from a full training. A more recent American study, however, absolves the selectors and trainers from at least part of the blame for this repeated lack of correspondence between personalities and jobs. It shows how in American industry the number of jobs demanding medium to high intelligence and other qualifications falls far short of the number of workers available for them; the deficiency is not merely in selection but in the design of jobs.

In a way, one might almost speak of the 'discovery' in these various enquiries of personality and the problems it presents for industry. No doubt managers have always needed and had a good deal of craft skill in dealing with these and related matters; the problem of older workers, for example, or of new entrants to industry. But now these problems have moved out of the realm of 'hunch' into that of accurate measurement and deliberate planning. They are perceived in a new way, and their solution calls for a new skill in direction. They contribute in that way to the new, more complex outlook on the problems of social and especially economic control in recent times.

Readiness to accept this very complex outlook has been helped by certain changes which have taken place in personality patterns. Kurt Lewin, comparing typical American and German personality patterns, comments on how the former take a shape particularly favourable to the continual adjustments of a society in a state of change. A 'typical' American, he suggests, is distinguished from an equally typical German by a much higher degree of flexibility in relationships not central to his personality, combined with much firmer attachment to a small hard core of central beliefs. This, it will be noticed, is a personality pattern corresponding closely to the 'Anglo-Saxon Protestant ethic' as described above. Those who have such a personality pattern are likely to find it relatively easy to adopt the balanced and well-directed and yet at the same time flexible and dynamic approach to economic or other social problems with which this book has been concerned. This pattern has, in fact, been at least partly accepted by wide sections of the British people: though as yet with reservations. Zweig, in his *British Worker*, comments that 'in regard to operations and processes the managers form what may be called the adaptive class, while the working classes represent the established and traditional forces intent to keep things as they are.' But, he adds:

'Everyone is conservative in some things and an innovator in others. I would say that the working man is strongly conservative in industrial processes, in the workshop, in his union, in his way of life, but is an innovator as regards the social framework as a whole.' (p. 82.)

That is probably a fair enough summary of the extent to which flexibility has entered into British personality patterns: halfway, perhaps, but not so far as the United States.

There is also, of course, the more fundamental and also more difficult question of how far British people possess the hard central core of ethical norms which this personality pattern requires. It certainly existed in the nineteenth century. It is more doubtful whether it does so today. Rowntree and Lavers concluded, in their massive survey in 1951 of *English Life and Leisure*, that Britain is, in fact, 'living on the spiritual capital of the past' (pp. 226 and 372). The hard core is still there; but it is in danger of crumbling away. But this whole matter requires far more detailed investigation than has yet been made.

There are other more tangible tendencies in personality patterns in Britain. People in Britain have become predominantly middle class (Table 1), about two-thirds of all working men being in the

TABLE 1.   Class structure in Great Britain, 1951

Males, aged 15 or over: percentage in each social class

Class	Percentage of all males, 15+	Occupations typical of the class
I	3·3	Judge, priest, army officer, graduate engineer, physicist, company director, administrative Civil Servant
II	14·8	Shopkeeper, teacher, social worker, manager, executive Civil Servant
III	52·5	Foreman, pattern-maker, barber, bus driver, clerk.
IV	16·4	Machine minder, platelayer, loco fireman, barman, general farm worker.
V	13·0	Labourer, watchman, office cleaner.

From the *Census of Population*, 1951 (1% Sample)

The classification is, of course, to some extent arbitrary. It is questionable for example, whether 'general farm workers' should not be in Grade III.

range from (inclusive) skilled workers, foremen, or clerks, up to teachers, managers, and executive grade civil servants. If the upper middle class is included the proportion goes up to 70%. They have, by world standards, high and assured incomes, wide opportunities and high social mobility. It is not surprising that, when Zweig contrasts working-class 'Peter' of the last generation with 'George' of this, he makes 'George' talk about the blooming boss and the bloody job in the authentic accents of that fine old middle-class figure John Hampden; if not perhaps with as fine a command of pure English. The worker today:

'regards himself more as a junior partner entitled to voice his opinions on all basic issues which involve conditions of work or the prospect of employment. The workplace on which his lot depends is *his* workplace; it is a social unit of the first importance. He has acquired a new sense of his importance and he asks that his dignity shall be respected . . .'. (*The British Worker*, 1952, p. 122.)

This has been a powerful influence, as Zweig points out, in the development of consultation within the firm, and, in general, in forcing managements to take a broader point of view than that of their nineteenth-century predecessors.

A particularly important change—or rather tendency to change, since it is still incomplete—has been the professionalisation of management, that is the adoption by managers of the personality pattern which has traditionally characterised professional men. A professional man, judging by the experience of the older professions, can be recognised by two criteria. He practises a complicated technique, designed to cope with the full complexity of a problem. And he practises it with full regard to the complexity of the problem; he respects, that is, the claims of consumers, his own colleagues, and all others involved, and does not seek only his own self-interest. For practical purposes the existence of professional men implies that of a professional organisation, which sees to the teaching and development of its members' technique and enforces professional ethics. But we are concerned here not with this institutional side but with the outlook of the men within the institution.

In one rather obvious sense management has been becoming professionalised for some time. Lawyers, accountants, scientists, and members of the various technical professions have played an increasing part in it (Table 2) and brought their outlook with them. But this is a case of importing a professional outlook from outside. More important and fundamental is the change which has taken place in the outlook of business men themselves.

The point is not, as it is sometimes said to be, that the individualistic qualities needed to survive in the intense economic competition of the nineteenth century are no longer called for today. It remains true of even the largest concerns, public or private, that— to quote a former Research Controller of Imperial Chemical Industries on the way a new product comes to be taken up—'one or two men must stake their reputations whilst everyone else sits upon the

THE CHANGING BACKGROUND

TABLE 2. Directors of 436 British public companies, 1936

Companies with capital of:	Directors qualified as lawyers, accountants, and technicians	
	Per 100 directors	Per 100 firms
Under £100,000	5·8	11–14
£100,000–500,000	9·7	23–25
Over £500,000	11·8	29–53

Florence, in *Journal of the Royal Statistical Society*, 1947.

fence'. But the environment in which these qualities are exercised has changed. The British business man today finds that his choice of a service to render to the public, and of ways and means of rendering it, depends much less than a hundred years ago on the simple ability to persuade consumers to buy and the owners of labour power or raw materials to sell, in an open competitive market. He has still to do this. But to keep in business he has also to adapt himself to a considerable amount of direction—over wages and working conditions, for instance, or building licensing, the control of location, or the rationing of products or raw materials—and to consultation with the government, labour, and other firms in his industry. The same applies within his firm, where he is more likely than in the past to be not an owner with full personal control but a managing director responsible to a board, composed, more often than not, principally of his own colleagues. And he has to attend much more than he did to the structure of formal and informal relationships within his firm—the political and social sanctions—as apart from purely economic questions of wages, salaries, and dividends. He tends everywhere to become a *professional* manager, skilled in using all three major types of sanction, and of mechanisms of social control. And he becomes used to using them in the interests of *all* the groups connected with his firm.

This situation is most marked in large-scale industry, where ownership is often split up so small as to be ineffective and the full responsibility for policy-making is thrust on the professional executive. Studies were made just before and during the war, on the 176 largest independent American companies outside the fields of banking and finance. In at least one-third of these companies, and probably about two-thirds, no shareholder or group of shareholders was in a position to exercise active control. About half the members of

283

boards of directors were executives of the companies, and many even of the remaining members—possibly most—were in effect appointed by the executives, who were in the best position to promote nominations and collect the proxy votes of otherwise unorganised shareholders. A post-war survey by Hargreaves Parkinson of thirty large British companies, having between them about 10% of the paid-up capital of public companies in Britain, arrived at the similar conclusion that:

'Majority voting control by large holdings is the exception, and not the rule. And instances of control in a few hands (where a company is a parent and not a subsidiary) are hard to find.'

The two most substantial exceptions, among the thirty firms, were Morris Motors and Woolworth's. In neither the American nor the British case do such conclusions imply that shareholders' interests are neglected. They may be; but the financial Press, resting on skilled and informed opinion, will usually see to it that glaring neglect is discovered and publicised. But consideration for owners' interests is one thing, and active control by owners is another; and in the biggest of big businesses the latter exists in only a minority of cases.

This is not, of course, true of medium and small business, where ownership and management continue to go together; and the importance of small business, if it diminishes at all, certainly does not diminish fast. Probably about three-quarters of the whole British economy (see below) is still dominated by firms of 'owner-manager' size. But the difference between the owner-manager of the small firm and the managing director of the large is, it must be remembered, one mainly of their *internal* situation within their respective firms. The owner-manager, or member of a partnership, if he and his partners do actually own the majority of his firm's capital, need be answerable within the firm to no higher authority. As owner, he may find it easier than a manager (one executive among others) to assert this authority against his colleagues; and all the more so as he has a smaller body of men to deal with, and can afford to be less bound by rules and precedents. To this extent, he can afford to be more individualistic, more exclusively concerned with economics, or competition, or some other sanction or mechanism, or with his own personal gain. But when it comes to external relations, or even to internal relations outside the circle of managers and owners— management-worker relations, for instance—the influences affecting managers and owner-managers are much the same. When, for instance, R. A. Gordon notes the tendency in the United States in recent years for the influence exerted on firms' policies by financiers to diminish and that of government and labour to increase, it is certainly not only to big business that this applies.

Moreover, the business man has his own life to live. He is a consumer as well as a producer; and the cultural changes recorded above apply to consumption, as well as production. Here again is an influence which applies to small and to big business alike. When the business man has managed to keep in business and render successful service, he finds that the type of reward which carries most public esteem, and so (other things being equal) gives him most satisfaction, is much less a matter of multiplying wealth than it was a century ago. The business man of the 1850's no doubt found it difficult, in a country like Britain with an older, eotechnic, aristocratic tradition, to buy his own way into the best society. But he could buy a way for his children, who had the education he lacked; and, meantime, in contrast to today, his unlimited accumulation of wealth was a ground, in the circles whose opinions then counted, for admiration rather than for suspicion. Today an income has to be equitable; not necessarily low, since a touch of magnificence still becomes the managing director; but conforming to all the canons of a just price, not merely to that which prescribes that incomes shall reflect the value of work. And there are signs, as has just been said, of a return to eotechnic conceptions of quality and skill in expenditure, though at the new levels appropriate to the more equitable income distribution of the neotechnic world. The business man finds himself expected to take account of the total, not merely the financial, situation surrounding him, not only in deciding his production policy but in limiting the amount of the rewards which are to emerge from it and setting standards for the way they are to be used.

In short, the business man, like the rest of us, is a social animal, and responds to cultural influences. The socialist age has largely socialised the business man, along with everyone else. The farmer learns to work with his colleagues in the National Farmers' Union, and within a close framework of government regulation and policy. A generation of business men grows up since the Second World War accustomed and willing to cooperate in measures of government control; as, thirty or forty years earlier, another generation grew up to whom, to the alarm of their forefathers, trade union recognition and collective bargaining seemed as natural as the day. And, if present trends in the teaching and practice of management are any guide, the federalist age promises now to equip the business man with an acute awareness of the problems of group relationships.

INSTITUTIONS

The institutions with which economists are concerned change in some ways surprisingly little, or at least surprisingly slowly. The broad distribution of workers among British industries, for example (Table 3), was much the same in 1951 as in 1911; between a third

TABLE 3. Persons (including out of work) engaged in main categories of industry, England and Wales and Great Britain 1911–51

| | Per 1,000 of all occupied | | | |
| | England and Wales | | Great Britain | |
	1911	1931	1931	1951 [1]
Agriculture and fishing	77	56	60	45
Mining and quarrying	69	64	64	38
Manufacturing	326	333	332	376
Building, contracting	53	56	53	62
Service trades	449	482	482	474
Other and not stated	26	9	9	2
Total	1,000	1,000	1,000	1,000

[1] Excluding out of work.
From *Census of Population*.

and two-fifths in manufacturing, around 45% in professional and service occupations, 5–6% in building, and the balance in mining and agriculture. Within this framework there had, of course, been important changes. The proportion of workers in textiles, clothing, and shoes, for example, was halved, whereas that in chemicals and the metal industries went up by nearly two-thirds. Domestic service went down, and public utilities, shopkeeping, and government service went up. But the broad frame remained as it was.

The size of firms has also remained surprisingly stable. The common impression that the medium to small owner-managed firm is disappearing from the scene is very far from the truth. In the United States at the end of the 'thirties about a fifth of the national income, other than that from banking, finance, and government activities, seems to have come from the country's two hundred largest corporations; about 40–45% from smaller corporations; and no less than 35–40% from businesses too small to constitute themselves as companies. These were principally in farming, retailing and the service trades, and building. Though wars and slumps favour big firms, the pattern of concentration even in manufacturing, where the opportunities of lowering costs by increasing the scale of employment and investment are exceptionally great, remained recognisably the same in 1937 as in 1914, and had changed very little indeed since 1919. A fall in the number of manufacturing and building firms from 1929 to 1939 was offset by increases in road haulage, retailing and the service trades.

In Britain in the 'thirties there were rather over two million businesses, including individuals operating on their own account. A third were in trade, principally retail, and about 66% of all national sales of consumer goods in 1938 were handled through independent unit shops, most of them very small indeed. Some at least of the department stores and multiples which handled a further 24%—the balance being supplied by cooperatives—were also small enough for easy owner-management. A further quarter of all businesses were in the predominantly small-scale service trades and the professions. In order of the number of businesses in each group, these included hotels, boarding-houses, and cafés; the professions; hairdressing; entertainments; and laundries. Another quarter were in manufacturing and building, principally (again in order) in building, the clothing trades and shoe-repairing, baking and food processing, carpentry and furniture, and such metal and engineering trades as garages, blacksmithing, electrical wiring and contracting, and watch and clock repairing. Here again, owner-management was not confined to these very small-scale businesses. About 60% of the employment in manufacturing and building in 1935 (Table 4 (a)) was given by firms employing fewer than five hundred workers, including about 10% from firms employing fewer than eleven. Finally, the balance of about one-sixth of all the businesses in Britain were in farming and fishing, where the vast majority of employment is given by what in manufacturing would rank as very small concerns indeed.

The number of very small businesses has dropped since the 'thirties (Table 4 (a)), but remains substantial. The proportion of the national income earned by small (unincorporated) businesses in Britain today remains as high as in the U.S.A. in 1937. The number of very small farm holdings, of twenty acres or less, fell between 1920 and 1947 (Table 5 (c)), but the number and size-distribution of farms in the range which accounts for the main bulk of British agricultural output remained unchanged. The typical farmer continues, as before,

287

TABLE 4. Firms

Number of employers, managers (other than branch and department managers) and persons working on their own account

	1951			1931		
	Employers and managers	*Own account*	*Total*	*Employers and managers*	*Own account*	*Total*
(a) *Number (thousands)*						
Farming, forestry, fishing, etc.	118	229	347	191	182	373
Manufacturing and building	208	209	417	245	265	510
Trade and finance	194	374	568	244	471	715
Professions and services	122	311	433	165	351	516
Other (including mining and quarrying)	3	2	5	5	3	8
Total	645	1,125	1,770	850	1,272	2,122
(b) *Percentage increase or decrease, 1931–51*						
Farming, forestry, fishing, etc.	−38	+26	−7			
Manufacturing and building	−15	−21	−18			
Trade and finance	−20	−21	−21			
Professions and services	−26	−11	−16			
Total (including 'other')	−24	−12	−17			

From *Census of Population*, 1931 and 1951 (Great Britain).

TABLE 5. Size of firms and industries, Great Britain

(a) Firms—manufacturing, mining, building, and public utilities, 1924–35

Firms employing	Number of firms [1]		Number of workers in firms of each size ('000s)	
	1924	1935	1924	1935
0–10	199,191	204,151	682	827
11–99	52,000	41,215	1,676	1,452
100–499	11,100	9,722	2,284	1,993
500–1,499	1,700	1,684	1,362	1,385
1,500 plus	600	596	1,984	2,373

[1] *Census of Production.* 1924 figures relate to the number of *returns*, and may slightly exaggerate the number of firms. In 1935 there were some 1,959 *units*, that is firms or *groups of firms* under one legal control, employing 500 or more. They employed 49% of all workers in these trades. Leak and Maizels, *Journal of the Royal Statistical Society*, 1945.

(b) Factories (Great Britain) employing

No. of workers	1935	1952
11–99	37,614	42,644
100–499	9,750	11,543
500–1,499	1,314	2,451
1,500+	266	
Total	48,944	56,638

Census of Production, and Ministry of Labour Gazette, Dec. 1952.

(c) Agricultural holdings of:

Acres:	1920	1947
301 plus	16,017	14,681
151–300	43,747	40,250
101–150	38,352	36,790
51–100	70,828	69,955
2–50	324,947	273,847
All	493,983	435,683

From *Agricultural Statistics,* Ministry of Agriculture.

(d) Industries

See Chapter V, Table 4, (p. 74).

to work with only family labour or with from one to four workers. In retailing and the service trades it seems, at what is frankly little more than a guess, that the number of independent concerns rose in the first three decades of the twentieth century and then fell slightly to 1939. It fell, in many cases sharply, during the war. In some at least of these it had not fully recovered by 1951. But it is notable how in the grocery trade, for example, for which full statistics exist, though the number of shops fell from 191,400 in 1940 to 146,300 in 1949—the whole of this being accounted for by a drop in the number of independent retailers, as apart from department stores, multiples and cooperatives—the proportion of rationing registrations held by the independents was actually greater in 1949 than in 1940. In manufacturing and building the number of employers and 'workers on own account' remained practically constant from 1924 to 1935. A marked drop in the number of firms employing from eleven to 499 was offset (Table 5(a)) by a rise in those employing up to ten. The number of *firms* dropped by a fifth or a sixth between the 'thirties and 1951. The number of *factories* per 10,000 employed or unemployed workers seems, however, trade for trade (the qualification is important, as demand favoured the big-factory industries during this period), to have been about the same in 1952 as in 1935. In manufacturing, building, and retailing, as also in farming, the very small business, the individual working on his own account or with one or two employees, has tended to be pushed out to the advantage of the slightly larger concern employing up to a dozen. On the other hand, the shortage and high cost of labour, and improvement of labour-saving equipment, has led many farmers, and probably shopkeepers, to dispense with hired help which they would have employed to secure a comparable output before the war. This may sometimes, as in farming, add more to the number of 'workers on own account', by transfer from the category of employers and managers, than are taken away by the tendency to squeeze the smallest small men out.

There are sectors of the British economy where business of the size suitable to the owner-manager counts for little: insurance and banking, the national and local government service (including defence, education, and the hospital service), and the nationalised mines, public utility services, transport and telecommunications. These sectors account between them for 20–25% of all employment. In the other three-quarters of the economy, 'owner-manageable' firms are still able to carry on most of the nation's work. And this state of affairs seems likely to continue for as far ahead as the evidence as yet to hand makes it possible to foresee.

But this apparent stability in the main institutions of the economic world is deceptive. For the problems of these institutions, like those of personality, have come to be seen with new eyes, and have changed immensely in both character and complexity.

For one thing, 'federalist' conceptions have been gaining ground here as elsewhere. Economic courses and text-books twenty years ago—and they were not entirely out of touch with practice in this respect—taught a great deal about the firm and its relation to other firms, but remarkably little (I write from personal memory) about what went on inside the firm, or about the industry. There was an earlier phase, dominated by the thought of Alfred Marshall, when the industry was (correctly) seen as an extremely important unit of economic organisation: important, notably, for the theory of competition. But in the 'thirties it figured as not much more than a conventional frame for assembling Census of Production statistics.

Whoever looks at business today will get a very different impression. Just as the State is being displaced from its dominant position in political thought, to the advantage of both higher (international) and smaller social groups, so also the firm appears today as merely one step in an ascending scale of industrial organisation. At the lower end of the scale, the working group has now acquired a whole literature and set of managerial skills of its own. A 'working group', for this purpose, exists wherever half-a-dozen or a dozen workers are associated together round one job. It may consist of a managing director and the half-dozen managers under him, or it may be a gang on a quay-side or a building site. Either way, it—its little social system, the sanctions and mechanisms used to maintain it, the resistance it sets up against outside interference—has come to be seen as of key importance for industrial efficiency, above all in cases calling for change in the social structure. The theory of competition itself, as developed notably by Andrews, begins to turn around the problem of change and adaptation among the small group of people who in practice make up the market for most firms. A firm today appears, not as a monolithic unit, but as a complex assembly of small living cells. And its problems and difficulties are as likely to be those of the cells as of the firm as a whole. The cells were, of course, there all the time. But they were often ignored, suppressed, or broken up through misunderstanding of their importance. Now that their importance is beginning to be understood, an important part of managerial skill is coming to consist in ensuring them a healthy, satisfactory, and even—one might almost say, looking at certain schemes for group contract—a chartered existence.

At the other end of the scale, the industry has also come to be seen with new eyes. In the theory of competition, as outlined in Chapter 2, it figures today in the same essential function originally marked out for it by Marshall. It is the assembly of firms which are qualified by experience and equipment to enter one another's markets if they see good competitive reason to do so. Statistically, Florence defines an industry as a group of firms 70% or more of whose output is of a certain kind, and which between them produce 50% or more of the national output of that product. Of some 133 divisions and sub-divisions of British industry recognised by the

Census of Production of 1935—omitting very small industries, and certain partly nationalised groups for which full statistics were not then available—130 passed this test.

On the side of direction and consultation, the industry has come into its own within the last generation both as a means of guiding and helping firms and as a link between them and the State. The nationalised industries have each a single, statutory, central management with more or less far-reaching powers. A typical private industry today has one or more trade associations, busy with wage negotiations, government relations, information and help on export and import problems, and a mass of other matters of information or action of interest to member firms. There may be a development council under the Industrial Organisation and Development Act of 1947, or a voluntary body with similar functions; with power, in any case, to raise a compulsory levy for research and other common purposes of the industry. There will often be a cooperative research association, set up in collaboration with the Department of Scientific and Industrial Research. There will almost always be one or more joint bodies bringing together managements and trade unions. And often there are other miscellaneous institutions: an export group, for example, or a technical institute.

Trade union problems, meantime, have also come to be seen in a new light. Some of these problems are internal to the unions themselves. Union membership is not very different today from what it was thirty years ago; it was nearly 8½ millions in 1920, and 9½

TABLE 6.   Trade Unions

(a) Number of members

| 1938 | 6,053,000 |
| 1953 | 9,460,000 |

(b) Size of unions (1946)

Membership of unions	Number of unions	Percentage of total membership
0–1,000	460	1·4
1,000–25,000	245	14·3
25,000–100,000	31	17·4
100,000 and over	17	66·9[1]

[1] In 1951 the 17 largest unions had 66·5% of the membership.
Source: Ministry of Labour.

millions in 1953. But in this time the number of unions has been practically halved: two-thirds of union membership (Table 6) has come to be concentrated in some seventeen unions with memberships of 100,000 and more; and what in effect is a whole new top layer of union organisation has come into existence through the growing influence and functions of the T.U.C. These changes have faced the unions with many of the same problems of direction as occur in the nationalised industries and other giant industrial concerns. In facing these, unions have been handicapped by a number of other changes which have tended to weaken, not so much the general loyalty of their members, but rather their detailed understanding of and responsiveness to union policy.

'The trade union meeting house,' to quote a first-hand account recorded by Sidney and Beatrice Webb sixty years ago, 'is the recognised club for the men in the craft, and thus presents many social attractions. Friendships are made and numerous sing-songs and smoking concerts arranged; and the joke and friendly glass, the good cheer and the conviviality, all present great attractions . . .' (History of Trade Unionism, 1920 ed., p. 444ff.).

It was the employment exchange and the Ministry of Pensions and National Insurance rolled into one. These functions have largely gone, and with them has gone one of the most powerful links between union officers and members. And much union work today takes place in offices and behind closed doors, where members' interests are served as effectively as ever they were at the factory gate or on the quay-side, but in a way far less easy for members to appreciate, understand, or help.

But over and above these internal problems unions are faced today with a new problem in their relations with firms. If workers today are, as Zweig says, partners whose views and voice cannot be ignored—partners who have, whether they want it or not, a large share of responsibility for the good running of industry—then in what way is this responsibility to be expressed in the policy of their unions? The unions exist as advocates of a particular class: a class, that of the men and women who take rather than give orders, which will always need advocates in the face of the superior power and authority of managers. Is it consistent with their position as advocates that they should take formal responsibility, jointly with management, for the running of a firm or industry? Experience would suggest that the answer is 'no'. They must, of course, act responsibly as advocates, just as counsel in court must remain within the framework of the law and the rules of court. But he remains counsel, committed to present the views of one side. And that seems also to be the right view for a union to take. In the London docks, for example, the fact that unions have shared with management responsibility for discipline has certainly not helped them to keep their members' confidence. When counsel for the defence starts to make the prosecutor's speech as well, his client is unlikely to be satisfied that justice is being done; and the client will be quite right.

Does this mean, then, that ideas of workers' control, of giving workers a direct power over and responsibility for the policy of the concern they work for, must be buried for ever? Is that consistent with the idea of the worker as a 'partner'—bearing in mind the very different conclusion drawn in democratic political practice from the fact that the worker is a partner in the State? Or can formulas be found which will allow workers to attain the equivalent of full citizenship in industry, and yet will leave the chief working-class organisations to act in their proper role as advocates, committed to no interests but those of their clients?

This question ties up with a number of others raised by the new appreciation of the role of the working group, the industry, and the relation of firms to the State. A firm today appears as a bundle of interests and activities arising from many sources, proceeding to many ends, requiring (the theme of this book) very different techniques of control, as difficult and, on all these counts, as complicated to govern as the State itself. The interests and contributions of owners, managers (top, middle, and junior), of rank and file workers and their unions, of other firms and groups in the industry, of customers and suppliers, and of the local and national community have somehow to be woven together in such a way as to produce a coherent policy reconciling the interests of all groups, and effective machinery for carrying it out.

In the State, the corresponding problems are solved by the complicated provisions of the British Constitution. The Cabinet is at one and the same time responsible to the 'customers'—the electors —and to the members of its own 'firm' or party. It is also responsible for reducing public policy to a coherent form and for seeing to its execution. Through their party, the leaders of the Government are also required to pay attention to various class or other special interests which, like the trade unions, cut across the divisions between parties or 'firms'. Some of these inter-party interest groups, such as the Welsh Party, have an organised existence in Parliament itself.

Can industrial management be put in the same place, in relation to its customers and collaborators, or to inter-firm interest groups like the unions, as the Cabinet occupies in politics? A number of extremely interesting experiments in defining and codifying industrial constitutions on these lines have begun in recent years, the most far-reaching to date being that of Glacier Metal Ltd. It seems likely that these experiments will increase and multiply in future. And it is certainly desirable. For the constitution of the firm is the focal point of the whole complex problem of modern industrial government, and one where clarity is specially necessary.

R. H. Tawney pointed out a generation ago that there is a close parallel between these problems in industry and those of the relations between King and Parliament three or four hundred years ago. It was, for instance, then the custom for the King to pay for both public activities and his own private needs out of a single fund, into which went all such revenues as came his way. The consequence, Tawney pointed out, was that suspicion and jealousy over the King's private expenditure led Parliament to refuse funds urgently needed for public purposes. Only when clarity was restored by drawing a sharp distinction between the Privy Purse and the public funds was it possible to escape from this dilemma. Confusions and suspicions of this sort, Tawney rightly insisted, abound in the field of industrial relations, and lead to similar conflicts and disregard of the common interest. And, as he added, the solution of these industrial conflicts would seem to lie in constitution-making of the same sort as ended the political conflicts of the past.

Among the many other changes in institutions in recent years, the one most relevant to economics is probably the new attention which has begun to be given to the family and its environment in the local community.

Mocking laughter echoed through the academic halls of the Anglo-Saxon world when in 1930 Dr. Abraham Flexner (of Columbia) revealed in his book on *Universities* the title-page of a recent thesis at Chicago:

THE UNIVERSITY OF CHICAGO

A TIME AND MOTION COMPARISON ON FOUR
METHODS OF DISH-WASHING

*A Dissertation Submitted to the Graduate
Faculty in Candidacy for the Degree of
Master of Arts*

With this went such other titles as 'A study of controlled conditions in cooking hams' and 'Style cycles in women's undergarments', a fascinating topic to which the econometrician's eye has been unaccountably little drawn.

In these latter days the design of machines for living in has become as reputable among housing authorities and architects as the design of atomic bombs among scientists and in Whitehall. The laugh is on Dr. Flexner, not on the pioneers of stop-watched dish-washing. For the family does, in fact, hold, directly or indirectly, a key position in a very wide range of economic as well as non-economic activities, and deserves to be studied accordingly.

Indirectly, the family affects economic life through the size of the population and the quality of personality; for it can be shown that the family has an effect in forming personality far and away greater than that of any other agency. Directly, it has a substantial influence on production and an overwhelmingly important influence on consumption and savings. Activities within the family add at least a fifth, and probably more, to the national income. The product of these activities is directly consumed by families themselves. In addition, families account for four-fifths of all consumption of purchased goods and services, and two-fifths of all purchases of durable goods other than buildings and works. Family housing (exclusive of any consequent work on public utilities) accounts for about two-fifths of all new building work, and a rather higher proportion of repairs.

Key points for the influence of the family on economic life include:

(1) Its size.
(2) Its share in the national income and wealth.
(3) The quality of its internal relationships.
(4) Its external relationships, notably with the local community.

Each of these points has received an increasing amount of attention in recent years. The average size of a family in Britain (Table 7) was halved between 1850 and 1950; the economic issues arising out of this, some of which were touched on above in Chapter 12, seemed important enough by the 'forties to justify a very full survey by the Royal Commission on the Population. The Royal Commission recommended far-reaching measures to equalise the standard of living of large and small families, additional to those—tax and family allowances, social services, advantages in the rationing of food and houses—already made available before and after the Second World War. These proposals have since been taken up and elaborated by the Royal Commission on Taxation. Studies by Duesenberry, Katona, and others have underlined the importance which this equalisation of incomes may have in altering norms of expenditure and saving; for these depend a great deal on the shape of the income distribution within a given social class. Detailed studies (of which Dr. Flexner's dish-washing thesis was an early

TABLE 7. The British Household

(a) Persons living in private households, England and Wales

	Percentage of:		
	All households containing the given number of persons		All persons living in households of this size
	1931	1951	1951
1	6·7	10·7	3·4
2	21·9	27·9	17·5
3	24·1	25·0	23·5
4	19·4	19·1	23·9
5	12·4	9·5	15·0
6, 7	11·4	6·3	12·4
8 or more	4·1	1·5	4·4
All	100	100	100
Total number of households	12,115,000	13,043,500	

From *Census of Population*, 1951.

(b) Average number of children born to women married in:

1851–5	5·40 (England and Wales)
1900–9	3·37 (Great Britain)
1925–9	2·19 (Great Britain)

From the *Report of the Royal Commission on the Population*, 1949, Cmd. 7695.

example) have begun to be made of various factors affecting family income and expenditure, including the services which the family produces for itself. The scope for improvement is illustrated by American studies of housewives' work, showing, for four-person families in homes with American standards of household equipment, typical working weeks of 47–61 hours. These figures are for the housewife alone, and do not count pauses, interruptions, or time contributed by other members of the family.

More attention has also been given to the quality of families' internal relations. The results of this examination have been disturbing. On the economic side alone, to say nothing of other fields, the family has to solve on its own microcosmic scale the full range of problems of production, consumption and provision for the future with which this book has been concerned. No one will expect a married couple to step down from the altar equipped with the full range of skills they will need from the wedding reception to the grave. But they should at least have the ability to acquire these skills as they need them. The founder of the Marriage Guidance Council, summing up his own and his colleagues' experience, comments on the general state of family knowledge as follows:

'Again and again the marriage counsellor will encounter almost incredible ignorance—ignorance of the proper place of sex in marriage, ignorance of the meaning of the emotional interactions between husband and wife, ignorance of the principles of parentcraft and home management . . . This goes on happening every day . . .' (Mace, *Marriage Counselling*, 1948.)

Finally, families' external relations have been worked on from two quite different points of view. On the one hand, sociologists, town planners, community association leaders, and social workers have tried to design and set up an environment in which the family can develop the best of which it is capable. The founders of the Peckham Health Centre gave a useful lead here by pointing out that the problem of 'social poverty', that is of defective social relations in the local community, is not only or even mainly one of the relations between the community and the individual. It arises first and foremost out of the lack of a satisfactory place within the local community for the family *as a unit*. The question of what sort of local community can offer it a satisfactory place has been a thorny one. What makes a good neighbourhood unit in town or country? It seems clear at least that the old 'closed' village or neighbourhood in which people lived and worked among themselves and apart from the rest of the world is no longer satisfactory. In modern conditions social life needs to be, and with modern means of transport can be, spread over a much wider area, that of the town, or of the 'key village' or market town and its satellites. But discussion and experiment on this may well go on for another generation or more before fully satisfactory solutions emerge.

Quite a different approach to the external relations of the family is that of the family movements which have sprung up notably on the continent of Europe. They are, in effect, family trade unions, defending family interests and also providing for families a number of cooperative services. They represent, so to speak, the family coming of age and taking its own affairs in hand, and they have important possibilities for education as well as for external representation and defence. They exist so far only on a small scale in this country. Their nearest large-scale equivalent would probably be the Women's Institutes.

In these various new approaches to the problems of the family there may well lie the germ of a revolution in the direction and control of consumption and savings, as also in the shaping of personalities, as extensive as that which has occurred in the last two generations in the direction and control of production.

FURTHER READING

CHAPTER 1

For the earlier part of this chapter, see particularly:

MUMFORD, *Technics and Civilisation*, 1934: and *The Culture of Cities*, 1938. Sometimes rather speculative and high-flown, but still one of the best introductions to the particular problems of civilisation with which modern economists are concerned.

See also:

OGBURN and NIMKOFF, *Handbook of Sociology*, 1947, Part VII (on social change).

CHAPTERS 2, 3, 4

Theory

Setting out from the ordinary theory of perfect and imperfect competition, of 'private' and 'social' costs, as set out in studies by Pigou, Robinson, Chamberlin, Triffin, Keynes, or Hicks (*Trade Cycle*), these chapters draw especially on:

The development of Marshall's theory of competition by P. W. S. ANDREWS, *Manufacturing Business*, 1948, and earlier in HALL and HITCH, 'Price Theory and Business Behaviour', *Oxford Economic Papers*, May, 1939, and HARROD, 'Price and Cost in Entrepreneurs' Policy', ibid. See also HOOD and YAMEY, 'Imperfect Competition in the Retail Trades', *Economica*, May, 1951.

SCHUMPETER, *Theory of Economic Development*, 1939, and *Capitalism, Socialism, and Democracy*, 1942. The distinction between decisions involving and not involving changes in the social framework comes close to that between 'genuine' decisions, reached by reorganising a psychological field, and other decisions, in KATONA, *Psychological Economics*, 1951.

Factual material—general and industrial. Sources include:

DOUGLAS, 'Productivity Functions', *American Economic Review*, March, 1948 (similar material is also summarised in CLARK, *Conditions of Economic Progress*, 1951 ed., pp. 514 ff).

FLORENCE, *Investment Location and Size of Plant*, 1948, and *Logic of British and American Industry*, 1953. The definition of an industry implied in the text is that given by FLORENCE, *Investment, etc.* pp. 4–5: a group of plants at least 70% of whose output consists of a characteristic product, and which makes 50% or more of the national output of that product.

ANDREWS and BRUNNER, *Capital Development in Steel*, 1951.
Report of the Technical Advisory Committee on Coal-Mining (Reid Report), 1945, Cmd. 6610.
BURN, *Economic History of Steelmaking*, 1940, Book III.
ASTOR and ROWNTREE, *British Agriculture*, 1938.
ORWIN, *Country Planning*, 1944 (on competition in farming).
Nuffield Foundation, Agricultural Policy Group: cyclostyled memorandum by ENGLEDOW and others.
Report of the Committee of Investigation into the Cotton Textile Machinery Industry, H.M.S.O., 1947.
FOGARTY (ed.), *Further Studies in Industrial Organisation*, 1948 (especially chapter by Mrs. H. EDWARDS on flourmilling. See also on this references in CARR-SAUNDERS and others, *Consumers' Co-operation in Great Britain*, 1938, pp. 427–8).
FOGARTY, *Town and Country Planning*, 1948, pp. 144 ff. (on the urban land market).
FOGARTY, 'The Incidence of Rates on Housing', *Review of Economic Studies*, 1942 (on landlords' and builders' price policies).
GRANT, *Capital Market in Post-war Britain*, 1937, Chapter II (the interrelation of prices in different sections of the capital market).
Second Interim Report of the Departmental Committee on the Patents and Design Acts, 1946 (Cmd. 6789), paras. 24, 27 (contrast this with the American evidence summarised in LYNCH, *Concentration of Economic Power*, 1946).
EDWARDS, *Cooperative Industrial Research*, 1950.
LUCAS, *Industrial Reconstruction and the Control of Competition*, 1937.
BRITISH ASSOCIATION, *Britain in Depression*, 1935, and *Britain in Recovery*, 1938.

And statistical data on the changing structure of British industry:

BEVERIDGE, *Full Employment in a Free Society*, 1944, appendix.
British and American productivity:
ROSTAS, *Comparative Productivity in British and American Industry*, 1948.

Distribution and retailing

BOARD OF TRADE, *Britain's Shops*, H.M.S.O., 1952.
The Home Market, 1950.
FOGARTY, unpublished investigation of small business mortality in six areas (Merseyside, Glasgow, Sheffield, Birmingham and district, Oxford and district, the Brighton conurbation) based on directories and shop-to-shop enquiries.
CHAPMAN, 'Convenience', in *Human Relations*, III (1), February, 1950.
SMAILES, 'The Urban Hierarchy of England and Wales', *Geography*, 1944.
GLAISYER and others, *County Town*, 1946 (Worcester).
Manchester Regional Plan.
GLASS, *Social Background of a Plan*, 1948 (Middlesbrough).

GREEN, bus-service maps in *Geographical Journal*, 1950.
BRACEY, *Social Provision in Rural Wiltshire*, 1952.
WEST MIDLAND GROUP, *English County* (Herefordshire).
Social Survey, reports on the Solway, Tweed, and Aberdeen areas.
KALDOR and SILVERMAN, *Statistical Analysis of Advertising*, 1950.
BIRMINGHAM SOCIAL SURVEY COMMITTEE, *Nutrition and Size of Family*, 1939 (a typical comment on the 'good use' on the whole made by consumers of their resources).
JOHNSON-DAVIES, *Control in Retail Industry*, 1943.
JEFFREYS, *Distribution of Consumable Goods*, 1950.
Report of the Committee on Resale Price Maintenance, 1949, Cmd. 7696.
Report of the Committee on Cement Costs, 1947.
Report of the Linoleum Working Party, 1947.
Reports of the Monopolies Commission on dental goods, rainwater goods, etc.
Report of the Committee on the Distribution of Building Materials, 1948.
CADBURY, *Industrial Record*, 1919–39, Chapters III–IV.
LEVY, *Retail Trade Associations*, 1942, and *Shops of Britain*, 1947.
SMITH, *Retail Distribution*, 1948 ed.
ANDREWS, 'Some Aspects of Competition in Retail Trade', *Oxford Economic Papers*, June, 1950.

The labour market

LIEPMAN, *Journey to Work*, 1945.
BRITISH INSTITUTE OF MANAGEMENT: cyclostyled circulars on labour turnover.
NEWTON and JEFFERY, *Internal Migration*, H.M.S.O., 1951.
Discussions of 'stickiness' where a high degree of mobility is called for, in: Pilgrim Trust, *Men Without Work*, 1939; Manchester University, *Readjustment in Lancashire*, 1936; Mass-Observation, *People in Production*, 1942.
Social Survey, report on recruitment to farming.
YOUNGHUSBAND, reports on *Employment and Training of Social Workers*, 1947, and *Social Work in Britain*, 1951.
Report of the Committee on Higher Civil Service Remuneration, 1949, Cmd. 7635.
JEFFERYS, *Mobility in the Labour Market*, 1954.
GLASS (ed.), *Social Mobility in Britain*, 1954.
SEERS, *Levelling of Incomes since 1938*, 1951.
CARR-SAUNDERS and WILSON, *The Professions*, 1933.
S. and D. WEBB, *History of Trade Unionism*, 1920 ed., and *Industrial Democracy*, 1897.
SLICHTER, *Union Policies and Industrial Management*, 1941.
DUNLOP, *Wage Determination under Trade Unions*, 1950.
P.E.P., *British Trade Unions*, 1948.
COLE, *Introduction to Trade Unionism*, 1954.

FURTHER READING

FLANDERS, *A Policy for Wages*, 1950.
DOUGLAS, *Theory of Wages*, 1934. (Notably for estimates of the elasticity of demand for labour: estimated for the U.S.A. to be −0·3, so that a 10% rise in wages will tend to diminish the labour supply by 3%).
MAYO, *Social Problems of an Industrial Civilisation*, 1945 (see also references below to FOGARTY, *Personality and Group Relations in Industry*, and TAYLOR on group loyalty among workers).
Report on Social Insurance and Applied Services, 1942, Cmd. 6404 (*Beveridge Report*), especially para. 26.
STANSFIELD, *Levels of Expectation in Productivity*, paper to British Association, 1952.
See also CLARK, op. cit., Chapter X.

CHAPTER 5

For further study of wartime experience of direction, see:
DEVONS, *Planning in Practice*, 1951.
ROBBINS, *Economic Problem in Peace and War*, 1947.
FRANKS, *Central Planning and Control in War and Peace*, 1947.
WILSON, 'Programmes and Allocations in the Planned Economy', in *Oxford Economic Papers*, January, 1949.
CHESTER (ed.), *Lessons of the British War Economy*, 1951.
Particular fields of wartime experience are studied in more detail in the series of *Official Histories* of the war published by the Stationery Office.

For general and peacetime aspects of direction, see:
Economic Survey, 1947, Cmd. 7046, and MORRISON, *Economic Planning*, 1946, contrasted with *Economic Survey*, 1951, Cmd. 8195.
P.E.P., *Government and Industry*, 1952.
LEWIS, *Principles of Economic Planning*, 1950.
BALOGH, *Dollar Crisis—Cause and Cure*, 1950.
ANDREWS, *Manufacturing Business*, 1948, Chapters IV and V, and URWICK, *Problems of Growth in Industrial Undertakings*, 1949.
DIMOCK, *The Executive in Action*, 1945, especially Chapter VII.
MILWARD (ed.), *Large-Scale Organisation*, 1950.

For illustrations of the wide present responsibility of the Government for policy, as apart from operations, see:
White Paper on *Employment Policy*, 1944, Cmd. 6527.
Education Act, 1944, especially s. 11; Town and Country Planning Act, 1947, s. 5; National Health Service Act, 1946, s. 20.
Statement on *Personal Incomes, Costs, and Prices*, 1948, Cmd. 7321.
See also Chapter 10, on the Government's role in scientific research.

For the early breakdown of direction in the U.S.S.R., see the account of the New Economic Policy in such books as BAYKOV, *Development of the Soviet Economic System*, 1947, and Webb, *Soviet Communism*, 1935.

CHAPTER 6

Material on consultation in industry, at the level of the firm and the small working group, is summarised in:

FOGARTY, *Personality and Group Relations in Industry*, 1955
TAYLOR, *Are Workers Human?* 1950.

Other more specific studies include

JAQUES, *Changing Culture of a Factory*, 1951.
RENOLD, *Joint Consultation over Thirty Years*, 1950.
ROBSON-BROWN and HOWELL-EVERSON, *Industrial Democracy at Work*, 1950.
SCOTT, *Joint Consultation in a Liverpool Manufacturing Firm*, 1950.
SCOTT and LYNTON, *Three Studies in Management*, 1952.
DRUCKER, *Big Business* (General Motors), 1947.
LILIENTHAL, *T.V.A.*, 1944.
P.E.P., *Government and Industry*, 1952, and *Planning*, nos. 318 ('Government and Industry') and 326 ('Development Council').
POLANYI, *Logic of Liberty*, 1951, Part I.

CHAPTER 7

On the review of market practice

BRITISH
Monopolies and Restrictive Practices Act, 1948.
Annual Reports of the Monopolies Commission.
Reports of the Monopolies Commission on particular industries (Dental Goods, cast-iron rainwater goods, electric-lamp manufacture, etc.).

AMERICAN
C. D. EDWARDS, *Maintaining Competition*, 1949, pp. 37–42 and Chapter 8.
Temporary National Economic Committee Monographs, 1938–40:
16. *Anti-Trust in Action.*
34. *Control of Unfair Competitive Practices.*
38. *Construction and Enforcement of the Federal Anti-Trust Laws.*

GERMAN
LIEFMANN, *Cartels, Concerns, and Trusts*, 1932, Part IV.

On organisation and methods

SELECT COMMITTEE ON ESTIMATES, Session 1946–7, *Report on Organisation and Methods* (in the Civil Service).
Organisation and Methods Bulletin (the February, 1949, issue, for instance, reviews the development of organisation and methods in British industry).
HOLDEN, FISH, and SMITH, *Top Management Organisation and Control*, 1941, (big American businesses).

'Ad hoc' reviews from other fields

Reports of the Local Government Manpower Committee, 1950 and 1951, Cmd. 7870 and 8421 (see also D. N. CHESTER, *Central and Local Government*, 1951).

TRADES UNION CONGRESS, *Trade Union Structure and Closer Unity*, 1947.

MINISTRY OF AGRICULTURE AND FISHERIES, *Economic Survey*, No. 48, 1947 (Lucas Report on agricultural marketing).

Report of the Broadcasting Committee, 1949.

CHAPTER 8

General

DUESENBERRY, *Income, Saving, and the Theory of Consumer Behaviour*, 1949.

RIESMAN, *The Lonely Crowd*, 1950.

KATONA, *Psychological Economics*, 1951.

HELLER (ed.), *Savings in the Modern Economy*, 1953.

This chapter is largely based on FOGARTY, 'Consumption', in *Les Données Actuelles de l'Économie*, report of the Third Study Session of the International Union of Catholic Employers' Associations, 1951.

Statistical

The most reliable source for pre-war consumption and savings patterns in Britain is the series published by the National Institute of Economic and Social Research on *Studies in the National Income and Expenditure of the U.K.*, especially Vol. I, STONE, *The Measurement of Consumers' Expenditure and Behaviour in the U.K., 1920–38*. This has very full references to material and family budgets and to recent analytical work.

ORR, *Food, Health and Income*, 1936.

MCGONIGLE and KIRBY, *Poverty and Public Health*, 1936, Chapter VII (the Stockton case).

CLARK, *Conditions of Economic Progress*, 1951 (international data).

Articles on elasticity of demand in international trade by TSE-CHUN CHANG and MACDOUGALL in *Economic Journal*, June, 1946; December, 1951; September, 1952.

Since 1945, see:

SEERS, *Changes in the Cost of Living and Distribution of Incomes since 1938*, 1949, and *Levelling of Incomes since 1938* (no date).

Home Market (annual).

INSTITUTE OF PUBLIC ADMINISTRATION, *The Health Services*, 1951, p. 100 (estimate of proportion of incomes derived before and since the war from payments in cash and kind, earned income and social services, etc.).

Reports and papers of the Royal Commissions on:
Equal Pay, 1947, Cmd. 6937.
Population, 1949, Cmd. 7695; especially Vol. V of the Commission's Papers on *The Economic Position of the Family.*
ROWNTREE, *Poverty and Progress,* 1941.
ROWNTREE and LAVERS,
English Life and Leisure, 1951.
Poverty and the Welfare State, 1951.
ZWEIG, *The British Worker,* 1952.

For underdeveloped countries, the best general reviews are those in the United Nations reports (especially those of the Economic Commissions for Europe, Latin America, and Asia and the Far East, *Measures for the Economic Development of Underdeveloped Countries,* 1951, and *The World Social Situation,* 1952).

For Africa see also the reports of the Organisation for European Economic Cooperation, notably, *Investments in Africa South of the Sahara,* 1951.

On human needs standards
> BRITISH MEDICAL ASSOCIATION, *Report of the Committee on Nutrition,* 1950.
> MINISTRY OF HOUSING AND LOCAL GOVERNMENT, *Housing Manual.* Also CENTRAL HOUSING ADVISORY COMMITTEE, *Design of Dwellings,* 1944.

And approaches to standards of convenience and human relations in such works as:
> PEARSE and CROCKER, *The Peckham Experiment.*
> GLASS, *Social Background of a Plan,* 1948.
> CHAPMAN, 'Convenience', in *Human Relations,* III (1), February, 1950.

On the part to be played by various mechanisms in controlling consumption decisions
See the references to the general effectiveness of each mechanism in Part II, and

On competition and direction
> WOOTTON, *Freedom under Planning,* 1945.
> TWIGG, article in *The Cooperative Movement in Labour Britain,* 1948.
> *Report of the Purchase Tax Utility Committee,* 1952, Cmd. 8452.

On consumer education
> BISHOP, *Ethics of Advertising,* 1949.
> TEMPORARY NATIONAL ECONOMIC COMMITTEE OF THE U.S. CONGRESS, Monograph 24, *Consumer Standards,* 1941.
> CONSUMERS UNION OF NEW YORK, *Consumer Reports.*

ASSOCIATION OF SCIENTIFIC WORKERS, *Spotlight on Shopping*, 1951.

MINISTRY OF FOOD, *Advertising, Labelling and Composition of Food*, 1949.

LEWIN, *Group Decision and Social Change* in Newcomb and Hartley, *Readings in Social Psychology*, 1947, p. 330 ff.

Chapters on 'Industrial Relations' and 'Personal Income Policy' in WORSWICK and ADY (ed.), *The British Economy 1945–50*, 1952.

CHAPTER 9

On the capital market

Report of the Committee on Finance and Industry (Macmillan Committee), 1931, Cmd. 3897.

GRANT, *Study of the Capital Market in Post-war Britain*, 1937.

HENDERSON, *New Issue Market*, 1951.

HARGREAVES PARKINSON, *Ownership of Industry*, 1951.

STEINDL, *Small and Big Business*, 1947 (useful summary of factors affecting the supply of capital to small businesses).

ZWEIG, *Labour Life and Poverty*, 1949, and *The British Worker*, 1952, has some useful comments on the small saver's or potential saver's attitude.

On factors affecting business men's investment decisions

In addition to the discussion in general text-books such as KEYNES, *General Theory*, see:

ANDREWS and BRUNNER, *Capital Development in Steel*, 1951.

Oxford Economic Papers, Old Series, Nos. 1 and 3. Articles on business men and the rate of interest: and New Series, 1, ii, article by R. S. HOPE illustrating the 'rule of thumb' element in, e.g., dividend decisions.

P.E.P., *Planning*, 308 ('Economics of the Council House'), and Jarmain, *Housing Subsidies and Rents*, 1948, on factors affecting investment in this sector.

On government control, see:

P.E.P., *Government and Industry*, 1952.

CHAPTER 10

General discussion

POLANYI, *Logic of Liberty*, Part I, 1951.

KILLEFFER, *Genius of Industrial Research*, 1948.

Research in industry

EDWARDS, *Cooperative Industrial Research*, 1950 (outstanding economic analysis).

HILL, *Cooperative Research in Industry*, 1947.

FEDERATION OF BRITISH INDUSTRIES:
Report of the Conference on Industry and Research, 1946.
Scientific and Technical Research in British Industry, 1947.
Research and Development in British Industry, 1952.
MANCHESTER JOINT RESEARCH COUNCIL:
Research and the Smaller Firm, 1946.
Industry and Science, 1954.

Government research relevant to industry

Government Scientific Organisation in the Civilian Field, H.M.S.O., 1951.
SELECT COMMITTEE ON ESTIMATES, *Report on Expenditure on Research and Development*, Session 1946–7: especially pp. 39 ff. ('D.S.I.R.') and 84–5 ('University Grants Committee').
Reports of the Department of Scientific and Industrial Research and the National Research Development Corporation.
Science at War, H.M.S.O., 1947.
Atomic Energy (U.S. Government, reprinted by H.M.S.O.), 1945, especially Chapters III and V.

Universities and miscellaneous research organisations

NATIONAL INSTITUTE OF ECONOMIC AND SOCIAL RESEARCH, *Annual Register of Research in the Social Sciences*.
Report of the Committee on the Provision for Social and Economic Research, 1946, Cmd. 6868.
Report of the Committee on Scientific Manpower, 1946, Cmd. 6824.
P.E.P., *Planning*, has a number of broadsheets on problems of research and the universities.
FOGARTY, *Plan Your Own Industries*, 1947, on regional development councils.

CHAPTER 11

Education

NUFFIELD COLLEGE, *Statement on Industry and Education*, 1943.
CAMBRIDGE UNIVERSITY APPOINTMENTS BOARD, *University Education and Business*, 1946.
FEDERATION OF BRITISH INDUSTRIES, *Report of the Universities Conference*, Ashorne Hill, 1952.
ANGLO-AMERICAN PRODUCTIVITY COUNCIL, series on training of operatives, supervisors, and managers, and on the universities and industry.
YOUNGHUSBAND, reports on the training of social workers, Carnegie Foundation, 1948, and 1951.
GRAY and MOSHINSKY, article in Hogben, *Political Arithmetic*, 1938.
MINISTRY OF EDUCATION, Annual Reports and *Education 1900–1950*, Cmd. 8244.

FURTHER READING

UNIVERSITY GRANTS COMMITTEE, *University Development 1947–51*, 1952, Cmd. 473.

Report of the Working Party on University Awards, 1948.

EDWARD CADBURY CHARITABLE TRUST, *Eighty Thousand Adolescents*, 1950.

KOTSCHNIG, *Unemployment in the Learned Professions*, 1937.

Medical and Environmental

HALLIDAY, *Psycho-Social Medicine*, 1948.

P.E.P., *British Health Services*, 1937.

NUFFIELD PROVINCIAL HOSPITALS TRUST, *Report for 1939–48*.

INSTITUTE OF PUBLIC ADMINISTRATION, *The Health Services*, 1951 (especially article by F. LAFITTE).

SELECT COMMITTEE ON ESTIMATES, reports on:
The Administration of the National Health Services, 1949.
Regional Hospital Boards and Hospital Management Committees, 1951.

WINSLOW, *The Cost of Sickness and the Price of Health*, 1951.

See also on particular aspects:

BRITISH MEDICAL ASSOCIATION, *Report of the Committee on Nutrition*, 1950.

ORR, *Food, Health and Income*, 1936.

Royal Commission on the Distribution of the Industrial Population, 1937–40, evidence of the Registrars-General on health of different classes and areas.

INDUSTRIAL HEALTH RESEARCH BOARD, *Industrial Health in War*, reprinted 1940 (hours of work: compare with actual hours, *Monthly Digest* or *Annual Abstract of Statistics*).

DURANT, *Watling*, 1939.

DANIEL, Article in *Oxford Economic Papers*, February, 1940 (Welsh in Cowley).

FOLEY, *Irish Workers in Birmingham*, 1951 (cyclostyled, Young Christian Workers: summary in FOGARTY, 'Strangers from Ireland', *Commonweal*, March 26th, 1954).

The reference to the 'tired community' is quoted from LYND, *Middletown in Transition*, 1937, pp. 254–6. See also PILGRIM TRUST, *Men Without Work*, 1938.

See also references in Tables.

Community-building services

Reports of the National Council of Social Service and National Council of Community Associations.

WHITE, *Community or Chaos*, 1950 (and other reports by this author).

PEARSE and CROCKER, *The Peckham Experiment*.

KUPER (ed.), *Living in Towns*. 1953.

See also generally:

HALL, *The British Social Services*, 1952.

CHESTER, *Central and Local Government*, 1951.

309

Reports of the Local Government Manpower Committee (on central-local relations).
Statistical summary of the cost of the social services in *Monthly Digest of Statistics*, May, 1952.

CHAPTER 12

On world resources and population

UNITED NATIONS
Demographic Year Book
Report of the Scientific Conference on the Conservation and Utilisation of Resources, 1950.

On the geographical distribution and movement of population

(1) *International movement*
ISAACS, *Economics of Migration*, 1947.
THOMAS, *Migration and Economic Growth*, 1954.

(2) *Movement within one country*
Articles in *Oxford Economic Papers*, Old Series, 1–4 (1938–40), by DANIELS and by MAKOWER, MARSCHAK, and ROBINSON.
NEWTON and JEFFERY, *Internal Migration*, H.M.S.O., 1951.
Report and Papers of the Royal Commission on the Distribution of the Industrial Population, 1940, Cmd. 6153.
References in FOGARTY, *Prospects of the Industrial Areas of Great Britain*, 1945. (Statistical data): *Town and Country Planning*, 1948: and article on 'Location of Industry' in WORSWICK and ADY (ed.), *The British Economy, 1945–50*, 1952.
MUMFORD, *Culture of Cities*, 1938.
DURANT, *Watling*, 1939.
ECONOMICS RESEARCH SECTION, UNIVERSITY OF MANCHESTER, *Re-adjustment in Lancashire*.
ORLANS, *Stevenage*, 1952.
FOLEY, cyclostyled memorandum on 'The Situation of Irish Workers in Birmingham', *Young Christian Workers*, 1951 (summary in FOGARTY, 'Strangers from Ireland', *Commonweal*, March 26th, 1954).
WARNER and LOW, *Social System of a Modern Factory* (1947). See also the other volumes of their Yankee City series, dealing with the social life and status systems of the community and the special problems of ethnic groups.

(3) *Some international conventions*
INTERNATIONAL LABOUR OFFICE, *International Labour Code*, 1951.
UNITED NATIONS, *Convention Relating to the Status of Refugees*, 1951.
Treaty establishing a European Coal and Steel Community, 1951 (English translation published by British Iron and Steel Federation, 1954).
Draft Statute of the European Political Community, 1953.

FURTHER READING

On the size and regulation of a country's population (primarily economic aspects)

Report and Papers of the Royal Commission on the Population, 1949, Cmd. 7695. Especially the report of the Economics Committee (*Papers*, Vol. III) and of an investigation of the cost of bringing up a family (*Papers*, Vol. V).

RATHBONE, *Case for Family Allowances*, 1940.

MYRDAL, *Nation and Family*, 1945.

INTERNATIONAL UNION OF SOCIAL STUDIES (Union of Malines), *Statement on Population Policy*, 1954

CHAPTER 13

Documents on post-war trade and investment policy

Bretton Woods Agreement (International Monetary Fund and International Bank for Reconstruction and Development), 1944, Cmd. 6546.

Washington Loan Agreement, 1945, Cmd. 6708.

General Agreement on Tariffs and Trade, 1947, Cmd. 7258.

The Havana Charter for an International Trade Organisation, 1948, Cmd. 7375.

UNITED NATIONS, *Report of a Committee of Experts on Measures for the Economic Development of Under-Developed Countries*, 1951.

ORGANISATION FOR EUROPEAN ECONOMIC COOPERATION
(1) *History and Structure*, 1953 (refers to other documents on O.E.E.C.).
(2) *Code of Liberalisation*, 1953 ed.

Treaty Establishing the European Coal and Steel Community, 1951.

Draft Treaty embodying the Statute of the European Political Community, 1953.

UNITED STATES OF AMERICA. Reports of the Paley Commission (*Raw Materials*, 1951) and the Randall Commission (*Foreign Economic Policy*, 1954).

BALOGH, *Dollar Crisis—Cause and Cure*, 1950.

WORSWICK and ADY (ed.), *The British Economy*, 1945–50, 1952.

NURKSE, *Problems of Capital Formation in Underdeveloped Countries*, 1954.

STALEY, *Future of the Under-Developed Countries*, 1954.

For general discussion of all this, see notably the series of articles by KEYNES, MACDOUGALL, and BALOGH in the *Economic Journal*, 1945 onwards. Also P.E.P., *Britain in World Trade*, 1947, and later broadsheets on trade, development, technical aid, etc., in *Planning*; and *Government and Industry*, 1952.

Factual and statistical material (international)

CLARK, *Conditions of Economic Progress*, 1951 ed.

UNITED NATIONS, reports of Economic Commissions for Europe, Latin America, and Asia and the Far East.

Reports of the Organisation for European Economic Cooperation and the European Payments Union.

Reports of the Colonial Development Corporation, and on the progress of the Colombo Plan (both H.M.S.O.).

And pre-war material in such sources as

LEAGUE OF NATIONS, *Annual Review of World Trade*, and *Europe's Trade*.

HAL B. LARY and others, *The United States in the World Economy*, U.S. Government (H.M.S.O., 1944).

NATIONAL INSTITUTE OF ECONOMIC AND SOCIAL RESEARCH, *Trade Regulations and Commercial Policy of the U.K.*, 1943.

LEWIS, *Economic Survey*, 1919–39, 1949.

HEXNER, *International Cartels*, 1944.

BEVERIDGE, *Full Employment in a Free Society*, 1944 (appendix on fluctuations in international trade).

I.L.O., *Inter-Governmental Commodity Control Agreements*, 1943 (full bibliography in footnotes).

FRANKEL, *Capital Investment in Africa*, 1938.

BAYKOV, *Foreign Trade of the U.S.S.R.*, 1946.

CROWTHER, *Money*, 1940 (useful short account of international monetary problems).

Inter-regional trade and development (especially the problem of the British depressed areas)

The policy followed in 1944–9 is nowhere adequately written up. See, however:

Official documents

Reports of the Commissioners for the Special Areas in England and Wales, 1935–9.

White Paper on *Distribution of Industry*, 1948, Cmd. 7540.

Summary of pre- and post-war policy discussions in

NUFFIELD COLLEGE, Social Reconstruction Survey, *Britain's Town and Country Pattern*, 1943.

FOGARTY, *Prospects of the Industrial Areas of Great Britain*, 1945, last chapter: and chapter on 'Location of Industry' in WORSWICK and ADY (ed.), *The British Economy*, 1945–50, 1952.

See also:

LILIENTHAL, *T.V.A.*, 1944 ed.
FOGARTY, *Plan Your Own Industries*, 1947 (regional and local development councils).
LUTTRELL, *The Cost of Industrial Movement*, 1952.
FLORENCE, *Investment Location and Size of Plant*, 1948.

CHAPTER 15

Accountancy

Useful historical material for Great Britain in:

CARR-SAUNDERS and WILSON, *The Professions*, 1933.
URWICK and BRECH, *Making of Scientific Management*, 1949, Vol. II.

See also:

BRADSHAW, *Developing Men for Controllership*, 1950.
BRAY, *Precision and Design in Accountancy*, 1947.

And on particular aspects referred to in the text:

INSTITUTE OF CHARTERED ACCOUNTANTS IN ENGLAND AND WALES, *Development in Cost Accounting*, 1947.
INSTITUTE OF COST AND WORKS ACCOUNTANTS and INSTITUTION OF PRODUCTION ENGINEERS, *Measurement of Productivity*, 1951.
PARKINSON, *Accountancy Ratios*, 1951 (on the accountant's interpretative role).
Report of the Linoleum Working Party, 1947 (a good example of old-fashioned obscurantism).

Econometrics

TINBERGEN, *Econometrics*, 1951.
STONE, *Measurement in Economics*, 1951.
DAVIS, *Theory of Econometrics*, 1941.

And for a couple of practical applications:

NICHOLSON, 'Rationing and Index Numbers', in Institute of Statistics, *Studies in War Economics*, 1947.
ROBINSON and MARRIS, *The Use of Home Resources to Save Imports*, *Economic Journal*, 1950 (and subsequent discussion).

Social accounting

UNITED NATIONS, *Measurement of National Income and the Construction of Social Accounts*, 1947.
MEADE and STONE, *National Income and Expenditure*, 1948 ed.
SHOUP, *National Income Analysis*, 1947.

20*

ECONOMIC CONTROL

On some problems of synthesis

BRAY, *Social Accounts and the Business Enterprise Sector of the National Economy*, 1951.

HICKS, *Problem of Budgetary Reform*, 1948.

And the series of contributions to the *Economic Journal* started by the publication of P. W. S. ANDREWS' *Manufacturing Business* (1949—economic analysis based on accountancy concepts). See notably articles by Wiles (1950 and 1954) and Edwards (1952).

CHAPTER 16

On the classical theory of the relation of economics to ethics

ROBBINS, *Nature and Significance of Economic Science*, 1935 ed.

KNIGHT, *Ethics of Competition*, 1935; *Freedom and Reform*, 1947; *Economic Order and Religion* (with T. MERRIAM), 1947.

and the criticism in

LITTLE, *Welfare Economics*, 1949.

See also:

POLANYI, *Logic of Liberty*, 1951, and *Science, Faith and Society*.

BARNARD, *Functions of the Executive*, 1938.

FOLLETT, *Dynamic Administration*.

The position taken up in this chapter is based primarily on the traditional doctrine of the natural law, useful short introductions to which are:

D'ENTRÈVES, *Natural Law*, 1951.

KEANE, *Primer of Moral Philosophy*, 1943 ed.

It is also influenced a great deal by the work of Talcott Parsons (*Structure of Social Action* and *Essays in Sociological Theory*) and R. K. Merton. Some of the issues raised are developed further in:

FOGARTY

The Function of an Undergraduate Department of Industrial Relations, 1953.

Personality and Group Relations in Industry, 1955, especially Chapter I.

CHAPTER 17

A number of the issues in this chapter are followed out in:

FOGARTY, *Personality and Group Relations in Industry*, 1955.

This contains book lists on:

Personality and industry.

The small working group.

Business as the meeting-place of many interests, and the professionalisation of management.
The local community.
The time factor in social change.

On the Marxist-Leninist theory of the three stages of development, see notably LENIN, *The State and Revolution*, 1917.

On the contribution of the Protestant ethic to modern social development, see:

Works by Weber, Tawney, and Fanfani on Protestantism and the rise of capitalism.

MERTON, 'Puritanism, Pietism, and Science', in *Social Theory and Social Structure*, 1949.

PARSONS, *Structure of Social Action*, 1937.

WEARMOUTH, *Methodism and the Working-Class Movements of England, 1800–1850*, and *Some Working-Class Movements of the Nineteenth Century*, 1948.

Generally, on changing cultural norms, see the suggestive if not always highly scientific analysis in such books as:

VEBLEN, *Theory of the Leisure Class*, 1899.

TAWNEY, *The Acquisitive Society*, 1921.

MUMFORD, *Technics and Civilisation*, 1934; *The Culture of Cities*, 1938; *The Condition of Man*, 1944.

SCHUMPETER, *Capitalism, Socialism and Democracy*, 1943.

Data on farming are taken from the *National Farm Survey*, 1946, and *Annual Agricultural Statistics* (both H.M.S.O.). Retailing data from *Annual Abstract* and BOARD OF TRADE, *Britain's Shops*, 1952

In addition to the references given with the tables and in FOGARTY, op. cit., use has been made of the collection of American data in STEINDL, *Small and Big Business*, 1945.

INDEX

Expenditure,
 basic elements in, 121
 maximum, 123, 124–5
 pattern of, 103ff
 public authorities' share in, 55–7
Experiment, cost of, 27

Factory Acts, 181
Family, the,
 average size, 297
 economic importance, 295ff
 and income distribution, 208
 internal and external relations, 297–8
 movements, 298–9
Farmland, diversion of, 222
Federal Trade Commission, U.S.A., 93
Federalist age, 275–6
Finance and Industry, Committee on.
 See Macmillan Committee
Firm and industry, relation, 291–2
Firms,
 expenditure and income, relation, 258
 new, life of, 50–1
 new small, financing of, 153ff
 size of, stability in, 286–7
Flexibility of economy, 38
Flexner, Abraham, 295
Florence, 291
Food and Agriculture Organisation, 242
Food supplies, and population, 195–6
Ford Motors, 79
Foreign trade, monopoly, 221
Foremen and management, consultation between, 86
Forest Products Research Laboratory, 167
Forestry Commission, 222
Framework, social, 11, 47
 effects of changes in, 49ff
Franks, Sir Oliver, 69
Free trade, 221
Fuel crisis (1947), 60
Fuel and power resources, 197
Furniture Development Council, 34

Geddes, P., 3
General Motors, 79
Geneva Agreement on Tariffs and Trade, 99, 234, 243
Geological Survey, 168
Glacier Metal Co., 84, 87, 295

Glasgow Industrial Finance Development Co., 155
Gloucestershire medical services scheme, 192
Goodwill,
 as barrier to market entry, 33ff
 importance in retailing, 34
 in labour market, 35
 reversibility of, 17, 19
Gordon, R. A., 284
Group pressures, and investment, 152
Group standards, and expenditure, 121–2
Groups,
 small, education of, 137
 social, solidarity of, 228

Haldane Committee on Machinery of Government, 96
Halliday, 171, 188
Handloom weavers, 51
Hankey, Lord, 172
Harvard Business School, 250–1
Havana Charter, 193
Health centres, 62, 192
Highlands and Islands scheme, 192
Hire-purchase, 154
History, relation to ethics, 272
Hookworm, 175
Hospital budgets, 191
Hours of work, 181
House ownership, 127
Household size, 206
Housing,
 expenditure on, 186
 and health, 181
Housing estates, direction and, 62
Human Rights, Charter of, 214

Ignorance, customer, 33–5
Imports, competition from, 26
Income,
 distribution of, 43, 111ff
 in rich and poor countries, 221
 inequalities, 114–16
 maximum, production and, 16
 national, 255
 growth of, 112
 stability of, 120–1
Industrial and Commercial Finance Corporation, 155